JOHN McCORMACK
HIS OWN LIFE STORY

JOHN McCORMACK

HIS OWN LIFE STORY

Transcribed by
PIERRE V. R. KEY

Edited and with an introduction by
JOHN SCARRY

With thirty-two pages of photographs

B
McC

VIENNA HOUSE
NEW YORK

RL-2254

INTRODUCTION

Most theatrical and musical figures never find
their Boswell, but it is an unusual performer who is
not the subject of at least one attempt to write his
Life during his lifetime. John McCormack was one
of these unusual artists, and during his long career
he was to find two biographers who would attempt
full length studies of his life and work. Three years
after McCormack retired from the concert stage
L.A.G. Strong published *John McCormack, The
Story of a Singer,*[1] a book that had its beginnings
in McCormack's own attempts to write his memoirs.
The tenor's impatience with the discipline of the
written word led to a collaboration with Strong; but
the result, as McCormack himself would later say,
was an anemic portrait. The singer's first biography,

INTRODUCTION

a 1918 collaboration with the journalist Pierre Key, began as an elaborate publicity effort by McCormack's manager but was soon modified by an adviser even closer to the singer. The present book is the product of these efforts, and when it originally appeared John McCormack was at the height of his popularity and very near the peak of his artistic success.

The John McCormack of 1918 had come so far in the musical world that a book describing his extraordinary rise to fame seemed almost inevitable. A singer's origins and early struggles are usually the stuff of legend, and here we have the McCormack legend in all its mythic outline and heroic detail: the humble birth, the hard work at school, the hope for a musical career, the momentary doubts, the first chance at success, eventual recognition. This McCormack biography has all of this and more, but the book becomes less mythic when the singer describes his initial success in Dublin in 1903 and his first visit to America the following year. These accounts, in addition to McCormack's descriptions of his student days in Milan and his early career in London, are among the best parts of the book; there is an immediacy of recollection in Key that is lacking in the Strong biography of more than twenty years later. McCormack's actual quotations,

iv

INTRODUCTION

given not long after the events he describes, make this book one of the most valuable documents we have of the singer's life.

McCormack's life was a combination of innate ambition, a willingness to work, and the good fortune to recognize opportunities when they presented themselves. His first success, winning the 1903 tenor competition at Dublin's Feis Ceoil, made McCormack aware that a singing career was a real possibility and he was shrewd enough to see that if he were to become a professional, this momentum had to be sustained. Young J.F. McCormack (as he was known in those early days) soon became a firm Dublin favorite, but local fame was not enough. McCormack's immediate acceptance of a contract to sing at the St. Louis World's Fair in the summer of 1904 indicates how quickly and how far his horizons had expanded, and reveals that, like every young immigrant, his hopes were for a career in the land of opportunity. He was at the Fair by June of 1904 but if, as seems likely, the fledgling tenor saw this engagement as the beginning of a career in America, he was wise enough to postpone it for an even greater opportunity. McCormack followed the advice that he should study singing in Italy, and the vocal training he would receive in Milan would in five short years bring him back to the United States as a leading member of Oscar Hammerstein's opera company. These 1909 appearances at the Manhattan Opera House marked the real beginning of McCormack's phenomenal success in America. Had he not been willing to undergo serious training in Italy, McCormack might have remained in America, a comparatively unschooled Irish tenor, and would most likely never have achieved an international reputation.

It was as a tenor of the *bel canto* school that McCormack was trained, and his vocal preparation was for a career in opera. Vincenzo Sabatini must have heard promise in the voice, but McCormack's first recordings (made in London late in 1904)[2] reveal little more than an attractive vocal quality; it is doubtful whether the maestro ever envisioned the career this young Irishman was to enjoy. The period of study under Sabatini was too short and this, coupled with McCormack's youth when he made his Savona debut—he was not twenty-two when he sang in Mascagni's *L'Amico Fritz* on January 13, 1906—made for a less than sensational first performance. Irish friends and English impresarios would see however that this young tenor had sung in Italy in grand opera, a fact that should open some doors. It did not; nor did a return trip to Italy offer any hope of building a reputation with which to ap-

INTRODUCTION

proach the directors of Covent Garden. London was the citadel to be taken and the Royal Opera was the immediate goal, but McCormack found that aggressiveness and an emerging talent were not enough to get him even an audition at Covent Garden. It took Sir John Murray Scott's influence to arrange for McCormack to be heard, and Murray Scott's prestige was a major factor in the singer's being given a contract; at twenty-three, he was the youngest principal tenor ever engaged at Covent Garden. McCormack's début was announced for October 1907, and Turiddu in *Cavalleria Rusticana* was to be his first role at the Royal Opera. There were several reasons for this choice. McCormack's understandable nervousness as he appeared before his first London opera audience would be lessened by the fact that Turiddu's first aria, which opens the opera, is sung behind a lowered curtain. In addition, the opera was short, then as now sharing the bill with *Pagliacci*. Finally—and perhaps most importantly—McCormack was no stranger to the role, having sung Turiddu in Dublin with Barton McGuckin's opera company in May 1907. The tenor also sang Faust during that engagement, and it was a more experienced McCormack who returned to London in the late spring of 1907. By the time he was heard in *Cavalleria Rusticana* on October 15, McCormack's voice had also matured dramatically but recordings made about this time and the contemporary reviews of his singing demonstrate that he was not really vocally prepared for the London operatic stage. Once he was on that stage, however, he kept his promise that nothing would get him off, and until the outbreak of war in 1914 he remained a regular member of the company, specializing in a lyrical repertoire that was especially suited to his voice: *La Sonnambula, Rigoletto, Lucia di Lammermoor,* and *La Traviata* were among his favorite operas. It was during this period too that McCormack's finest operatic creation emerged and was perfected: his singing of Don Ottavio in Mozart's *Don Giovanni.*

McCormack never had a very robust voice, and in opera he was hardly serious competition for a Caruso. Knowing that his strength lay as a *tenore di grazia* of the De Lucia and Bonci variety, the Irish tenor chose his models and style accordingly. It was partly for reasons of this finished lyric style and partly because of the natural lightness of the McCormack voice during these early years that Tetrazzini and Melba both chose him as their partner in opera. Neither of these brilliant songbirds wanted stentorian competition from their leading man, and McCormack was the perfect tenor for their common purpose. Tetrazzini's spectacular success at Covent Garden had come on November 2, 1907, less than a month after McCormack's own début, and in January 1908 she was to take New York by storm. The coloratura needed a tenor for her return to America the following year and McCormack was her choice; Hammerstein reluctantly carried out the wishes of his new soprano. Tetrazzini was genuinely fond of McCormack, professionally and otherwise, and their association began as early as 1907 when he sang the Duke to her Gilda in a November 23 performance of *Rigoletto*. They were to sing several Covent Garden seasons together, appearing regularly in such operas as *Lucia di Lammermoor, Lakmé, The Barber of Seville,* and *La Traviata,* a repertoire that was repeated during their one season together in America under Oscar Hammerstein's aegis. The other prima donna who selected McCormack as her leading tenor was Nellie Melba, a soprano even more famous than Tetrazzini but not nearly so affable. Melba was accustomed to having her own way, and as the tenor favored by her to be chosen to accompany the grande dame on her triumphant opera tour of Australia in 1911, McCormack was at first in no position to openly defy her. He had watched her take solo curtain calls when they sang together at Covent Garden in 1910, but when they reached

INTRODUCTION

Melba's native Australia in the summer of 1911 McCormack realized that the enthusiastic reception he was receiving could not be denied.

McCormack's contract called for his singing in three operas a week, but as John Hetherington reports, "After eyeing the packed houses he contrived to find the Australian climate so hard on his voice that his third weekly appearance nearly always became impossible unless he was compensated by an extra fee of £100."[3] Hetherington adds that since a part of Melba's income from the engagement depended on the season's profits, the extra £100 meant she was losing money, a fact which did nothing to endear McCormack to her. The combination of McCormack's Irish temper and Melba's prima donna temperament would permit neither to forget nor forgive, and their uneasy association resulted in some glorious singing and several memorable quarrels. Years later, when McCormack was about to sing in Dublin's Theatre Royal, he happened to see a large photograph of Melba mounted on the wall near the artist's room. The tenor exploded, announced he would not sing until the picture was removed, and only when workmen were called and the portrait dismantled would McCormack go on. Even the absent Nellie Melba could cause tempers to rise.

INTRODUCTION

McCormack's appearances with Tetrazzini in America two years earlier had been as much a personal as an artistic success. Cleofonte Campanini, who acted as Tetrazzini's spokesman in the negotiations to convince Hammerstein of McCormack's abilities, had predicted that an Irishman singing Italian opera in New York would take the public by storm. The conductor's comment was a shrewd box office prophecy; Campanini knew that thousands of Irish immigrants in America would be a natural following for a handsome and talented young Irish tenor, and McCormack also was aware of the potentially enormous following awaiting him. In his first American newspaper interviews the tenor was careful to give some refreshingly unexpected opinions and seemingly unrehearsed answers. His favorite tenor was Caruso, there was nothing he liked better than a few rounds of boxing, and when could he hear some orchestral concerts in New York? New York was charmed, and from the beginning McCormack had a good press. His November 10, 1909 début in *La Traviata* with Tetrazzini met with restrained but positive critical reviews, while his Edgardo in *Lucia di Lammermoor* was better received; only his Tonio to Tetrazzini's Maria in *The Daughter of the Regiment* was pronounced a failure. From November 1909 until the spring of 1910

INTRODUCTION

McCormack sang some fifty operatic performances with the Manhattan Company, many of them in such centers as Philadelphia, Washington, and Cincinnati; but when Oscar Hammerstein sold out to the Metropolitan Opera on April 26, 1910, McCormack had to look elsewhere. Although he continued to make regular appearances with the Chicago and Boston Opera Companies and would eventually sing some performances at New York's Metropolitan, the break signalled by Hammerstein's withdrawal from opera was almost symbolic for McCormack whose increasing attention to recitals was meeting with a growing success. The tenor who had never been comfortable in opera came to recognize the concert platform as his true home. From 1911 on, his operatic repertoire would continue to provide money and prestige, but McCormack the recitalist would reach a wider audience and would earn larger fees than any opera singer could ever hope to command. On May 24, 1917 the *Musical Leader* could report that McCormack had arranged to sing five performances during the upcoming season at the Metropolitan Opera, "this being all the time he was willing to take from his concert engagements." It was becoming clear that such appearances were exceptions to what was by now the rule, and the magazine report added that the tenor's concert engagements "promise to be more engrossing than ever next season." As Pierre Key writes at the conclusion of this book, McCormack's decision to devote himself to the concert platform would give him "a career unapproached by any singer since Jenny Lind." Jenny Lind had also left opera and turned exclusively to concert singing so the comparison was apt, but the rest of the Irishman's career would lead the chroniclers to search for superlatives: John McCormack was to become the highest paid singer in history.

* * * * *

By 1918 McCormack had been enjoying nearly a decade of uninterrupted success in America, and his manager Charles Wagner felt it was time for what he calls "a dose of press agentry—a sugar-coated publicity stunt" in the form of a book length account of McCormack's "unusual rise to artistic heights."[4] In his memoirs Wagner alludes to an unauthorized life of McCormack that had begun to appear about this time in a Boston newspaper. Presumably this was a spur to Wagner's own press agentry, but the manager fails to mention another journalistic stimulus for his project, a lengthy article published in the *Musical Leader* of June 14, 1917. The piece, entitled the "First Authentic Story of John McCormack's Life and Career," was by Florence French, editor of the magazine and a good friend of Wagner's. Mrs. French was the right person to present this detailed account of McCormack's life; it was she who had introduced Wagner to John McCormack in St. Paul in January 1911. It was also timely that the interview appeared on McCormack's thirty-third birthday, and as the caption under the cover photograph of the singer announced, in three days McCormack would receive a doctorate in literature from Holy Cross College. McCormack was a regular subject for articles in the *Musical Leader,* and the fine hand of Charles Wagner may be seen behind this lively and direct interview, so evidently a custom-made press agent's product. This special McCormack issue helped Mrs. French to boost the sales of her magazine while it also served as a special favor for Charles Wagner.

This 1917 *Musical Leader* interview is important for a number of reasons, one of which is that it provided a working model for the 1918 biography. Wagner saw that the McCormack articles and interviews which had been appearing regularly in the magazine were effectively exploiting his tenor, and he realized that an expansion of the same formula

INTRODUCTION

would make a good popular biography. Wagner undoubtedly envisioned the book as a literary "publicity stunt" based on his managerial efforts which
had been tried and found true in the pages of newspapers and magazines throughout the country, and
an examination of the Key book bears this out. The
manner in which Key arranges some of his chapters
and divides some of the smaller sections of the
book is remarkably similar to the arrangement and
treatment of the material in Mrs. French's interview: McCormack the book lover and art collector,
the candidate for American citizenship, the defender
of his choice of songs, and the somewhat chauvinis-
tic critic of song programs in foreign languages. In
this area of song repertoire, at least one other *Musical Leader* interview with McCormack seems to be
related to a part of the Key biography. In the
March 8, 1917 issue of the magazine McCormack
pronounced Schubert's "Die Allmacht" to be "the
greatest song ever written" and the terms of his enthusiasm for it are virtually identical in the article
and in Key; the singer's second song choice, "Die
Mainacht" of Brahms, and his estimate of it are also
the same in both pieces. McCormack's patriotic
comments, recorded at length throughout chapters
XXV to XXVII in Key are also anticipated in the
June 14, 1917 *Musical Leader*, when the tenor

boldly announces that "the nearest to the solution of the world's political difficulties likely to be found this side of heaven is the American government." Such simplistic politics were understandable in the America of 1917, but it makes us grateful that McCormack's 1938 announced intention to run for the presidency of Ireland never got beyond the proposal stage.

McCormack's statements in the *Musical Leader* interview are at times remarkably frank, and from the first the tenor strikes an honest note: "My father," he announces to Florence French, "told me I should never amount to anything in the world," and after the young man failed to win a scholarship from the Royal College of Science in 1902, Andrew McCormack was "disgusted" with his son. McCormack is also very straightforward about some of the circumstances leading to his 1909 Manhattan Opera appearances in New York with Tetrazzini; in the interview the tenor freely admits that "Hammerstein kicked against my engagement. And this is how he objected: 'An Irish tenor in opera? I don't think so!'..." The same incidents are reported in Key with something less than equal fidelity to the facts: McCormack describes his father as "stern enough, but I like to feel it to have been more a quality of dignity," and Hammerstein's reluctance to hire him is never even mentioned; "I shall never cease to be grateful to him for the opportunities he so freely gave me," is the singer's most direct comment on his association with the impresario although Campanini's role as McCormack's champion in the negotiations with Hammerstein is clearly indicated. There is no indication, however, of Tetrazzini's desire for the services of the young Irishman.

In the spring of 1918 Wagner approached Pierre Key and the Boston publishing house of Small, Maynard & Company and arranged for the writing and publication of the book. Early in June, Key met with McCormack for the first time. The journalist was not the only visitor that summer at Rocklea, the singer's Noroton Connecticut home; Michael Curley, McCormack's boyhood friend was also there on a visit from Florida. Not yet forty and already Bishop of the diocese of St. Augustine, Curley had maintained his early friendship with the singer and had become a confidant of the McCormack family. It was as the singer's literary adviser that Bishop Curley saw himself when Key began work on the book in June 1918. Wagner reports that Bishop Curley's role as consultant in the writing of the biography had one immediate result: the "entire idea was altered. What was intended to be an authentic story turned out a very sentimental and unreal account." In addition, according to Wagner, "Key was obliged to change his writing style and the Bishop edited the copy for John." Directly and indirectly Bishop Curley dominates the book, and McCormack was apparently satisfied with the arrangement. Curley makes his first appearance early in Chapter I, providing a romanticized portrait of the young McCormack that cannot be taken seriously as a picture of the singer's early life; and his attempts to make McCormack the above average schoolboy into McCormack the brilliant student are equally unconvincing. Bishop Curley's presence is less direct but just as evident in a later chapter, "Pope Pius X Confers a Blessing." McCormack always considered himself a staunch Catholic, and throughout his career he received several papal honors, the greatest of which came in 1928 when the singer was rewarded for his contributions to the Vatican by being made a Count of the Holy Roman Empire. The tenor's strong religious sense, however, does not explain the fact that the whole of Chapter XVI is devoted to a 1909 Rome visit by the McCormacks; this emphasis most likely originated with the Bishop, not the tenor. Long before the penultimate chapter ("Reflections"), Curley's presence is an established fact and we are not surprised to find the Bishop as visible at the end of the book as he was

at the beginning. In the "Conclusion" we have confirmation of Wagner's comment that Curley edited
the text for McCormack: "Bishop Curley sent back
his last batch of proofs," the singer announces to
Pierre Key during their final meeting, "He made a
few changes, but he approves what we've done. I'm
glad of that." Key is less than convincing when he
adds that they were indeed "fortunate" to have had
the "sympathetic guidance of His Lordship, as editor." Wagner, no doubt realizing that Bishop Curley's influence with the singer far outweighed his
own, recalls that he himself "remained silent," but
the manager's influence in the preparation of the
book was far from nullified by the clergyman's edi-
torship.

The Wagner-inspired *Musical Leader* interview
gives us a clear idea of the type of biography envisioned by McCormack's manager, and it identifies
rather accurately those parts of the Key book Wagner considered good "press agentry." As we have
seen, most of the chapter headings in Key follow
the topics and divisions found in Mrs. French's interview, and "Songs for the Concert Programme"
and "McCormack on Critics" (Chapters XXIX and
XXX in Key) are very much in keeping with Wagner's desire to project an image of a McCormack
whom the manager describes in his memoirs as "a

singer of the classics" and "an indefatigable student
and workman." The chapters "McCormack for
American Citizenship," "McCormack and American
War Funds," and "Selling Liberty Bonds" (XXV to
XXVII in Key) provide an expansion of that section
of the *Musical Leader* interview in which the singer
described at length his patriotic feelings and his decision to become an American citizen. The article
even reproduces a photograph of the tenor's declaration of intention to become a citizen.

In addition, Wagner would not have objected
to the singer's restating in the Key book his account
of Oscar Hammerstein's lack of interest in him; the
story would only tend to confirm Wagner's image as
the man who almost singlehandedly made McCormack into America's greatest concert attraction,
producing what he refers to in *Seeing Stars* as,
"Box-office records of the century." Nor would
Wagner have found any reason to change McCormack's admission in the *Musical Leader* that after
he decided to leave St. Louis in 1904 and study in
Italy, he looked for a way "to get out of the engagement." In these and many other instances, however, it is evident that Bishop Curley did have objections, and with the omission of certain facts, the
softening of McCormack's usually frank manner,
and the nearly monotonous religious overtone, the

Bishop made his influence felt throughout the
biography. Curley carefully avoided or eliminated
those elements which he felt might reveal McCormack to be less than virtuous or even less than
lucky. In the Key book there are no references to
Andrew McCormack's lack of faith in his son;
McCormack's sole reason for wanting to break his
contract at the St. Louis World's Fair was his disgust with the stage Irishman; and Oscar Hammerstein did not hesitate for a moment to engage the
tenor. Curley's determination that McCormack
should be seen as a loyal Irishman nearly upstages
Wagner's desire to have his tenor presented as an
American: "Irishman that he is," Key writes, "and
with a true Irishman's love for his land and its
people, McCormack is also an American." Similar
statements throughout the book were in every sense
dictated by Bishop Curley who felt compelled, even
in the chapter entitled, "McCormack for American
Citizenship," to emphasize McCormack's Irish origins. Such an emphasis would certainly appeal to
the large Irish-American population, but we may be
sure that Charles Wagner did not approve. As Wagner recalls, McCormack's early managers in America
had "emphasized his nationality—an unnecessary
tactic. John McCormack never belonged solely to
the Irish race; he belonged to the entire musical

world." The American manager and Irish-born Bishop were often at cross-purposes during the writing of the biography, and the subject himself almost became lost under the combination of managerial ideas and Curley-inspired rhetoric.

McCormack's manager remembers that when the book was finally published it was "damned with faint praise" and the singer "bought off the publishers and withdrew the entire edition." The speed with which McCormack had the biography withdrawn is indicated by the fact that until the present edition, the book has remained a musical rarity, sought after as the first full length document of McCormack's life but virtually unobtainable except through rare book dealers. Wagner's desire to disassociate himself from the writing of the biography—through it all he "remained silent"—cannot conceal the fact that the larger portion of the book is modelled on an obviously Wagner-inspired account of McCormack's life. Wagner is also silent on the fact that control over the writing of the book passed from his hands to Bishop Curley's; McCormack's manager probably did not like to admit that the singer was more easily influenced by a Bishop who was also a boyhood friend than by a man whose interests were almost purely commercial and with whom the singer had already had some inevita-

INTRODUCTION

ble differences of opinion. McCormack's indication of the extent of Bishop Curley's influence over the writing probably came as a relief to Wagner. Long before the book was finished Wagner had lost his desire to be associated with it, and the fact that the manager's original structure was so modified by Curley must have had a great deal to do with this attitude. Charles Wagner and the critics were hardly sensitive to the documentary value of what Key had transcribed; they were too distracted by Bishop Curley's overblown prose style and Victorian pieties to realize the inherent value of the book. For us, Wagner's preconceived notions and Curley's interference scarcely hamper this first effort to document McCormack's career and we only wish that the legendary tenor Rubini, or his successor Mario, or some of McCormack's immediate Victorian predecessors, had been allowed to record the highlights of their early lives, training and first recognition from a similar vantage point: with this McCormack biography we have a personal account of a currently successful career, not nostalgia for one that was over. This note of youthful confidence in present and future success gives this McCormack biography a special authenticity and an unmistakably enthusiastic tone.

* * * * *

INTRODUCTION

It was fortunate for McCormack that he was so successful in America during these years; he would need all of his natural energy and optimism shortly after the war ended. The singer's first intimation that the world and his position in it had changed came in the summer of 1920, when he signed for his third tour of Australia. McCormack was scheduled to sing in Australia from June to November, with concerts in England early the following year. By August, however, the prejudice against the tenor's American citizenship was being openly expressed at concerts in Sydney, Melbourne, and Adelaide, and by early October feelings were running so high that a planned confrontation between native Australians and the large Irish colony was avoided only by the cancellation of the rest of the tour. England was even more hostile to the singer who had been given his first big opportunity at Covent Garden and who had established a British reputation before America had lured him with its financial rewards. McCormack dared not announce a London recital, and late in November 1920 he arrived in Paris.

McCormack's decision to go to France was born of exasperation, but his success in two charity concerts in Paris in December marked the beginning of the singer's only period of extended success on

the Continent. We can only guess what his reputation in Europe would have been had he been able
to fulfill the Salzburg engagement of 1914, but late
as it was, this 1920-24 period with its series of almost uninterrupted triumphs is a dazzling chapter in
McCormack's career. If McCormack was cheered by
his ovations in Paris he was positively elated when
Raoul Gunsbourg, the director of the Monte Carlo
Opera, asked him to do a season in Monaco. The
singer's repertoire at Monte Carlo was predictable—
Tosca, The Magic Flute, and *The Barber of Seville*
—and his reception was good, with high praise coming from the elderly Jean de Reszke. The great
Polish tenor heard McCormack's Count Almaviva in
an April 1921 performance of *The Barber of Seville*,
and wrote to him that he was "the true redeemer of
bel canto," a compliment which apparently would
not have been so deserved when the singer returned
to Monte Carlo the following season. By early 1923
Edwin Schneider was reporting to Charles Wagner
that there was much criticism of McCormack's singing; the accompanist concluded that the tenor was
out of place in opera and his art was lost. Schneider's comments reveal that McCormack's voice was
changing, and a comment made to Walter Legge by
the singer himself probably dates from about this
time. McCormack told Legge that when he was

practicing one day the top notes suddenly ceased to respond; the singer recalled that he "went down from the music-room to my lovely Lily and said: 'I've lost the trick. The soft high notes don't come any more...' "[5] At that point McCormack must have realized his days in opera were numbered. In concert he could transpose songs down to suit his vocal range, a practice not possible in opera. In addition, to have his less than robust voice continuing competition with an orchestra would be vocally ruinous. McCormack's March 17, 1923 singing of Gritzko in Mussorgsky's unpublished *The Fair at Sorotchinsk* at Monte Carlo was his last role in opera. With his upper register gone opera would not miss McCormack and the fact that he was by his own admission a bad actor made even less difficult his decision to leave the opera house. As far back as the early Covent Garden days Tetrazzini would complain that during the love duets she had to whisper to McCormack, "Hold me tighter!" to give some impression of a histrionic effort. The intervening years had done nothing to make him less wooden, and we may be sure that a sense of relief was prominent among McCormack's mixed feelings as he left the opera stage. Years later, when the tenor's role in the 1930 film *Song O' My Heart* was being discussed, some of the Fox Studio writers suggested a leading romantic role for him. McCormack would have none of it. "I had to do too much lovemaking for too many years in opera," he announced, and for once the reluctant Romeo had his way.

If McCormack had any regrets in leaving opera his phenomenal concert tour of Middle Europe in the spring of 1923 was not only consolation, but confirmation that the recital stage was his true *métier*. During the singer's tour, Denis McSweeney wrote to Lily McCormack that "the whole business seems like a dream," McCormack was enjoying unprecedented success, and "the ovation...in Berlin was simply colossal. I don't think I have ever seen our tenor so deeply touched."[6] The Berlin concert McSweeney referred to took place in April, and when the Paris *New York Herald* reported that the scene at McCormack's second Berlin Recital on May 2 "resembled a football rush," Paris was prepared to be as enthusiastic as ever when McCormack returned there for a charity concert on May 8, followed by another appearance at the Théâtre des Champs-Elysées ten years later. McCormack's last Paris recital would come the following year in a Beethoven Festival organized by Walter Damrosch. McCormack's contribution to the series, his singing of the recitative and aria from *Christ on the Mount of Olives* and the Beethoven song "Adelaide," on May

20, 1924, shows the tenor at the height of his powers and enjoying the same overflow audience and
critical superlatives he had enjoyed at other concerts
in other capitals.

McCormack must have found this Continental
atmosphere congenial. Most of his American audiences would wait impatiently until the singer had
gone through his formal program; then they would
demand the popular songs and ballads he always
gave as encores. A wry shake of his head or a good-
natured growl of "Shame on you!" would reveal
what he thought of these popular requests but he
always complied, and generously. McCormack's
matchless talent for communicating the meaning of
a song and his ability to reveal to sophisticated and
unsophisticated listeners alike some hidden beauty
in the humblest ballad were two of the more obvious secrets of his success. Equally obvious and
equally important was his sincerity, and he brought
as much depth of feeling to his singing of Bach as
he did to the ballad of the hour. Walter Legge recalls that McCormack had "no illusions about the
musical inferiority of much of his repertoire" but
he also observes that the tenor could sing the "poor
or vapid or sentimental verses so well because he
was in the depths of his being a very truthful man"
who sang all of his repertoire "with all his instinc-

tive sincerity." McCormack the musician knew the best music and could sing much of it supremely well, but he also knew what the many in his audience wanted and he gave it to them without hesitation, but only after—to the pleasure of the few—he had sung his classical repertoire. That his generosity with the many also made him a very wealthy man does not take away from the fact that, from the classical opening to the popular close of every McCormack recital, the singer was always a musician. At times the musician's peculiar situation would amuse the singer. Shortly after his first Berlin concert in 1923, McCormack wrote to his wife that "the first thing handed to me in the artist's room... was a card asking wouldn't I *please* sing 'Mother Machree?' I really laughed picturing to myself the expression on Bruno Walter's face if after Beethoven I had started 'Mother Machree.' " Serious musicians found themselves torn between admiration for the singer's abilities and amazement at some of his repertoire. The singer himself, just as serious a musician, remained amused while he gloried in his own versatility.

In the summer of 1924 McCormack and his advisers decided that the time had come for him to regain his English reputation. London was once more the citadel but this time McCormack was presenting himself as an established artist, fresh from his triumphs on the Continent, not as the immature singer of 1906, hoping that a few Italian engagements would bring him to the attention of the right people at Covent Garden. McCormack's artistic maturity was beyond question but his new political allegiance was not. "Although six years had elapsed since the war," L.A.G. Strong writes, "there was still a considerable amount of feeling against him." As October 5, the announced date of the concert, drew near, tension ran high in London and the singer was threatened with demonstrations and possible violence if he dared to appear. It was at this recital that Walter Legge heard McCormack for the first time, and he admits to being disappointed: "The voice was evidently a bit threadbare at the top and, as it must always have been, whitish in color. The diction was as always extraordinarily almost uniquely clear but the mannerisms...irked me." The critics noticed this loss in the upper register and others pointed to the singer's somewhat diminished volume, but these became minor points in the general enthusiasm for the singer's greater musical intelligence and the fact that, in the ten years since he had been heard in London, the tenor had become a supreme classical artist. McCormack's concert at Queens Hall was not marred by any incident; there

INTRODUCTION

were no demonstrations against him, and the audience welcomed the singer back with genuine enthusiasm. The recital was almost as much of a personal as an artistic triumph.

Grove's *Dictionary* (5th edition) states that, after 1924, McCormack could no longer be taken seriously as a musician, but the contrary is true: during the 1920's and beyond, the singer became even more aware of his musicianship although the people who knew the extent of McCormack's artistry remained a comparatively small group; the few were as few as ever. The critic and Wagnerian scholar Ernest Newman may have been influential in McCormack's decision to record an aria from act two of *Tristan und Isolde,* although the tenor himself had briefly toyed with the notion that he was Wagnerian material. He recorded an unorthodox but successful "Prize Song" in 1916, and in the Florence French *Musical Leader* interview of the following year he announced that the part of Tristan "might tempt him," but "his one great ambition" was "to sing the part of Walther in *Die Meistersinger.*" Fortunately, McCormack was content to leave such roles to tenors of the Melchior variety, but his interest in German music did lead him to some significant achievements in lieder. McCormack began to study German songs during the war years in America, and he wisely approached Schumann, Brahms, and Wolf by way of translation; in the early 1920's he felt sufficiently fluent in German to sing lieder in the original and by 1923 his confidence was such that he was presenting some rare Schubert songs in German to Berlin audiences. McCormack the lieder singer was never fully secure in German, however, and his coming so late to the language prevented him from mastering the pronunciation (the umlaut gave him particular trouble). His lieder was never fully accepted by native speakers of German, although his musicianly approach to the form was widely admired and cherished by the specialists. Shortly after Walter Legge founded the Hugo Wolf Society in the summer of 1931, he arranged for McCormack to record two songs for the group. The result was the preservation of the singer's finest achievement in lieder and perhaps his finest recording: his inspired interpretation of Wolf's "Ganymed." During the late 1920's and into the following decade the bringing together of voice and musicianship became increasingly difficult for McCormack. The 1932 "Ganymed" had caught him in good voice, and his recording of the recitative and aria from *Christ on the Mount of Olives* made two years earlier is remarkably beautiful, both in tone and in the precision of his attack, while the

manner in which he sustains the vocal line is a revelation. But after 1924 performances such as these
were exceptions to the rule; McCormack's muscian-
ship grew, but his voice changed dramatically and
the youthful freedom, that extraordinary flexibility
which at times astonished the tenor himself during
his vocal prime, were gone.

During the late 1920's and until his retirement
in 1938, McCormack's career was chiefly in England
and the United States but after 1929 the singer's
American popularity began to decline. The stock
market crash led to a sharp drop in record sales and
the tenor's only starring film, *Song O' My Heart*,
was a box-office failure the following year. The
signs of his loss of popularity were becoming evident, and when after his retirement in 1938 his last
accompanist, Gerald Moore, asked him why he had
retired from the concert platform in America, the
singer answered without hesitation: "Because I lost
my public." Ironically, the public he had lost for
ten years and had won back only with some difficulty were the most loyal to him; the British could
hardly believe the announcement that November 27,
1938 at London's Albert Hall would see McCormack's last recital. It was indeed his farewell, and as
the London *Times* observed the following day, the
singer "carried his great audience with him unfail-

INTRODUCTION

ingly through a programme of quiet, elegiac songs...
an anthology of 'songs of farewell'." Officially the
singer had retired, but he continued to record for
His Master's Voice and when the war began he went
on tour for the British Red Cross. More recording
activity and several broadcasts for the BBC followed, but at the end of 1942 the voice gave out.
McCormack made his last home in Dublin, where he
died on September 16, 1945.

* * * * *

We shall never know what the great singers of
the distant past were like; their voices have come
down to us only in written descriptions, and we
must depend on a Hogarth or a Chorley for our im-
pressions of a Malibran or a Mario. Even those singers of the late Victorian era who lived to see the
invention of the phonograph and became convinced
of its value often regretted their longevity when
they heard the results of their efforts to preserve
their voices. By the time Adelina Patti was finally
persuaded to make records her voice was less than a
golden echo, and when Jean de Reszke recorded in
1905 his voice was in such serious decline that the
legendary tenor decided to remain a legend by not
permitting any of the discs to be released.

INTRODUCTION

John McCormack has left us a complete history of his voice, from his first attempts in 1904 before a primitive recording horn which caught little but his youthful effort, to his last records made in 1942 before a microphone which captured every nuance of his vocal deterioration. McCormack's first recording contract of any consequence came just after his return to London from Italy in 1906, and we are justified in concluding that the results of his Italian training were not immediately apparent. Nor is his vocal progress really audible at the time of his Covent Garden début. It is not until 1909 and the final Odeon records that we have the sense of a singer approaching his maturity. His first Victor discs were made in 1910 and they indicate dramatic progress, but 1913 and 1914 show the voice in its prime; in the ten year period from 1914 to 1924 the McCormack tenor is in full bloom, and the combination of youthful flexibility, beauty of tone, diction, and the ability to communicate the essence of a song in an irresistibly and unmistakably heartfelt manner makes McCormack one of the greatest interpreters of song in the history of the phonograph. The McCormack discography is vast. The songs and arias he has left number nearly six hundred, and L.A.G. Strong rightly observes that "none will be able to doubt him, as we doubt the Victorian tenors."

INTRODUCTION

Strong's mention of the race of the nineteenth century tenors is appropriate; McCormack was very conscious of his predecessors and their reputations. During his early days in London, he would ask Sir John Murray Scott about Mario, and the older man would assure him that when Mario and Patti had sung together, the tenor had been as flexible as the soprano. The young McCormack also listened attentively to Lady de Grey as she gave her minute descriptions of Jean de Reszke in all of his characteristic roles. McCormack's own place in this line of great tenors was given some significant definition when he met Mario's daughter, Mrs. Godfrey Pearse. She paid him the compliment of noticing a similarity between his voice and that of her father. McCormack must have had an even more direct sense of this legendary past when he sang with the great Patti herself at a London concert in 1908. McCormack recognized that the nineteenth century tenor was a rare singing type; just before his Manhattan Opera début in November, 1909 the singer told a *New York Times* reporter that "the coloratura parts written for men in some of the older operas show that the singers of the old school were far more proficient than those of today. There are some tenor parts which I believe cannot be sung today the way they ought to be sung." McCormack

INTRODUCTION

undoubtedly believed this, but he also believed that his talents and training made him a part of this great tradition and he did not hesitate to sing some of the opera roles favored by the great *bel canto* tenors of the last century, and even items taken directly from the soprano repertoire, in addition to some of the opera roles favored by the great *bel canto* tenors of the last century. No other tenor—and few sopranos—have brought such a chaste, unbroken line to Handel's "O, Sleep! Why Dost Thou Leave Me?" McCormack's approach to the aria is pure *bel canto* and his trill—a genuine one, not merely the usual pronounced vibrato—shows how completely he could lavish appropriate stylistic graces on already demanding material. Critics frequently pointed out McCormack's ability in this area, and after a November, 1923 Youngstown concert one reviewer noted that when the tenor sang two Handel arias, "he executed the roulades with the skill of an expert coloratura soprano." McCormack's recordings of Handel's "Come, My Beloved," and Lotti's "Pur Dicesti" are also evidence of the tenor's brilliant virtuosity with classical material.

McCormack's awareness of vocal legends did not lead him to neglect living models, and no less a connoisseur of singing than James Joyce was able to recognize one of these influences. After hearing his fellow countryman sing in Paris in December, 1920, Joyce wrote him a letter of congratulations and noted that, "no Italian lyrical tenor that I know (Bonci possibly excepted) could do such a feat of breathing and phrasing to say nothing of the beauty of tone..."[7] Since Joyce was commenting on McCormack's singing of "Il Mio Tesoro" from *Don Giovanni,* this was high praise indeed. Allesandro Bonci was one of McCormack's major models, and Fernando De Lucia was another. The young singer first heard De Lucia in 1905 and remained a great admirer of the older *bel canto* stylist. McCormack would never reach De Lucia's level of acting, but he could and did adapt the Italian's *legato* and smooth, polished vocal line. During his early years McCormack's admiration for his Italian models—they included Caruso, as well as Bonci and De Lucia—was hardly selective, and at that point he evidently hoped to make up in enthusiasm what he still lacked in originality. L.A.G. Strong describes the singer listening to his own recording of Tosti's "Ideale": " 'Ah,' he exclaimed after one note, 'imitation Caruso'; in another place, 'Vulgar! imitation De Lucia!' Then, when the young tenor slurred from one note to another, 'Ah, God, Man—make up your mind!' "

INTRODUCTION

It did not take McCormack long to evolve his individual approach to song; we can hear the beginnings of his mature style even in some of the early Odeons. No number of critics or connoisseurs, however, looking for historical predecessors or stylistic influences, could explain the utterly unique hold McCormack had over his audiences. The singer gained their attention with his beautiful voice and extraordinary diction, and he maintained it by singing what his listeners wanted. McCormack's recording output reflects all of this. Popular songs and ballads dominate the McCormack discography, much to the exclusion of opera, oratorio, and art song. Beethoven, for example, is represented only by the recording from *Christ on the Mount of Olives,* a performance only recently released; we have no examples of the reputedly brilliant oratorio singing of his vocal prime, although his excellent 1917 recording of "Champs Paternals" from Méhul's *Joseph* does give us a valuable clue as to the oratorio style of his youth. The tenor recorded no Bach until 1941 when little besides vocal style was left to be appreciated; and even his operatic records are hardly representative of his work in that area. We do have the tenor's definitive "Il Mio Tesoro" but, incredibly, there is no recording of any other Mozart aria; there are some exquisite duets with

INTRODUCTION

Lucrezia Bori, and a few rather poor ensemble pieces with Melba, but no duets with Tetrazzini and no recordings at all of McCormack singing from his roles in *La Sonnambula* or *The Tales of Hoffman*.

The singer's reputation as a lieder singer also suffers from this lack of documentation. If McCormack had recorded only Wolf's "Ganymed" (or only "Il Mio Tesoro" for that matter) he would be assured of a place in vocal history, but in the area of lieder, the singer did not try to leave a truly representative sampling of what he could do with German song. There are only two Schumann songs, and they remained unreleased; the singer's famous interpretation of Schubert's "Der Jungling an der Quelle" has suffered the same fate, and one of his most praised efforts, Beethoven's "Adelaide," was apparently never recorded.

We have enough of McCormack's repertoire on record to realize that he was one of the supreme Handel stylists of his time, and we have the evidence that he was the best Don Ottavio of his generation and the perfect Mozart singer for any era. We know that his study of Wolf and the other German songwriters led to some wonderful efforts, and there is some evidence that indicates that he was indeed very good in oratorio. But it was in song, English song, the songs of his native Ireland, that

INTRODUCTION

McCormack was without peer. No one, high brow or low, could resist the expression and near pathos McCormack infused into "The Snowy Breasted Pearl" or the note of Celtic sadness he achieved in "My Lagan Love." His other accomplishments notwithstanding, McCormack was known throughout his career as a singer of Irish songs. From the stirring "Avenging and Bright" of the early Odeon days, to the more quietly patriotic "She Is Far From the Land" to the elegiac "She Moved Through the Fair" of his last recording sessions, we can trace the evolution of a sensibility that was at once national and personal and that touched everyone in McCormack's audiences as a note that revealed at once the essence of the singer and the heart of the song.

McCormack's position as one of the great tenors of this century is beyond dispute, but the manner in which the singer has left us the evidence of his greatness is still the subject of debate. In the process of enriching himself by making recordings of the popular ballads of his day, the singer cheated posterity. His musicianly approach to these ballads delights us almost as much as it delighted his original audiences, but we do not have the advantage of hearing the next group of songs on a McCormack program, or the promise of the concerts he would be sure to give the following season. John McCormack was never guilty of a lapse in taste; whatever he sang was enriched by his musicianship, but we can only regret some of the songs and ballads he chose to enrich. We would much prefer more Mozart and Handel, but economics largely determined what would emerge from the recording studios of Victor and His Master's Voice. As Walter Legge observes, McCormack "of his own volition and his desire for material success...sold a great part of his artistic inheritance [for all the] paraphernalia of evident success." But let us also allow Walter Legge the last word, a fitting tribute for this memorable Irishman: "he was a truthful man with a great heart."

JOHN SCARRY

NOTES TO THE INTRODUCTION

1. L.A.G. Strong, *John McCormack, The Story of a Singer* (London and New York, 1941).

2. For a complete listing of McCormack's recordings, see L.F. MacDermott Roe, *The John McCormack Discography* (London, 1972).

3. John Hetherington, *Melba* (London, 1967), p. 168.

4. Charles L. Wagner, *Seeing Stars* (New York, 1940), p. 159. This and subsequent quotations from Charles Wagner's memoirs are to be found in Part Two, chapter IV of the book, "Cashing High Notes into Bank Notes" (pp. 128-177).

5. Here I would express my deep appreciation to Mr. Walter Legge for sharing his recollections and opinions of John McCormack with me; much of this introduction would not have been possible as it stands without the information he so kindly supplied. Mr. Legge was a close friend of John McCormack, and supervised the singer's recordings from 1931 to 1942.

6. Lily McCormack, *I Hear You Calling Me* (Milwaukee, 1949), quoted on p. 129.

7. Richard Ellmann, ed., *Letter of James Joyce* (New York, 1966), III:32.

ADDENDA & CORRIGENDA

Page 16, lines 19-20: *For* I was entrusted when I was three and a half *read* nearly five years of age

Page 68, lines 13-14: *after* "the verdict...was mine" *read* A third piece, the singing of a test piece at sight, was required of all Feis participants.

Page 69, line 11: *For* May 14, 1903 *read* May 18, 1903

Page 117, line 20: *For* Fernindo De Lucia *read* Fernando De Lucia

Page 132, lines 25-26: *For* December of Nineteen Five *read* January 13, 1906

Page 144, line 2: *For* July second, Nineteen Six *read* July 20, 1906

Page 200, lines 21-22: *For* The Duke in "Rigoletto," *read* Don Ottavio in *DonGiovanni,*

Page 202, line 6: *For* 'Don Giovanni' *read* *Rigoletto*

Page 280, lines 16-17: *For* The Boston Theatre was too small for the audience that tried to get in; *read* The *Boston Herald* of March 30, 1910 reported that the seats of the theatre were only "nearly" filled.

Page 290, line 20: *After* "We gave 'Natoma' that season" *read* The first performance of Victor Herbert's *Natoma* was given at the Metropolitan Opera House in Philadelphia on February 23, 1911.

Page 408, line 1: *For* Franch *read* Franck

CONTENTS

CONTENTS

ILLUSTRATIONS

JOHN McCORMACK
His Own Life Story

CHAPTER I

THE BEGINNING YEARS

Faith, which burned in the heart of him, was the force that guided him on. It is unlikely, during those early Athlone days, that he was aware of his ultimate destiny or suspected how necessary he should one time become to the people of many lands. If he had known I doubt if he would have swerved from his course or exulted in what lay before.

It wouldn't have been his way—the way of John McCormack, who is what he is because of that quality which sets one man apart from others and makes him the exception.

His intimates understand this. When his audiences have pondered they, too, will understand. For the very quality I mention is what

1

they get when he sings to them—and creates that bond between.

Achievement seems to have been the actuating impulse behind the endeavors of the man. To do well a task to which he set himself appears to have been the thing he cared for most. Whatever accompanying rewards there were never concerned him at all—until at length he stepped back from the task to say mentally to himself: "It's the best I could honestly do."

McCormack does not sing, merely, because it is his profession to do so. Medicine, the law or any of the other learned professions might easily have been made his calling. His was the mind for any of these, and his education led straight to where he could have proceeded into whichever one his inclinations chose.

But when his college career closed it was the interpretative soul of the man that whispered a gentle wish to be tended. And because he had in him the breadth of simplicity John McCormack listened.

He began to sing, he sings to-day—and will go on singing until he dies—for just one reason alone: God meant that he should sing! He was born with the voice, with talent supreme;

and yet the seeming intervention of circumstance was all that diverted McCormack from the wrong course to the right.

Some provocative soul, with good intentions but an opaque mind, may suggest that if John had presented himself as he had planned for a certain Civil Service examination in Dublin he would have passed into governmental activities and out of music.

But did he forget? Or was his apparent idling hour on the Liffey's banks a response of the artist nature to a predestined call?

The hundreds of thousands who comprise the McCormack phalanxes will decide unerringly for themselves, because they have got the messages his interpretations revealed.

And that is the secret of it all, the why and wherefore of his being as a singer: which has made him a lyric star who puts truth and simplicity above all else, who feels with the heart, who sees with the mind and binds the two into one.

It is some years since this impression grew into a conviction and thus has become an accepted fact in our daily lives. But now that he has made himself an institution the public of every country wherein his voice is heard regards him as part of its own. And so it is appropriate to write of those things concerning him which these publics have the right to know—and to record faithfully the story John McCormack himself tells.

It is a fascinating story, too, as subsequent pages will show—a tale of an artist's rise to fame in a space of time so short as to savor of the Arabian Nights. For no other such individual meteoric ascendancy may be found in music's history. The probability is that none other will recur.

It is this amazing circumstance that gives pertinence to this volume. McCormack himself was opposed to its preparation and publication. When the matter was broached, two years ago, he strenuously objected. "I'm too young a man," he declared, "to be written about. The printing of the life and career of one barely past thirty whose professional efforts lie within a decade might impress people as premature."

That attitude is typical of McCormack. But his counselors, from their points of vantage, discerned what the tenor could not see. He has always been diffident; he still is. And nothing so offends his sense of consistency as a word or deed out of time and place.

His persuasion brought reluctant yielding, a final concession, I am moved to think, that the public to which he feels he belongs had to be considered. So the decision was made, and with an unassuming charm demanding emphasis at this point in the book, in order that those who read on may catch and hold to another strand of a sensitive nature which, in the face of surmounting success, continues upstanding and unspoiled.

It was a summer's day, with the sun shining, when we began. McCormack sat on the veranda of Rocklea, his Noroton, Connecticut, villa, gazing upon the waters of Long Island Sound. He had sat that way for some minutes; in a suit of tennis flannels, his stalwart body relaxed in an armchair. I waited for his opening words.

"What a debt a man owes his mother and father!" he said. "We never know, when we are young. It is only when time has passed, and the world gives us one thing after another, that their tending is felt. For what I have been able to accomplish I am obligated to many; very deeply to a generous few. But every year which

5

drops behind leaves me with a fuller consciousness of that unpayable debt to father and
mother."

He paused and lowered his chin upon one
tanned hand. He continued gazing over the
hundred-yards' stretch of lawn upon the waters
of the Sound. Yet I do not think he saw them
dancing under the sun's rays, which seemingly
turned them into bits of silver. He was in his
old home again; three thousand miles eastward,
in the historic Irish village of Athlone.

He sat in that contemplative attitude for half
a minute. "That's one of the great things,"
he announced.

I missed his drift, and told him so.

"Having made enough of myself," he explained, "to be a credit to my parents."

I acquiesced, in silence, with a nod.

"And," he added with a gratified smile, "being able to see they have some of the comforts
they deserved. I've been singularly blessed,
perhaps overmuch; but"—and here his voice
slipped a tremulous note—"no one thing has
filled the heart of me as making my mother and
father happy."

He said no more, after those words, for a long

time. He just sat there like the big and world-loving boy he is, sunk in the joy of having brought contentment to those who gave him life and care.

Those of you who thrill under the spell of the golden tone he spins and confess to an occasional glistening eye from the pathos with which he clothes some phrase need wonder no longer. He may be an actor—David Belasco asserts stoutly that he is—but what he puts into his songs is the real thing. No artistic veneer in any one of them. Finish of detail and style, yes, and much of it. Words, too, which you not only can hear distinctly to the last syllable but can also feel the subtlest meaning of—as John McCormack sings them.

For all of which there is reason, in abundance.

I should like, if such impossible thing *were* possible, that every man, woman and child who appreciates this tenor at his true worth could have seen him that June afternoon in Nineteen Hundred Eighteen and been close enough to him to have felt what I was privileged to feel.

"Do you know," he demanded suddenly, bringing himself out of the past with an internal jerk, "I'd not mind risking one of those aeroplane trans-Atlantic flights they're talking about—if we could start off now."

"Straight to the town of Athlone?"

He smiled. "Yes," he answered eagerly. "Right up the River Shannon from Loop Head to Athlone, and on past to Greystones, near Dublin, where my father and mother and sisters now live. Tell me," dropping into one of the roguish moods he delights in, "is there any chance, do you think?"

We laughed; and presently McCormack got back again to the subject.

"I was born on June 14, 1884, our Flag Day here in America. It was a Saturday. I was the fourth of eleven children, which is some indication of the burden my father bore in providing for his family's support.

"We were genuinely poor, as the goods of this world go, but fortunate in those things which create happiness in the home. Ours was a Catholic Christian hearth, and the guidance my brother and sisters and I received proved for our best good.

"Both father and mother held the natural parental anxiety for their children's welfare.

They reared us under close supervision, and strictly; but their companionship was something we always sought. I knew, well enough, the pathway of right and duty. Yet the wisdom of treating it was shown me in a tactful way. I realize that my disciplining was rigid, though it never held a harsh touch.

"Father was stern enough, but I like to feel it to have been more a quality of dignity; a reflection of his serious outlook upon life and the responsibilities which were his. He was superintendent in a department of the Athlone Woolen Mills, and he worked hard, for which he received a salary of 'two-pound-ten' a week. Mother, too, was industrious; always gentle and a just arbiter of such disputes as we youngsters had."

It is an accurate picture McCormack drew of his early environment. The facts are attested by Bishop Michael J. Curley, of the Diocese of St. Augustine (Florida), who was one of John's Athlone playmates and who has continued through succeeding years a chum and valued adviser.

"He was a good boy," said Bishop Curley, "and very young to realize the dignity of the world. His own inherent qualities were of

9

course mainly responsible, but historic Athlone and its ways did their part."

Historic, Athlone truly is; and it has produced three illustrious sons: The Right Reverend Bishop Curley himself, youngest of Catholic bishops in America; T. P. O'Connor, one of Ireland's best loved statesmen, the "Tay Pay" of literary and journalistic fame; and John McCormack; a triumvirate, surely, which instills community pride into the nine thousand people comprising the population of this quaint town by the Shannon River.

"Andrew and Hannah McCormack did not wait long after the birth of their first son to have him baptised," said Bishop Curley; "he was only three days old when Father Donohue sprinkled drops of water on his head and pronounced him 'John Francis.'

"And it was a christening apropos of an occasion—that particular Tuesday being the feast of the nativity of St. John the Baptist. The ceremony took place in St. Mary's Church, where the boy afterward became a devout worshipper."

Bishop Curley related these facts during a lull in the story McCormack had begun to tell on that

June afternoon at Rocklea. The tenor, responding to Mrs. McCormack's summons, was on his way into the house just as Bishop Curley came out on the veranda. I could not well miss the looks these men exchanged as they passed; Bishop Curley's eyes shone as he took a seat.

He, too, seemed retrospective that afternoon. He sat there, looking westward much as McCormack had looked; with shoulders squared and his fine profile silhouetted against the foliage beyond. I was not long in discovering the brilliant mind of which John had told me. Bishop Curley talked easily, as an eloquent man will who is master of his subject.

"Athlone," he said, with a touch of pride in his voice, "was a garrison town. It has been that since the days of the contest between James II and William, Prince of Orange—when these monarchs clashed for no less a reward than the crown of England.

"John will tell you that some of his own bouts at fisticuffs with his playmates took place on identical spots where Irish soldiers of long ago stood shoulder to shoulder in battle for their rights. And like his dead and gone countrymen,

11

whose fortunes swayed first in the proprietorship of their native soil and then to its loss, John tasted both victory and defeat.

"I could relate much concerning those early events, and of moments wherein Norman settlers did their full share with the Irish. But out of those troublous times stands one on which Athlone's glory rests—the Fight on the Bridge.

"Its history all Ireland delights in; a proof of national courage and good red blood. King James II held Athlone, but the Prince of Orange's commanding general, the Dutch de Ginckle, challenged for its possession, and battle ensued.

"Colonel Fitzgerald, a junior commanding officer of the defending Irish forces, fought well, but he was outnumbered. And at last he made his stand, where General St. Ruth had ordered, at Athlone Bridge. A dragoon sergeant, and six of his men who volunteered, grasped axes and faced the musketry fire of the foe in an effort to smash an opening in the bridge that would check the invaders; but bullets sent them to an heroic death. Six more men volunteered to complete what had been begun, and four of this little band were leveled by de Ginckle's soldiers. Yet there was triumph for the two who lived—the bridge had been cut, the planking flung into the river and the enemy was stopped.

"A premature celebration, permitted that evening by General St. Ruth, proved disastrous, for de Ginckle renewed his assault upon his unsuspecting adversary, crossed the river and took the town. But the Fight at the Bridge still lives and will, always. It was put into verse by Aubrey de Vere, and John McCormack has recited his poem in the Marist Brothers' school, at Athlone; the lines are these:"

Does any man dream that a Gael can fear?
  Of a thousand deeds let him learn but one!
The Shannon swept onward, broad and clear,
  Between the leaguers and worn Athlone.

"Break down the bridge!" Six warriors rushed
  Through the storm of shot and the storm of shell,
With late, but certain, victory flushed
  The grim Dutch gunners eyed them well.

They wrenched at the planks 'mid a hail of fire;
  They fell in death, their work half done;
The bridge stood fast; and nigh and nigher
  The foe swarmed darkly, densely on.

"O, who for Erin will strike a stroke?
  Who hurl yon planks where the waters roar?"

Six warriors forth from their comrades broke,
  And flung them upon that bridge once more.

Again at the rocking planks they dashed,
  And four dropped dead and two remained;
The huge beams groaned, and the arch down-
    crashed—
  Two stalwart swimmers the margin gained.

St. Ruth in his stirrup stood up and cried,
  "I have seen no deed like that in France:
With a toss of his head Sarsfield replied,
  "They had luck, the dogs! 'Twas a merry
    chance!"

O, many a year upon Shannon's side
  They sang upon moor and they sang upon heath
Of the twain that breasted that raging tide
  'Mid the ten that had shaken hands with Death!"

Bishop Curley told, also, of the romance that
steeps Athlone, of other traditions than those of
clash and strife and of the learning in which it
abounds. It was in such an atmosphere that
John McCormack thrived, where man's fibre and
his mind count for most.

CHAPTER II

EARLY SCHOOL DAYS

"I suppose Bishop Curley has been telling every secret of my past," announced McCormack, as he came out of the house and over to where we sat on the veranda. He looked down at us, a twinkle lurking in the corners of his eyes, and put an arm on the shoulder of his old-time comrade. "Run on into the house, now, like the good man you are; there's a little lady waiting, and her name's Mrs. McCormack."

Bishop Curley smiled and got up. The tenor watched him until he passed through the doorway from his sight. Then he turned to me. "A great man," murmured John, "and—friend."

He dropped into the chair he had left and extended his legs straight before him. "Where did we leave off?" he queried.

"Well, you were about to undertake a hazardous aerial cruise; but Bishop Curley turned back your life's history a few pages. Suppose you

15

recount some of those experiences which began at school."

"Ah," observed McCormack, "prying into the extent of my education?"

"The early part, first, if you don't mind."

"Of course not," he conceded, drifting quickly with innate courtesy from his humorous turn to the serious. "I was a lucky lad, though I didn't grasp it all at once. Most boys don't. Still, I think I was not overlong in making the discovery. There was the preliminary home training, painstakingly given; then the day of my advent in school. And in this I was more fortunate than the vast majority.

"You have heard of the Marist Brothers. They were skilled educators—sons of the saintly 'Champagnat'—whose influence upon the community of Athlone none can overestimate. To their care I was entrusted when I was three and a half, and with them I remained until the age of twelve."

In that portion of his story, however, McCormack did not particularize as to certain essentials which his public should know. But Bishop Curley informed me; explaining how exceptional a mind the then youthful John disclosed, the talents he evidenced at many a turn, and the intellectual advancement gained when his tenth birthday anniversary arrived.

"He was passed at that time into the Intermediate school," said the Bishop, "and became absorbed in his studies. He could not have been otherwise, for entering upon the competitive sphere of Irish examinations he became, at twelve, a Burser. At thirteen he gained the coveted title of Exhibitioner, which carried with it college scholarship rights and a cash prize of twenty pounds; that, I can assure you, is an honor.

"This was an introspective period in John's life. Boy that he was, nothing appeared comparable in interest to that contained in the classic teachings he received. Unconsciously, he was establishing an intellectual foundation for the future which he little suspected.

"But there were dream days, and many of their hours John spent strolling and singing through grass-waving meadows along the Shannon's banks. He was a normal lad, who loved a game with his companions, and while many may not have suspected his natural gifts and brilliance there were those who did know, and who watched admiringly his progress. For he knew very little outside the Catholic church, his school and humble living."

I brought to McCormack's attention some of these essentials which, in his narrative, he had omitted. "Bishop Curley does not exaggerate, I take it."

"Well," said John hesitatingly, "I would not like to contradict the Bishop, but—does it occur to you that he might be prejudiced?"

It was the McCormack way, again; another instance of his inclination to slip over matters which put him in a favorable light and which he prefers to let others relate.

"I admit I liked to study," he confessed, pushing on in an amusing effort to escape the issue introduced. "And I liked, then as now, to play. You know the adage about the effect too much work had on Jack, and Jack's my name—as you know.

"I had no objections to a fling, for I was healthy enough and fond of anything athletic. I enjoyed, also, those pranks towards which boys, the world over, seem by nature to drift. I'd have been a queer lad if I had held no such inclinations. But there wasn't any meanness in me. I tried to be above-board in what I did."

People generally will no doubt think more of McCormack in knowing that he was no different, in most ways, from other humans. No analysis will yield any different conclusion. Yet his capricious moments did not appreciably expand until he entered college—at the ripe age of twelve. Even then he preserved for some time the serious mien which had become habitual and was ingrained as part of him.

His entrance into the Diocesan College of the Immaculate Conception of Summerhill, at Sligo, on October 15, 1896, was more or less an event. For he had won a free place by competitive examination and was starting upon a phase of his youth in which a notable personality, Bishop Clancy, was to exert upon him a lasting effect.

Up to this point no word of his voice or singing had come from the tenor's lips. I purposely avoided any suggestion. To let him relate his story, in his own way, was my desire—for spontaneity's sake. Small need to fear that his logical reasoning would make a slip in the sequence. He would reach the beginnings of his singing impulses, I figured, in due time; and my assumption proved not at fault.

From the roadway, back of us, came to our ears the musical sound of an automobile warning. It was one of those chiming affairs, made of tubes of brass. McCormack lifted his head to glance toward the strip of road.

" 'Tis a pleasant invitation, those chimes make, to get to somewhere out of the way. But perhaps the machine has a soft heart,—who knows? I remember my own heart was soft enough—the day I first sang before a crowd." He was getting to it.

"When was that?"

"Twenty-five years ago; I was nine and a slip of a lad and shy. It was in the Marist Brothers' school, on a feast day, when Dr. Woodlock, Bishop of Clonmacnoise, was the guest of honor. I'll not forget the sensation at hearing the words which Brother Hugh whispered in my ear. 'We want you to sing, John, for Bishop Woodlock.' With that the good man lifted me upon a table, and left me looking at the gathering.

"Like many another Irish boy I had sung: in my own room at home, or a snatch of some ballad as I walked outdoors. But never had I sung

20

seriously before what may be described an audience. Different persons had told me I had a
nice voice, which warmed me because I love
to sing.

"But there's a difference between singing for
one's self and singing to others, who may be
more or less critical—according to the mood and
capacity. Not that I expected to be severely
judged on that occasion, either. I daresay it
was no more than a natural feeling almost any lad
would have felt; a human sensation which comes
when one essays for the first time a task on
which judgment must pass. And the presence
of Dr. Woodlock was most impressive.

"A great deal flashed through my childish
mind as I was lifted to that table. As I stood
facing my auditors—the Bishop, schoolmates and
teachers—I felt queer around my middle. No
absolute fear, mind you; just a sudden consciousness that I wanted to do well—and wondering if I would."

He broke off, there, allowing himself a
reminiscent smile. He must have sung that
song, silently and to himself, quite through from
beginning to end, for it was a matter of minutes
before he again spoke.

" 'Shades of Evening Close Not O'er Us,' said McCormack softly,—"that was the song in which are the words, 'Absence makes the heart grow fonder.' Every one kept very still and attentive. I'd like to have a record made of that song, as I sang it that day—just for Mrs. McCormack and the kiddies and myself."

I sat studying him as his thoughts drifted, again, to that spot in the Marist Brothers' school. Presently John came out of his mental journeying.

"I think they must have liked it," he buoyantly announced, with a complete change of manner. "They seemed to." And I presume McCormack was right.

"I had no extensive repertoire," he informed me, "but what I knew I knew. And the singing spirit, I guess, must have been there. Like the man born to be hanged, I possibly was intended to sing."

There came, then, an interruption. John didn't seem to mind. He appeared rather to welcome it—in the form of a girl of nine, lithe and jubilant and affectionately inclined. And straightway Gwendolyn McCormack danced over to her father and mussed his hair in most familiar fashion.

In the case of Gwenny, photographs do not serve. They miss, for one thing, the spirit of Irish beauty which is hers and which, for full appreciation, must be seen in the flesh. The glint of her hair, too, is something for actual sight. An optimistic lass, with bubbling nature, a sturdy little body and unspoiled ways.

And for some reason—perhaps because she is his daughter—John appeared fond of Gwenny. I asked him why—and he grinned and replied: "Ask *her*."

But before I could this energetic miss was off and away and out of sight.

We followed as far as the edge of the veranda, and walked together across the lawn to the beach. The tenor became more concerned, at that moment, with nature. He cast about for wide, flat stones and finding them flung them zipping over the water's surface, in that process known to the youthful contingent as "skipping."

"How many can you do?" I wanted to know.

"I did eleven—once."

"El-e-ev-en?"

"Well, what's a matter of a few skips . . . between friends?"

"Oh, yes! What you might term skipping the count rather than counting the skips."

"Here, now," objected John, "you're not to put that in the book. *I'll* say all the clever things."

In the evening we resumed.

"It was a trim little stone house, where we lived," said McCormack,—"only six rooms, with a slate roof. But comfortable within, and very near St. Mary's Church. When the family was complete there were thirteen of us—eleven children: Mary Ann, who died as an infant; Peter, who also passed away when he was a baby; Isabella, who lived until she was sixteen; Jane, now married and living in England; John (that's myself); Mary Ann, whom mother and father cannot allow out of their sight without being unhappy; Andrew, a fine lad, who made this truly wonderful request of me on his death-bed, 'Put your head against mine, so it will rest against something hard, like the Lord's did, when he died'; Thomas, who died very young; James, now a wireless operator in the British Navy; Agnes, at present with my father and mother and waiting to be called to France, as a nurse, and Florence, who likewise is at the parental home in Greystones.

"Father was a true Irishman; he loved music. I well remember seeing him at the piano, picking out on the black keys with one finger 'The Wearin' of the Green.' So what piping I did, by way of singing at five and thereafter, he never minded. Nor mother."

"County Westmeath tunes, eh?"

McCormack laughed at this. "Yes, and tunes from other parts of Ireland, sung in those days in Westmeath; that's where the McCormack homestead stood."

"Not in Roscommon?"

John shook his head. "I'm aware of the discussions as to that, but we were on the Westmeath side of the Shannon whose swirling centre was the dividing line between the counties. No, I was born in Westmeath, and I should know —I was right there.

"Michael Curley—he's the eminent Bishop Curley now—was one of my earliest playmates. Older than I by four years and, bless him, a good influence, even then. He used to wait around for me at school when father first took me there, on his shoulders.

"Time brought us continually closer. We had much in common. He was an example in studiousness and character; a safe leader to follow. The Bishop—the Michael of those other times—always had a cheering word for my voice and singing.

" 'Sing on, John,' he would say, and thus encouraged I obeyed.

"The songs I knew then were good songs, though few. 'Believe me, if all those endearing young charms' was one. My mother taught it to me, and though I sing it to this day I have never found it necessary to change so much as a breath-mark in it. 'Annie Laurie' was another of my youthful songs; so was 'The Irishman' and yet another 'Jessie, the Flower of Dunblane,' which I shall some day put on my concert programmes.

"But the vocal part of my early schooldays was subordinated to the more serious duty of learning. The desire for knowledge was strong in our community, and those who commanded knowledge commanded, in corresponding degree, the respect of the citizens.

"Athlone, as the Bishop has told you, was a garrison town. Like all of its kind, it had a certain culture—despite the fact that the people were simple in tastes and felt the constructive effects of religion, in which the Catholic faith exerted a most beneficent influence.

"I would not change Athlone, if I could, nor were I living over again those days would I ask to have any altered in the littlest way. The town was kind to me, and though my disciplining was severe, it begets its reward and few suffer from its touch."

CHAPTER III

COLLEGE DAYS

John did not enter upon his college career in the propitious manner that prevails here in America. Andrew McCormack's meagre income, and the manifold needs for it, left only a few pounds a year to be sent the boy for his clothing. John's success in winning an allowance as an Exhibitioner provided for his tuition and left a small sum sufficient for other necessary expenses. But from October 15, 1896, to June 23, 1902, which marked his college days, economy was McCormack's watchword. Fortunately the purchasing power of money in Ireland, at that time, was large. " 'Twas lucky for me, else I should have fallen by the intellectual wayside," said John.

No more than a child when he passed his examinations, McCormack was strangely matured in his ways. The youngest of his classmates, he approached his studies with calm assurance,

28

and as he was one of the six Exhibitioners in Summerhill College he attracted the attention of the saintly Bishop Clancy himself. The ruler of the Diocese of Elphin had a scintillating mind, with keen perceptions. And observing this student he discovered more than the intellectual talents he possessed; he probed the soul of the lad, finding there a craving for song.

"Long before I was aware of it, Bishop Clancy was nurturing that part of me," declared John. "He did it with a subtlety such as few men could have known; for all the while my intellectual development progressed, and without consciousness of the process I was growing in two ways.

"Have you ever known homesickness? I experienced it in that fall of 1896. It came and stopped with me like an unwelcome relative who never knows when to go. Bishop Clancy effected my cure; his kindliness and the cheer of his voice and words seemed to start my heart beating anew. He was a stimulant, with an indescribably wonderful way.

"I worked," said the tenor, "very hard. And when homesickness was sufficiently dispelled the world breathed for me a new note. I decided to live a while longer, and to continue preparing for the career my father had his hopes set on for me. Yet there were doubting moments, with each day. The Church had its appeal, but I could not shake that vague questioning as to my fitness to be its servant."

Bishop Curley touched on this phase of churchly matters shortly before he left New York for St. Augustine again, not long after our conversation at Noroton. "There are some students for the priesthood whom it is better to dissuade from that wish," said he, "and others who eliminate themselves in a perfectly normal way. John McCormack was of the latter kind."

We were trudging along a Connecticut road, near Rocklea, during this period of McCormack's life tale. He's a free-swinging pedestrian, with a stride that gets somewhere. Nearing the tiny church which stands halfway between Noroton and Stamford, where the McCormack family worships, John came to a full halt.

"Now then," he began by way of opening his argument, "I ask if I'm not a greater help at pulling the boat than as a pilot? Bishop Clancy thought so, and his vision was clear."

McCormack stood in the roadway, disregarding the heat of mid-day, and gazing long at this particular domicile that helps foster the faith he was born in. "Yes," he said slowly, "I'm a good soldier; better that, don't you think, than a commonplace general?"

John was right. Bishop Clancy thought so; and Bishop Curley agrees, which should have some influence in the matter.

"There have been stories to the effect that my father was heart-broken over my not having entered the priesthood," said McCormack, "and they are wrong. It would have pleased him had I become a priest, that I know; but his ambitions for me were always of a different sort. He anticipated seeing me eventually launched in either medicine or the law. My having been placed in the Marist Brothers' school was a perfectly natural procedure on father's part. It was a wonderful educational institution, and though it offered exceptional facilities to whoever had leanings towards the Church, it was no less admirable for the professions. What is true of the Marist Brothers' school holds equally of Summerhill.

"That first college year at Summerhill was not easy," confessed the tenor. We were walking

31

again, McCormack dripping with perspiration and carrying his cap in his hand. "The next year came less hard—and the third—when I was fourteen—found my outlook broader.

"Bishop Clancy was responsible. The premier preacher in the entire Irish hierarchy, he was the most human man imaginable, with sympathies and an understanding for his fellow creatures which helped in making him the force he was. We were gradually becoming friends, and his friendship was a thing to cherish. I had become interested in the college life and in the whirl of intellectual pursuit. It was discipline, and it kept one's head up and let him look his neighbor in the eye.

"I won't bore you with the nature and extent of my studies except to state that they included those subjects incorporated in the legitimate classic course. They were sufficient, you may believe, and the lessons had to be well learned. Early to rise and early to bed—you remember that phrase? I reverse the usual order of the words, because it seemed to me that I was for ever getting up in my sleep. I think an Irishman thought of that saying and that Summerhill tried to stretch its usefulness.

"At any rate, we took time in that college by the forelock and were disinclined to let go. We relaxed, of course, and had our games and pleasures. Football—Association style—was popular, and I well recall that at one period of my college days I was more interested in making the team than in anything else. But handball was my forte and I gave it many spare hours."

"You organized a glee club, didn't you?"

"Never," answered McCormack. "Such a thing never existed at Summerhill during my time. It was a pity, too, because there was more than enough good natural musical material to be had. But no consideration was given music, nor is any given throughout Ireland to the youth of that country. I hope some day to see conditions changed, because there are so many fine voices amongst the Irish and they are so musical that with their opportunities the priests in Ireland could do a great musical good.

"Had my father and mother not been musically gifted my own progress would have amounted to nothing. It was their encouragement and their sensible, if non-technical, instruction, which supplied my initial impulse in music. Father

33

had a pure tenor voice and mother a very pleasing soprano.

"To sing was second nature to me by the time I was fourteen. I sang eternally—wherever and whenever I could—even during that period when my voice was changing. I realize that this will invite from experts expressions of surprise. Opinion has it that such a practice is dangerous to the voice, but it never seemed to injure mine. I would be singing, in my boyish soprano, when the tone would 'turn over' and sound a masculine timbre; a sort of 'mixed' tone, as it were. Then the soprano quality would creep back into the voice, and remain until the next moment of physiological disturbance. If I had forced, or sung with muscular constriction, damage no doubt would have been wrought. As events proved, I bridged the critical part of that period of my vocal development; in a few months the voice settled into the beginnings of the tenor it now is.

"I wouldn't describe that third year at college as one in which there was a division of effort, still the call to sing was loud in my ears and I was giving heed. My first paid engagement, by the way, materialized about this time, and this was the way of it.

"Father Hynes, one of the Summerhill instructors whom we boys adored, had arranged to give two concerts. He had the co-operation of citizens in the town of Sligo, and the proceeds were to be given to the temperance cause. I first learned of the project one afternoon, when Father Hynes stopped me on the campus and told me about it. He finished by saying to me, 'How would you like to sing at those concerts, John?' I wasn't certain, for a moment, whether my hearing had not played me a trick, but I was straightway reassured. The world thereupon assumed majestic proportions, with John McCormack conspicuous in their midst. I was to receive, for my services, the impressive sum of four shillings.

"I believe there is a tale to the effect that I stole out of my college quarters and slipped to the concert, and returned unobserved, but that is incorrect. Father Hynes secured for me the necessary permission to be absent on the two nights of the concerts, and I departed from and returned to college quite conventionally. My first appearance, however, carried the great appeal and found me in a state of suppressed excitement. I went to Sligo, sang in the concert, received from Father Hynes one-half of the agreed sum of four shillings and returned to my bed with the heart of me still singing. My mind, of course, was filled with mingled confusions; thoughts zigzagging without arrangement or order or very much definiteness, with but a single exception. And that recurred again and again until it became an obsession.

"External evidences had all contributed to a satisfactory achievement on my part. In the hall I had sung very sincerely each song, and the recognition encouraged me to believe that my honorarium was being earned. There were demands for encores which I was glad enough to grant, and the conclusion found me in a haze of happiness which did not lift until Maggie, the college cook, pushed through those congregated about me to add her congratulations to the rest.

"I saw her coming, her benignant face beaming and one hand outstretched. 'And did you like my singing, Maggie, really?' 'Sure, Johnny, darlin', but what did you want to show off your education for by singing in them furrin languages?' She meant to be kind, dear old Maggie, and yet that question was like a stab in my side. I'd sung nothing save English; English from the start to the close, which Maggie knew well. I laughed it off and my unconscious critic left me with a pat on my shoulder, but her query was a disturbing thorn in my momentary triumph. For if she had not understood my words there must have been others, too, in the audience similarly unenlightened as to the texts.

"This fact I cogitated as I lay between the sheets, and wrestled mentally with the possible consequences if I proved unequal to conquering what must be a defective enunciation. The words of a song are its soul and must be heard if the poet's message is to be comprehended. I had fancied, vainly perhaps, that articulation was an asset in my singing, for a large part of my attention invariably was focused upon this very element when I sang. Something, apparently, was amiss. An unintelligible word or two might be condoned, but to have everything I had essayed to convey to my listeners fall upon Maggie's ears as any possible language foreign to her learning—that was like a slap in the face, and far more humiliating.

"Thus, from a trivial episode, was I projected into a sleepless night. I would doze off, half in the lingering ecstasy of my début, only to waken with a jerk to stare into the darkness with eyes gazing on disaster. Nor could I escape from the reminders of my fault when daybreak came. But the lesson was worth learning, and I set at it —and still am. For never again do I wish such an experience as Maggie gave me. It disturbs one's pride."

We walked for some distance after that, McCormack having gone suddenly into a reflective mood. I forbore to interfere. I gathered that an objective avenue of thought had been opened to him from the incident he had told. But from time to time on that last half mile of our tramp I stole a glance at his face, though vainly, for it was as inscrutable as a mask of clay.

Across the lawn to the house we went, and entered. And there in the living-room a young woman, who had been seated before a desk, turned on hearing our steps and rose.

The pen of a Richard Le Gallienne would be needed to describe this charming lady, who is known to every McCormack "fan" almost as well as the tenor himself. But being only a prosy music critic all I can tell you is that she is very gracious, and lovely, and that one is at once impressed by her fine eyes.

I was nearing the door which leads to the veranda facing the Sound when Mrs. McCormack called to me. "Make yourself at home for a few minutes; it's just time for tea."

And in that phrase—if you analyse its inner meaning—you have Mrs. McCormack. Always thinking of the comfort of others. Not her children only (of whom she confidentially assures one that John is the littlest) but of all who cross the thresholds of her homes, and many who never have been inside them.

She is wife and mother and chum and counsellor, firm in her mildness, with a far-seeing worldly vision and an unselfishness which was sufficiently manifested the day she withdrew from an already established singing career to devote her life to John McCormack's. And should your intimacy with the tenor be such as to make the question no impertinence, and you put that question to him, he would tell you that what he has done professionally he could not have done without the aid of that selfsame little lady who charmed the music public of Great Britain and

39

Ireland under her maiden name of Lily Foley.

She busied herself, after a wifely conference with her husband, to see that her servants served the tea, and as they should.

Afterward, having done my duty by certain potato-cakes which literally melted in my mouth, I strolled off to the tennis courts, where John was industriously smiting the ball out of reach of a visiting neighbor who played well—but not well enough. And there, when the set was finished and the vanquished neighbor on his homeward way, McCormack finished for me the tale of his Summerhill College days.

"That lesson in the necessity of distinct enunciation which Maggie gave me was one I gave more thought to than anything else for the few days following my first appearance in public. Articulation became the subject more engrossing than anything else, and it was a matter of days before my equilibrium was restored sufficiently to allow me to resume, in normal fashion, the course of study and recitation.

"Aloud, and silently to myself, I would pronounce the words of a song—over and over again. It mattered not whether I was in the classroom or out of it; I had an objective and steered towards it with tenacity. My college mates, coming suddenly upon me when I plunged into this practice, were at first startled. From the looks some of them gave me there appeared a doubt as to my sanity; until I at length explained. Instead of laughing, as they might have done, they showed comforting sympathy. Perhaps their attitude may be interpreted as an instance of good wishes, for most of my associates were musical and not unwilling to have me sing to them whenever my fancy chose."

John might have said, had he been the sort to do so, that even as far back as in those times, he was more a hero to his classmates than anything else. He sang, but, also, he played the mouth-organ. He played that limited instrument, Bishop Curley informs me, upon slight provocation and with unremitting frequency. Apparently, too, he acquired a deal of technical facility in various styles of harmonic accompaniment to the tune of the moment. Runs, *arpeggios*, *staccati* and long-drawn and impressively held chords John introduced in his musical efforts upon this instrument; and part of his four shillings, earned from the singing engagement aforementioned, he put into several mouth-organs manufactured in different keys. His collection, it appears, at one time, included two which bore on their metal sides "Key of C," and others similarly branded with G and F.

Leadership in directions other than music was another McCormack tendency at the fifteenth year of his life. He was not only a football and handball expert, but had developed proficiency as a swimmer. And on rare occasions the boys revelled in their aquatic excursions with no less distinctive guest of honor than their beloved Father Hynes.

"We returned from one of these swims," said John, "to find the college president, Dr. Kielty, in a stern mood. He was a fine man, an able educator and a clear-minded executive; but I think he held a mild resentment for our fondness for Father Hynes. We paused before Dr. Kielty when we reached him, a dignified and imposing figure, standing under a tree on the campus. We paused, as I have said, frankly awed by his demeanor which portended something apart from the routine of the day. But his message threw us boys off our youthful balance, and brought a flush to the cheek of Father Hynes.

"In effect, he informed us that on the following day he, Dr. Kielty and no other, would accompany us to the point of departure from the river bank into the water; and having thus relieved his mind he stalked off, a dignified personality, leaving us to stare at one another openmouthed.

"The good doctor went out the following afternoon, to the appointed rendezvous; went there —and waited in vain.   For we boys rebelled at the affront to Father Hynes and remained to ourselves.

"So those college days passed, with interminable happenings in which the serious and sad and comic were intermixed.   And in my fifth and sixth years at college I found myself coming closer and closer to the great Bishop Clancy, whose counsel and encouragement spurred me to those achievements which I contemplate with some pride.

"But I must have borne scant resemblance to a student, for I remember—during one vacation when I was at home—being introduced to a visiting neighbour who greeted me, after introductions, with: 'So this is John Francis, the

Exhibitioner? I've heard he's clever, but he doesn't look it.' "

McCormack overlooked one achievement to his credit while at Summerhill. It might have escaped the telling if Bishop Curley, indefatigable soul, had not confided the facts. "It was final examinations week," said the Bishop, "and John was ill with a sty which rendered seeing not only difficult but painful. The boys sympathized, though they needn't have. For that week John made a record. His mark in Latin, in which 1200 was the highest mark possible, reached 1028; in French he scored 648 points out of a possible 700 and was perfect in algebra with an unblemished score of 600.

"He left behind a record which has never since been equalled. And I am glad, as he is, too, that competing with one hundred and sixty others for one of the twenty available places in the Royal College of Science he emerged number twenty-one. For had he been victorious his career would have been other than it has been, and the work he has done still have remained unaccomplished."

CHAPTER IV

EARLY DUBLIN DAYS

"At eighteen the determination to become a singer was a seed firmly implanted in my mind." McCormack made this declaration on a cloudy morning on the golf course of the Wee Burn Golf Club. "My college days were done, the retirement from endeavors in the direction of the priesthood accepted by my father, and Dublin was beckoning me onwards. Yet there were a few twigs that needed removal from my path. I sensed the trend of coming events, but even to myself admission was not quite complete. The hand of Fate may have been—doubtless was— leading me towards the starting mark whence I should take up that journey. Every obstacle I sought with full sincerity to remove in my struggle for the coveted positions, first of priest, then of Civil Service clerkship. I like to think that I fought as good a fight, and as fair a one, as was in me.

45

"Even the story Bishop Curley tells about my leisurely stroll in Phoenix Park that afternoon when the Dublin examination was taking place has its rejoinder.   In a sense the Bishop is right; he generally is.   I probably could have passed the examination.   But the postal clerkship, had I secured it, would have been mechanically filled. My alternate, if we may call him such, no doubt served the government more efficiently than I would have done."

McCormack teed his golf ball, after these remarks, and sent it down the fairway in a cleanly swung two-hundred-and-fifty-yard drive.   The effort seemed to rid him of some seething element in his system, for he relaxed after the blow and marking the ball with his eyes turned again to me.

"I cannot truthfully say that I studied like a fiend at Skerries Academy, in Dublin.   It was a school of specialization," he explained, "designed to prepare one for just such examinations as the Civil Service board prepared.   My entrance there came as an aftermath to my failure to be one of the twenty who contested for free scholarships in the Royal College of Science.   I really wanted that; but I finished number twenty-

John McCormack wearing the gold medal he won at the Dublin Feis Ceoil on May 18, 1903. A photograph taken in Athlone shortly after his Feis victory.

ANTIENT CONCERT ROOM
EXHIBITION OF IRISH
INDUSTRIES
AND
GRAND IRISH CONCERT,
TO-MORROW (Saturday) EVENING,
At 8 o'clock.

Artistes :—

Miss AGNES TREACY,
Miss OLIVE BARRY,
Madame HALL.
Miss WALKER (Marie Nic Shiubhlaigh).
Mr. J. C. DOYLE,
Mr. JAMES A. JOYCE, and
Mr. J. F. M'CORMACK.

Orchestra conducted by
Miss EILEEN REIDY, A.L.C.M., R.I.A.M.

Prices—3s. 2s. and 1s.

8019

A newspaper announcement (greatly enlarged) of the August 27, 1904 Dublin concert at which the young James Joyce appeared with John McCormack.

one—a single unit below requirements, which shunted me into the scientific discard. That, if you please to believe it, was a touch of Fate's hand. For had I won a place . . .

"I was disappointed. I dislike to lose, in anything. You've possibly noticed that."

I had noticed. John is a good sportsman, and a clean one; but he chafes under defeat. I have seen him grouch when beaten at tennis, and I admire him for it. Because it's a good sign in a man; a sign that he's for ever trying.

"Skerries Academy, because of that College of Science failure of mine, became a place of momentary refuge; and I think my mind found relief from the accusations of that failure in the work which I feverishly sought. But instead of studying, as had been my custom up to that time, I evaded study. My parents had found a place for me to live in the home of a worthy woman, who was charged to see that I went regularly to Skerries Academy. So far as the lady knew I did go there; at least, she saw me leave her house each day, ostensibly bound thither, and I returned at a proper hour. It is fortunate, for her peace of mind, that she did not know that in those hours of absence I was chiefly concerned with anything which had no direct connection with Skerries.   Those first weeks at the academy seemed bleak and dry and forlorn.   Singing, and all thoughts of singing, I put from me resolutely in that subconscious way one will when there is an inner gnawing of self-censure.   It may have been foolish, doubtless it was, but it acted as a mental tonic.   For I began, as time passed, to restore my equilibrium and to renew my interest in what had lain dormant within me during those disturbing weeks.

"Aroused from its siesta, my passion for song seized me more firmly than ever.   One month gave way to another, and all the while I sang and practised distinct enunciation of the texts of those songs which I was learning in a way to make them part of me.   There was no relaxation in the academy schedule; rather an acceleration of my musical nature, which was crystallizing fast.

"My mind is by no means clear upon the facts of that examination day for the second division clerkship.   I waked in a perfectly normal mood and proceeded about the morning's business with no qualm as to the outcome of the approaching competition.   The day was fine, with clear skies and a beaming sun.   The examination was easily within my abilities to pass and I knew it. So there was nothing to prick my concern.   In such a frame of mind I turned to Nature, as was so frequently my way, for those delights she always gave.

"It is quite probable that in this relaxed and imaginative state the balance which preserves that nice adjustment between one's practical and æsthetic sides swung too far to one way.   Unquestionably I drifted away from the one and very near the other.   At luncheon I was abstracted—that much I recall.   Afterward came the desire to walk abroad by myself, which I indulged.

"I concede the danger I was in, but, frankly, I did not sense it.   There was ample time for a walk, and Phoenix Park lay at no considerable distance.   As I had often done before, I gravitated in that direction by force of habit.

"Once within its verdant boundaries, one forgot the rest of the world.   There was peaceful quiet; a solitude that soothed and encouraged. Tree-branches seemed to nod at me, and the windblown grass and the flowers bent in my direction as if conscious of how I felt.   The hum of Dublin was far removed: no hurry of pedestrians dodging the grind of traffic, nor newsboys' cries of their wares nor other sounds of worldly strife of the day. Only a tranquillity of which I continued to drink. No one was near; I began to sing. . . ."

"Then you really forgot?"

We had been walking, all this time, in the direction of that excellent drive of his. McCormack stopped before the little sphere of white and dropped the head of his brassie alongside an inviting lie. He looked up at the question—but past me, into the distance. The barest inclination of his head was his sole assent.

So I respected his mood by moving leisurely off, and to one side, as if to allow him full play in the next stroke. He was almost staring at me as I turned round; and I fancied his eyes held an appreciative look, a mute endorsement of my act which left him free of any explanation he did not care to voice.

A week or so later, however, and with startling unexpectedness, John mentioned the Phoenix Park incident again. Very briefly, 'tis true, but in words. "I became absorbed, that afternoon, and forgot." That was an end to it, and I never referred to the occurrence thereafter.

"Do you believe in suggestions?"

"What sort?" I countered.

"Other people's?"

"For instance?"

"Well," he replied, then, after a long pause—"being told that you should do so-and-so; that the world offers a chance in some particular direction, in the performance of a particular capacity for which you seem to have a special aptitude.

"Without a doubt. Nearly every one is influenced by what the world says and thinks. And no man, or woman, is free from being affected—positively or the reverse—by what friends suggest."

"Same here," agreed John; "it was that way in 1903, in Dublin. After the Dublin postal clerkship fiasco—if we may term it that—I took singing by the hand and gave it a sound shake. It was as if we were pals joining forces with a resolution never to part. The whole circumstance had come about so naturally that I felt no blame. Perhaps it was the feeling that it was all for the best, as it has since proved.

"It was about that time that my friends, one after the other, began proffering advice. They all agreed. I was destined to have a singing career and was a fool not to see it. There was power in these suggestions, a world of it; and I was not insensible to entertaining a fondness for hearing what they said. I was heeding, too, more willingly than I knew; for directly I let myself fall into the ways of their thinking and before winter passed music had me for a life votary.

"One man drove the last spike in my rail of decision—Vincent O'Brien. I said earlier in our talks—if you remember—that I felt deeply obligated to a very few. Well, one of those few is Vincent O'Brien. He was organist of Marlborough Street Cathedral, in Dublin; a splendid musician, a fine man, and a staunch friend. He had vision and appeared, intuitively, to feel that all I needed was study and opportunity to achieve a goal worthy of serious aspirations. It was good to feel, as I often did, that he was right; yet I dared not allow myself to share the hopes, in so positive a manner, which O'Brien consistently held. He never wavered, and his convictions buoyed and steadied me mightily in my doubting moments. I was the tenor in O'Brien's choir, at one hundred and twenty-five dollars a year, and it was this that caused me to ask myself occasionally if my organist-friend was not over-prejudiced.

"The manner of how it all came about is, I conclude, in order. Dr. Dudley Forde did me the service of introducing me to Vincent O'Brien, and many's the time I've breathed for him my everlasting gratitude. The doctor was house surgeon in the Mater Misericordiae Hospital, of Dublin; a lover of singing and considered a judge of it. That I had attracted his favorable notice was a comfort to me, though it was some time afterward that I was to discover how much that was to mean.

"Shortly before Dr. Forde introduced me to Vincent O'Brien I had had a talk with a young Athlone attorney named John Walsh, whose attainments and personal charm made him, at twenty-seven, one of the most influential and best loved men in the city. He was forever doing something for others; an altruist, if ever there was one. It was in December, 1902, soon after my unintentional deviation from the Civil Service examination, that Walsh said to me: 'Mac, why don't you run up to Dublin to see Charles Manners, of the Moody-Manners Opera Company? Your voice ought to fit there like a glove.'

"I explained my inability, through lack of funds, and like a shot he retorted, 'That's easily fixed.' He slipped into my hand the money for the journey, gave me a push and a slap on the back. His words, 'Good luck, Mac,' were the last I ever heard him say. For, before I returned, he was taken ill with typhoid fever and died shortly after I reached Athlone, being *in extremis* when I reached home. It wrung my heart when I learned that, in his last hours, he kept asking for me. 'Is Mac back, yet?' he would repeatedly inquire. 'How did he come out?' Poor boy; perhaps he knows, now, what his friendship did for me. I carried with me, and do to this day, the influence of his staunch faith and comradeship.

"The interview with Charles Manners led to nothing. He was a precise man, on the lookout for a bargain which he concluded lay neither in my throat nor in my soul. I sang to him, then walked into the front of the house for his verdict. He sat curled up in one of the chairs in the theatre, his face pushed into the fingers of his right hand. But his interest was mild. The best he could offer me, he said, was a place in the chorus.

"Although I had not imagined that a contract would result from my Moody-Manners expedition, the rebuff discouraged me. The position he offered was of course the cause. And then, it was the first occasion of such indifferent treatment. I spent the time during the railway ride back to Athlone debating inwardly the extent of my capacities, and speculating upon the exact value of my friends' encouragements. But that faith which I had in myself—a faith I honestly feel to have been something remote from conceit—never ceased its silent endeavors to buoy me. I am not a fighter, in the physical sense. It is only when there is a mental encounter that I seem not to waver or lack the fortitude to meet an issue. Descending from the railway carriage at Athlone station I found this to be my mood. And I hurried to Walsh's home, where they told me the sad news."

The tenor reached for a handkerchief to wipe the moisture from his face, and I wondered, seeing the bit of linen across mouth and nose and eyes, if it were due to the heat—and nothing else.

"Let's see," said McCormack, with assumed gruffness, "I'm playing four here, am I not?"

"Yes."

"Well, watch me hole out." He was twenty feet from the cup, but the ball rolled true as a die to its mark. His partner, from his place at the edge of the green, exclaimed in disgust: "For sheer luck—"

"—And putting skill," reminded McCormack, as imperturbable as if such a feat were a common occurrence.

"—you Irish beat us southerners."

John admitted the superiority and demanded solemnly of me, as scorekeeper, how many up he was. After that incident he played the next two holes in silence; nor did he complain when, attempting an awkward recovery from a lie against the outcropping root of a tree, he split the club, —his pet spoon,—with a stroke that sent it spinning yards away. He didn't thaw into a talkative mood again until we had finished our lemonades—John drank his without sugar—and had left the club-house for the tenor's waiting roadster. With the whirr of the motor, spun into life by the self-starter, he spoke.

"Dr. Forde took me to Vincent O'Brien soon

after that cheerful trip to see Charlie Manners,"
announced John. "O'Brien needed a tenor,
and the doctor had suggested that he hear me.
The experience was a horse of another color.
O'Brien was as positive as Manners was nega-
tive; so much so that he volunteered to have
Edward Martin listen to my voice. Martin, an
Irish playwright of means whose fad was music,
had endowed the Marlborough Street Cathedral
choir, and out of courtesy O'Brien wished to con-
sult him before engaging so important a member
for the organization (which it then needed) as
a tenor.

"Martin came over to the cathedral, and I
sang to him, in the choir room. It was a good-
sized place, but my voice—though smaller than
it is now—was telling in quality. I watched my
critic while I sang for some sign of approval;
but Martin allowed me nothing, from any outward evidence, on which to base a hope. And
when I had finished what do you suppose he
said?"

I said I had no idea.

"He said," replied McCormack, with a laugh,
"that my voice, he feared, was too large for the
choir."

That *did* seem odd. "Then he turned you down?"

"No; O'Brien explained that in the auditorium of the cathedral the voice would not give such an impression. This appeared to satisfy Martin, and he told the organist to go ahead, if he liked, and engage me. I walked out of the cathedral a happy young man. I had a choir position, a salary of one hundred and twenty five dollars a year, and the music road showed clear ahead."

CHAPTER V

He was swimming, just beyond the end of the McCormack pier, with a double over-arm stroke; a smallish figure, like a boy's, from the spot where I stood watching. He turned, presently, to retrace his course, and as he swam nearer I saw he was a boy. He came on, using a narrow kick to his legs that drove him at a considerable speed through the choppy brine. At the ladder he stopped, trod water for a moment, and then ascended leisurely to where I stood.

"Good morning, Cyril; how's the temperature?"

"F-ff-i-i-ne!" announced the scion of the McCormack household, at the same time kicking alternately with right and left legs to dislodge the remaining drops of water from his ears. "Go ahead," he suggested, "and get into your bathing-suit; the water's great."

He appeared to me, as he stood there with a smile on his face, a likely-looking boy. Eleven

59

and very self-contained. And with no trace of affectation, such as might be expected in a youth whose father's celebrity had been thoroughly dinned into his impressionable mind. A clean-limbed youngster, too, rather deep of chest and with a pair of shoulders that will some day rival his father's. I was not sorry, as I stood there looking into his eyes, which returned my gaze with easy frankness, that Cyril has a well-balanced little brain. For he's more than ordinarily good-looking.

John arrived at this juncture, in a particularly jubilant mood.

"Come on, Pop; come on in," said McCormack junior, who leaped then to the rail of the pier, poised there impudently and dove. He cut the water as a knife cuts butter, and went from our sight, leaving behind him on the surface only the tiniest splash.

"The little dare-devil," commented John (with some pride, too). "What did he think, that I'd follow with my clothes on?" But he obeyed Cyril's demand by starting for the house for apparel suitable for the swim he takes each morning. "Come on yourself," he said to me, "and don't take all day."

We passed Mrs. McCormack, Gwenny, and Miss Josephine B. Foley (Mrs. McCormack's charming sister) on their way to the beach. They were clad for bathing, too, and added their suggestions to Cyril's that we lose no time to join them in a forenoon dip. A quarter of an hour later found us in the Sound, an amphibious sextette, and making a great to-do about the matter.

When we had finished and dressed again and were seated on the veranda, McCormack resumed his narrative.

"I feel almost as happy, this morning, as the day I got that Marlborough Street Cathedral job," confided the tenor; and he looked it.

"The good fortune interfered with that night's sleep," he went on, "but I got up unfatigued; excitement has its virtues. I met O'Brien and went with him into executive session. He wanted to know if I read music. I admitted that I could not. 'All right,' he replied, 'come on up to the house, and we'll see how well you can do in a first trial.'

"He propped a piece of music on the piano rack and we began. I estimated the distance between notes, and as my musical instinct was

61

strong I did fairly well. 'Hm,' mused Vincent, 'some lessons wouldn't hurt you any.' He gave me one then—and I continued with him in learning the tonic *sol-fa* system. Up to that moment my father and mother, as I mentioned once before, had been my sole instructors, and their musical knowledge, as you may have guessed, was not extensive. So this advantage which O'Brien laid before me was invaluable; it meant the start of a foundation I have since tried to make secure.

"Within a few weeks I again met Dr. Forde. 'How goes it at the Cathedral?' inquired the good doctor. Then, before I could answer, he said: 'That reminds me, why don't you enter in the Feis Coeil?' This, as you are doubtless aware, is an Irish musical festival in which competitive singing between individual types of voices—sopranos, tenors and so forth—forms the principal interest. The winner in each division receives a gold medal and considerable prestige. I knew that the list of entrants had been completed and so informed the doctor.

" 'That is true,' he admitted, 'but an entry can be made, even after the closing date; it merely requires a fee of ten shillings.' Ten shillings! It might as well have been a hundred. Dr.

Forde saw my look, and interpreting it aright
asked if I hadn't the necessary money. I nodded
my head. 'Don't worry,' he said comfortingly,
'you enter and I will supply the ten shillings.'

"Of course I went at once to Vincent O'Brien.
'There'll be two compositions every tenor will be
obliged to sing,' was the information he gave.
They were Händel's 'Tell Fair Irene,' an aria, by
the way, which I but recently felt I sang well
enough to put on my concert programmes, and
'The Snowy Breasted Pearl.' There wasn't
much time for their preparation. O'Brien intimated as much and directed me to get the music
and bring it to him. 'I'll teach you,' he said.
'But—I have no money with which to pay you.'
'Who asked you to pay me?' he gruffly demanded.
'I said I would teach you; wait till I ask you for
money before you talk about it.' I felt rather
meek at that, but too grateful to venture any expression. I hurried to a music store, got the
songs and Vincent began to coach me.

"He is one of the finest accompanists alive:
a thorough musician, with rare feeling for a composition, a subtle understanding of the singer's
intentions and superlative skill in giving one the
musical and moral support in the interpretation.

John McCormack, a photograph taken perhaps during his first visit to London in 1904.

John McCormack (seated) and his brother James in London, probably taken in 1904.

Edwin Schneider, my present accompanist, is such another.

"O'Brien was very patient in the coaching; and just as thorough. Over and over again he would drill me in a phrase until I was able to approach somewhat nearly to what he sought. I will not say that he was satisfied; but when the task was done he said to me: 'Sing those songs as well at the Feis as you just sang them and you will win.' I felt my breath catch at his prediction—I really did not believe I had more than an outsider's chance."

Mrs. McCormack, Miss Foley and the two children interrupted the story at this point by commanding us to luncheon. And during that, and other meals served in the McCormack household, I marvelled at the tenor's rigidity at denying himself those things of which he is fond—pastries and such, which he contends he is better off, as a singer, without. The duty of eating concluded, John strolled out upon the veranda. He lighted a cigarette and, comfortably ensconced in his favorite chair, he resumed:

"The hall was packed that first Feis afternoon," he said,—"several thousand people, many of whom had come miles to Dublin for that occasion. And every tenor and baritone and soprano and contralto had 'rooters'; but silent rooters, for applause was forbidden. I made my way to a spot in a corner of the hall, not far from the stage. In half an hour the judges called the first of the fourteen tenors who were competing, and the content was on.

"Eight of these tenors sang, and none of them disturbed materially my peace of mind. Three of the remaining five, however, did, one especially. This chap was William Rathborne, a matured singer and very evidently, by the actions of the audience, the favorite. He sang both songs very well, I thought; yet some of his phrases would not have got by Vincent O'Brien if O'Brien had been coaching him. Rathborne finished and stepped down from the platform. As he passed down the aisle toward the dressing-room, which brought him near me, I saw him take his left hand in his right and press it with congratulatory fervor. It may appear to have been a presumptuous act; I thought it such, and was inclined to smile. Also, that act of Rathborne's of shaking hands with himself on his assumed victory struck me as a trifle previous. It made something inside me rebel, and straightway there was born a resolve to teach him a lesson—if I could."

"Put you in a properly scrappy mood, was that it?"

"I daresay. At any rate, all the undesirable part of my long-continued nervousness promptly vanished. And I walked, as my name was called, to the platform and over to the piano where Hamilton Harty sat waiting. Harty, now a distinguished composer, was the official accompanist for the Feis. But when my turn came he was tired. There is a point, however, which demands relating before I tell about how I sang.

"As Rathborne passed me I heard a familiar voice, just back of me, say: 'W-w-w-willie, you r-a-an away with it.' I recognized the speaker to be J. C. Doyle, Dublin's popular baritone, who stuttered. He had heard me sing, and when I caught what he said I quailed. If that were Doyle's belief my chances, probably, were small. Then the baritone spoke again, and turning my head our gazes met. 'What, you here, Mac? Gad, W-w-willie, wait a minute, n-o-ot yet. There's a dark horse who's likely to spoil your afternoon.'

"So you may imagine I walked over to Harty

with some feeling of confidence. Well, we finally began. But Harty, as I intimated, was physically worn out. He wanted to get through, and quickly; and he played the introductory measures of 'Tell Fair Irene' as though he had a train to make. It was a tempo twice as fast as O'Brien had taught me was the correct one; a tempo, likewise, too rapid to permit of good singing, to say nothing of interpreting Händel's music as he intended.

"There was only one thing to do and I did it. I turned around and informed Harty I had learned the aria in a way different from the way he was playing it. 'Please take it just half as fast,' I requested. Instead of objecting he only smiled. He probably thought: 'The poor boy, well, let him have his way.' But I hadn't gone far before Harty settled down and played for me one of the finest accompaniments I have ever sung to. He was a sportsman to the tips of his talented fingers, and he gave me all there was musically in him.

"With my last note there came from the audience a volley of applause; one of those spontaneous demonstrations which one gets intuitively to reflect the feelings of an audience. Perhaps it was the pure quality of my voice, or my youth, or both that prompted it. They forgot for the moment that they were breaking a rule of long standing. At any rate, the applause went on for some moments—nor did the judges interfere.

"You may believe that the incident heartened me; no doubt it had its effect upon the jury, which was one of the reasons for forbidding that very thing. I began, then, 'My Snowy Breasted Pearl,' which I may have sung better than 'Tell Fair Irene.' "

"And the verdict?" I queried.

"The verdict," responded the tenor, "was mine."

He rose, then, and went to meet Bob, his gardener, who was busy on another part of his estate cutting hay. I did not see McCormack for several hours. He came across to the tennis courts, where I sat watching two amateur cracks at play, with the collar of his outing shirt open and evidences of having participated in manual labor.

" 'Tis an easier game, tennis," he declared, "than pitching hay. But my muscles still cry out for exercise, so I'll take on both of you." He did, and beat them.

FIRST MUSIC STUDIES

It was while we were running along the Connecticut shore of Long Island Sound, in McCormack's motor-driven fishing dory, that he proceeded with the story of his life. The sun was low in the west, the sky forbidding with a vault of low-lying clouds. It looked stormy and John put about and headed for Rocklea.

"The gold medal I was awarded as winner of the tenor contest at the Feis decided my future. I determined to abandon all efforts at anything else; so May 14, 1903, may stand as the pivotal date in my career. As the competition was an open one to all residents of the British Isles some reputation attached to the winner in each division. I profited; and another profited, a young soprano, Miss Lily Foley, whom I had never met. Miss Foley had surpassed her rivals with astonishing ease: her lyric voice (one of the smoothest I've ever heard) and breadth of style and finish were used in a way to let none who heard forget. As I listened to her, at the Feis, I thought to myself, 'I'd like to sing with her.' And in the fall of that same year I had my wish.

"Up to then," explained the tenor, "I had never heard an opera. Though I was nineteen my understanding of this form of musical art was

69

nil; I hadn't so much as a bowing acquaintance with anything or anyone operatic, much as I yearned for both. It was in that year, 1903, that I listened to and saw my first opera; it was a performance of 'Cavalleria Rusticana' and 'I Pagliacci,' those two works which usually are presented in what is known as a double-bill. The Moody-Manners Company gave the performance, in Dublin. 'Cavalleria' was the first offering, and my attention centered quite naturally on the tenor. He was an American, Francis Maclennan, and he had a clear, ringing voice, a convincing style and has acquired just fame as a fine Wagnerian exponent. I could scarcely sit still in my excitement and when the curtain dropped on the opera I was trembling.

"I sat through the intermission living over again the performance of Mascagni's opera and only emerged from my ecstatic daze when the overture to 'Pagliacci' began and the baritone came out to sing the prologue. Philip Brozel was the *Canio* in this opera, and I consider him one of the best I have ever heard in the rôle. I left the theatre in some mental confusion, for, though impressed, I was by no means convinced

70

that opera represented the highest form of either art or singing.   Since then I have come to know that opera really is a hybrid—being neither one thing or the other, but a mixture of elements which tend to restrict its freest utterances in music, text, acting and pictorial illusion.   And nowhere is the singer so handicapped as in opera, as I shall show later on.   Nevertheless, on that evening, I envied the two tenors, Maclennan and Brozel, and fell to wondering if I should ever find myself doing what they were doing so well.

"After a summer's vacation, spent with my parents in Athlone, I set about finding work for my voice and such art as I commanded.   Engagements came, and not so many, either, at insignificant sums: ten, fifteen, twenty shillings each.   But my musical equipment grew.   I found in Vincent O'Brien an efficient instructor, and the music we performed in the cathedral was an education in itself.   Palestrina compositions were freely used; others by illustrious composers, also, so that much of the best to be had became necessary for me to learn, under careful guidance.   So my abilities steadily grew.   And as I obtained concert appearances, in other cities and towns besides Dublin, I acquired by degrees further security and was enabled to provide increasing satisfaction to my hearers.

"But my income was small, and the stretching of financial ends to make them meet something of a job. Still, I persisted. My faith endured. And one day I was summoned to appear in a concert which William Ludwig—one of the most distinguished baritones Ireland has produced—was preparing to give.

"I was recovering from a cold the morning I went to rehearsal and was coughing. Ludwig, as bluff in his manner as his heart was big, did not approve of the cough. My boyish appearance doubtless stirred in him a fatherly concern, for he gazed in assumed sternness at me and said: 'John, I don't like that cough. You need somebody to take care of you, and here's the girl to do it. Let me introduce you to Miss Lily Foley.'

"That was the way of it; the precise manner my wife and I met. I was a bit bashful in those days and must have blushed. Lily's cheeks, too, showed a hint at more than the color I had beheld—for I'll admit I had seen her some moments before being introduced, and had utilized each moment. She had a reputation, you must know, as something more than a soprano singer. I'll not equivocate: she was called a beauty."

"So you decided, then and there, to make her Mrs. McCormack?"

"Wait, man! Not so fast. There were others who had plans to marry the lady, as I'd been told. No, indeed. I made no such decision as that. I was more concerned over disposing of my hands, which seemed suddenly to have grown and gotten discomfortingly in my way."

"But you—"

"It was to be an important concert," said McCormack, conclusively, and he lighted another cigarette.

"—admired her?"

"I did," he admitted, having been brought to a reply. "I did and do and shall so continue. But let me proceed. There was a notable Dublin audience for that concert; many people from other places who anticipated an event. Miss Foley sang, in that glorious lyric soprano of hers, and I listened and was glad. Others appeared glad, also, if their applause may count as the measure of their gladness. But for me it was her art and the finished authority she displayed.

73

It seemed so very easy, as she sang; none of the facial distortion or writhing of body which is too customarily to be seen. She just stood there, like a feminine Irish rose, and brought everyone to her feet.

"It is a just tribute to one of the greatest singers Ireland ever produced to say, at this point, that William Ludwig was a supreme artist. A Mr. Walker, an accompanist whose father knew Mendelssohn well, tells of having played for Ludwig the song, 'There is a Green Hill Far Away.' When the baritone reached the phrase which runs 'There was no other good enough,' Walker says that he was so completely under the spell of Ludwig's art that he stopped playing, the better to listen. He stopped his accompaniment mechanically, and neither he nor the audience was aware that for some time there was no piano, so marvelous was the reality of Ludwig's singing."

Other concerts in which McCormack and Miss Foley appeared followed that one. And the months passed, carrying John from one place to another, with voice and experience expanding and his faith expanding, too.

Then came the day of a certain Mr. Riordon,

from St. Louis, Missouri, U. S. A. It was an
April day with summer approaching; a period
unproductive in the earning capacities of the
tenor, who was giving that matter thought.
Riordon represented the owners of The Irish
Village, then being built at the World's Fair, at
St. Louis, and among other needs were those for
two of Ireland's representative singers. Many
he met, but the two whose recommendations impressed him most were John McCormack and
Lily Foley.

"The wind was glowing gustily the morning
Riordon came to see me," said McCormack.
"He was one of that direct type of man, who
curtails whatever preliminaries another might
indulge. He was willing, he stated, to furnish
me transportation to St. Louis and return to Dublin, pay me ten pounds a week and guarantee an
engagement of six months. In return for all
this—which loomed a fortune to me—I was to
appear twice a day in the performance to be given
in the Irish Village, a performance partly musical
and partly theatrical. Some of it, I was to discover, was not considerate of the Irish people.

"Riordon was a plausible man and the thought
of a visit to the United States anything but dis-

tasteful. Friends, whose advice I sought, influenced me to accept, which was what I was moved to do. I consequently signed the contract Riordon prepared.

"Miss Foley had already sailed—for she, too, had succumbed to Riordon's offer—so my journey to Queenstown and across the Atlantic was a lonesome affair. I felt the pangs of homesickness before I was fifty miles away from Dublin, but they were as nothing to those destined to come. And I never knew until my return that my father would have prevented my going to America had the gang-plank not been thrown off from the tender the moment it was. 'Two seconds more, John,' said my father afterward, 'and I shouldn't have let you go.' The steamer I sailed on was the *Lucania,* a boat on which I made subsequent trips between America and Ireland."

CHAPTER VI

EARLY AMERICAN DAYS

"Never will the first sight of New York, and the harbor, fade from my memory. The thrill of it still lingers. Our ship moved up the bay, very slowly as if impressed as I was by the view which lay before and which caught and held my gaze till I blinked. It was like nothing I had seen or imagined before: a sweep of broad waters ahead, with the shorelines of Staten Island and Long Island to left and right, and dead forward of our bows the Statue of Liberty. All this I saw first. Then my gaze, elevated, fell upon lower Manhattan, upon the peaks of its towers that were made peaks by mortal hands, not by Nature. And as I leaned there against the ship's rail, my feet hard upon the deck, I wondered what that land held in store for me—if anything.

"I have been called psychic; perhaps I am. But whether or not, I experienced a strange sensation as of good and ill meeting and refusing to merge. I remained there, my arms leveled on the rail, for as long as it took to move past the Battery and on up the North River to the ship's berth. I roused, then, went below and at ten o'clock on the morning of Friday, June 7, 1904, I set foot for the first time on the soil of the country which is now my home; the country I love and of which I shall be a full-fledged citizen in January, Nineteen Nineteen."

"The first sight ashore that caused my jaw to drop was the breadth of West Street and the jam of its traffic. I dimly remember getting into a cab with friends and a careening ride, punctuated with numerous abrupt stops at street-crossings, which terminated at some hotel, I know not where. I was in New York for two days, which I spent in strolling about in wonderment at the unusual sights. Then I was taken to the old Grand Central Station and boarded a train that pulled slowly towards St. Louis.

"Hundreds of thousands of miles I have ridden on railway trains since that day, most of it in the United States. But practice has made me no more willing traveler than I was then. I dislike it, immensely; nor would I yield were it not for my audiences, who are so many and so widely apart that I can go better to them than to ask them to come to me.

"But—to get into the story again—I was on my way; in a curious turn of mind if not exactly rejoicing. And some thirty hours later I alighted in the Union Station in St. Louis, weary, dirty, I fear, and in need of refreshing. I was taken to a boarding-house where accommodations had been reserved for me (those were not days of sufficient affluence to permit the luxury of a first-class hotel); and my first efforts lay in the direction of soap and much water.

"I felt better when I had tubbed, but there was another craving to grant. I needed a shave. And there came to me, in the room of that St. Louis boarding-house, a longing to slip into a barber's chair and have another perform the task. The more I considered it the stronger the desire grew, and I ended in an establishment which looked invitingly clean. It was clean; that must have been the proprietor's axiom; to clean cleanly those customers of easy guile. For they charged me, for a shave and the polishing of my boots, the not inconsiderable sum of one dollar and sixty cents."

"You're not in earnest; you don't mean I'm to swallow such a yarn as that?"

"It's no yarn," said John severely, "but the truth. A dollar and sixty cents, that's the amount. And at the end of the week my opinion of the United States got another shock. I had accepted the tender of ten pounds a week. Well, in my mind a pound in English money is five dollars in America's; so I naturally expected to receive fifty dollars. But what do you suppose that business-like Riordon paid me?"

I had not recovered sufficient breath to reply, so McCormack supplied the answer without any request on my part.

"He paid me, the stingy beggar, forty-eight dollars and a half; that's what ten pounds came to, figuring the prevailing rate of exchange."

"Very nifty."

"Very nothing," retorted the tenor. He hadn't recovered from his disgust; it is probable that he never will. "But," he went on, "I realized Riordon was within his rights. We argued the matter. When I saw his determination I knew it was no use. And that incident, with the other of the barber shop, left I can assure you a most unfavorable impression of America upon my unworldly mind. Of course," he supplemented, "it was transitory. I've laughed since—as you laughed about the one-sixty—yet I still have a sympathetic feeling for that lonely boy, John McCormack; only nineteen, in a strange land thousands of miles from home and being mistreated."

"But you had—Miss Foley."

"I had nothing of the sort. To speak truthfully, Miss Foley never so much as left the stage, where she was rehearsing, when I first saw her in the Irish Village. I recall, distinctly, that she only waved her hand and called down to me: 'I hope you saw father before you left. Did you have a nice trip?' Oh, no! So far as I was then concerned Miss Foley was a most exclusive young person."

"When did you propose? It happened in St. Louis, I believe."

"Yes, though some weeks later, when my courage was nearer par. But before I asked her," said the tenor, "I found myself mechanically repeating what Forbes Robertson had said to me, when I asked him how it happened that Tony Navarro was so blessed as to win for his wife Mary Anderson, whose friendship I so dearly

cherish.   Robertson had replied to my question:
'He had to wade knee-deep through admirers.'
Well—*I* had to wade knee-deep through admir-
ers to win Lily Foley.

"In the meantime—to go back—I went about
the Fair Grounds and became acquainted with
the theatre in the Irish Village where I was
to appear.   It was attractive enough; cheaply
built, of course, but sufficient for the purposes.
I pulled myself together and a few days later began my work.

"But there was something askew.   Perhaps
intuition flashed a message that trouble lay ahead.
I only know that one afternoon, six weeks after
commencing that engagement, I saw something
on the stage of the theatre that aroused my Irish
blood in hot resentment.   The Irish people are
my people, and I'll not stand by and have them
mistreated or slurred.

"I was ready to go on, and stood to one side
in the wings, when one of the members of the
company—a new member—passed me and
stepped before the audience.   He was made up
with red side-whiskers, a bit of putty on the end
of his nose to give it a further tilt upwards and
he wore a green coat.   From his mouth pro-

truded a clay pipe. My first impulse was to follow and forcibly remove this caricature of an Irishman from the stage; prudence, however, forbade. I stood for a few moments watching his clownish antics; remained as long as my patience endured, and then I sought the management of the theatre.

"I explained that this man was insulting a fine people, and requested that his 'act,' as it was called, be eliminated, or at least remodeled to truthful lines. The manager only curled his lip. 'He is amusing the people, and that's why we hired him.'

"I was furious to the point of being ready to fight. Again I demanded the removal of the offensive act, which was as positively refused. Then I played what I considered my trump card. 'Either he goes,' I said, 'or I go.' The manager inclined his head and replied, 'Very well.'

"I received what was due me, that afternoon, and never again did I sing in that place.

"Miss Foley, staunch champion of Ireland, too, said I had done exactly right. 'Go back home, John,' she counseled; 'I'll follow you soon.' I lingered a few days. I couldn't bear to leave the girl I loved, and to whom I was then engaged. But her salary—it was larger than mine—was something to consider; and she was gaining notable success. For she danced with the skill of a *première* and was an actress of such merit that she had attracted an offer from Will J. Davis to star her in light opera. So we agreed that it was wisest for me to sail home alone.

"But before I went I had a long talk with a Dr. Cameron, who was stationed there in his capacity of a United States Army physician in charge of the Philippine Marine Band. The doctor and I had had many visits, sitting together in the Irish Village after Miss Foley and I had finished appearing in the theatre. Dr. Cameron was one of those believed in me. I can hear his words, even now: 'You have a future, young man, but this climate isn't the best one for your voice. Italy is the place for you; Italy, with its balmy air —and the singing teachers. You mustn't stay here, lad, the climate will ruin your delicate voice. If you can't get out of this engagement I'll give you a doctor's certificate.'

"He reminded me, again, of Italy in that concluding talk we had. Somehow it made more of an impression that June afternoon, fourteen years ago, than ever before. 'You really think so, doctor?' I remember having said. And he answered: 'Some day you will find out for yourself.

"I have never seen Dr. Cameron since, though I've tried very hard to discover his whereabouts. I hope—should this paragraph ever reach his eyes—that he will communicate with me. For I feel that I owe him a debt, and that the period of payment is long past due."

At other times, previous to the official beginning of setting down the facts contained in this volume, McCormack had mentioned Dr. Cameron: once, nine years ago, in the lobby of the Manhattan Opera House, in New York, when the tenor was with Oscar Hammerstein, and as recently as last winter, after a performance of "La Bohême," in the Metropolitan. At neither of these moments, nor during other whose specific places I do not recall, did he seem so concerned. On that June afternoon, in the year Nineteen Hundred Eighteen, he was like one sorrowing for a lost friend.

Nor did John forget to mention, as an associate and dear friend at the Irish Village who was warmly received, Miss Marie Narelle, a soprano whose voice and singing have since been heard in some notable concerts.

We were not far from Rocklea, the fishing-dory bowling along at a good eight knots and rolling in the rising sea.   McCormack sat at the wheel looking shorewards under knitted brows that showed he had not done thinking about that United States Army physician who passed from the tenor's life as abruptly as he entered it.   He was too busy with his thoughts to notice my scrutiny; but I observed the gradual relaxing of his concern in the task of piloting his craft.

"I'm developing an appetite," he announced, as we rounded a point of land that put us into the lee of the wind and somewhat under the shelter of a part of Collander Point.   "I had one just like it the day I landed in Queenstown, after my first American visit, in the late summer of 1904. We'd had a good voyage.   And I was nearing my beloved Ireland, which helped to lighten the heaviness of my heart which beat for another heart in St. Louis.   But my experience had helped, and I really believe I had less diffidence than when my destination had lain the opposite way.   Perhaps it was the love I bore my native

land, which loomed so near; I was very agitated
—I well remember that.

"The possession of several pounds in money
gave me independence; not a great deal, but
enough to let me hold up my head with the consciousness that I was getting on. If my arms
had been big enough I would have taken the
whole city of Dublin in them the day of my return. Athlone, too, when I ran down to spend
some time with father and mother and the rest
of the family.

"They seemed proud of me, and we had a real
reunion. Father, always sympathetic because
he so thoroughly understood me, said: 'John,
you'll make your singing mark some day.' He
appreciated the value of my American trip and
he and mother and I talked extensively of my
future. I should have liked to stay long in
Athlone, it was so restful after the bustle of the
cities I had been in. But there was work to do,
and the day of parting came. We all were a
trifle misty about the eyes, so I broke suddenly
and left them."

John ceased his narrative for a spell, for Rocklea was a hundred yards off our starboard bow,
the pier drawing nearer and nearer. He shut off

the motor, threw the wheel over, and brought us to a landing pretty enough for any seaman. A man who had been waiting took charge of the dory and John and I climbed to the boards and stretched our legs.

"Rain's on the way," said the tenor, sniffing and casting an eye skywards. We proceeded towards the house, but slowly; McCormack clearly wished to finish that next episode of his story before we passed the lawn.

"That fall and winter of Nineteen Hundred Four and Five brought memorable events in my life," said he. "I heard Caruso for the first time, made some phonograph records—my beginning—and arranged to go to Italy to study. One thing crowded another, and with the few concert engagements I got those months were completely filled.

"But, first of all, I went to see my fiancée's father, Patrick Foley. I knew him, at that time, in only a slight way; but he greeted me like a son. He lived only two years longer, yet in those two years he unselfishly gave me assistance and counsel that could not have been more devotedly bestowed had I been his own flesh and blood. I thought I appreciated the worth of the man then. It has taken time, however, for that, a constant turning in my mind of what he was to me, his sturdy gentleness and infinite patience to point out what in his judgment was best for me. He was unfailingly right; God rest his soul.

"Well," said John, after an audible sigh, "we discussed many things. I had had two invitations to go to London to try for some record-making among the phonograph companies. 'Do you think a trip to London a wise plan?' I asked Mr. Foley. 'Go, lad, by all means,' was his answer, and I went.

"I'd never seen the world's metropolis. It lay, in my brain, an image of fancy, and during the railway ride I wondered if it would be at all as I had pictured it. In a way it was, with some spots very like those of my imagination. Instantly I was held by its reflection of material substance, the semblance of long and honorable upbuilding of a people who had built for all time.

"It appears that I had gained enough reputation of a certain character to filter up to London. Reports had it that there was a young tenor in Dublin named McCormack who had something of a voice and a way of singing that the people liked. And these two invitations—one from the

Edison Company, the other from the Gramophone Company—had come wholly unsolicited. I was pleased, yet I went to London in a humble spirit, glad of what offered and hoping it would lead to something of a permanent nature in the way of recording.

"There was a temptation to count unhatched chickens, but I stoutly resisted. I remembered the remark of my future father-in-law, who helped me in so many ways, to the effect—'Try, always, John, to make the best use of your time, but do not anticipate unwarrantedly.' I shall never forget another kindly suggestion he made to me when, one evening, as I slipped by him in a narrow passageway in a concert auditorium hastening after a friend, Mr. Foley called to me. 'Mac,' he said, and of course I stopped. 'It doesn't do you a bit of harm to say when you brush past an old man like me, "I beg your pardon." ' He wasn't an old man, but I never forgot.

"Well, I called on the Edison manager and made arrangements to return at a specified time to make the records for him, and left his office somewhat elated. Then I headed up Gray's Inn Road, towards the Gramophone establishment which, as you know, is the sister company to the Victor Talking Machine Company, of America. There, also, I was successful.

"It was gratifying to qualify with both companies, contracting with the Edison to do ten songs for fifty pounds and to record twenty-five songs for twenty-five pounds for the Gramophone. The difference in the fees I received was this: for the fifty pounds the Edison Company was to pay me I agreed to make as many matrices as might be necessary to secure ten perfect records; but my agreement with the Gramophone Company required only a single record for each song, regardless of whether a record might be slightly imperfect."

"Did you build any air castles?" I queried. John had stopped a few yards from the house to greet his Belgian sheep dog, Nellie, who greeted him with sharp yelps of joy, leaping the while towards his face which she was straining affectionately to caress.

"Get down, Nell! Sit down and compose yourself." Which the dog obediently did, though her tail wagged at a tremendous rate. "What mischief have you been up to?" he demanded, in a tone of canine understanding.

"Tell me!" Nellie barked joyously, and straightway came to all fours and leaped again. They frisked about together, master and dog, until interrupted by the appearance of Mrs. McCormack on the veranda.

We proceeded in a group—McCormack, and Nellie and I—to the house, where Mrs. McCormack showed a worried look. "I was wondering—" she began, when John stopped the sentence with a kiss.

"If I'd got back safe with the dory. That was it, wasn't it?" His life partner admitted her concern and present relief, and reminded us that the dinner hour was near.

"Five minutes more, then I'm free. He makes me work, this man; and in vacation time, too." Mrs. McCormack smiled indulgently. "Five minutes, then," she said, "but no more," and she left us.

"You asked me a question," reminded John, picking up the thread of our conversation where Nellie's impetuous arrival had sent it spinning. "Oh, yes, air castles. Of course I built them, and they were fine ones, with many rooms and exclusive furnishings—and works of art, which I revel in. Air castles? I should say; I reared and

92

demolished them and rebuilt them again. It's a pleasant labor, diverting and generally harmless.

"I built a dozen or two when, on reaching Dublin and talking with Mr. Foley, he told me he believed Dr. Cameron's advice about Italy should be heeded. 'You ought to go,' he decided, 'and we'll start planning a way.'

"Nothing definite was reached in that preliminary conversation concerning one of the desires my heart had been set on for several months. Mr. Foley had ideas, and one which ultimately proved practical under his guiding hand. Several days later he told me of it, and it was this. A testimonial concert was to be arranged; a concert on a pretentious scale which Mr. Foley assured me he would personally manage himself."

Although this volume is officially McCormack's own, some of the facts incorporated in it have been supplied by persons other than the tenor. And it is better so, because otherwise they would not have come to my, and the general public's, knowledge. For John has a way of often avoiding some incident that places him in an advantageous light; and then, another's viewpoint not infrequently brings to the surface some

element or climax which sounds better than it
would have sounded had it dropped from the ten-
or's lips.

Michael Keane, one of McCormack's staunch-
est admirers and a "booster" from the first moment he heard him, imparted the information of
the tenor's introductory appearance in London.
Mr. Keane—now American representative for
the music publishing firm of Boosey and Company—was at that time an associate of Robert
Newman, manager of Queen's Hall. As many
know, this auditorium was the London home for
the symphony and the ballad concerts, with a
seating capacity of some thirty-five hundred and
having back of it fine traditions.

I had gone to see Mr. Keane at McCormack's
request. In a few minutes we were in the heart
of matters McCormack; and in the snug little
New York office of Boosey and Company, in East
Seventeenth street, Michael Keane talked on for
hours, ignoring the approach and passing of the
luncheon hour. But it was time profitably
spent.

"None of us in London knew of John McCormack at the time he burst upon us at a concert
in Queen's Hall, in November of Nineteen Four,

given by the Gaelic League. The tenor had been heard by some of the gentlemen of the League, the afternoon he won the first prize in the Dublin Feis Coeil, and they concluded that his appearance at that important London concert would add to its interest. It certainly did.

"I chanced," continued Mr. Keane, "to be in the auditorium when John came upon the platform. He walked to a place near the piano with an agreeable unconsciousness we have since learned is characteristic of him, and waited for the accompanist to begin the prelude to that rare song, 'The Irish Emigrant.' Apart from showing a casual concern in an unknown Irish tenor I doubt," explained Mr. Keane, "if I held any special interest. Certainly, I had no idea that I should be so affected by what I was to hear."

"Then he made an impression?"

"Rather!" said Mr. Keane emphatically. "Personally, I was amazed. The voice, then, was what I term a pure Irish tenor; with the richness in the middle of it, and that delightful suggestion—just a suggestion, mind you—of nasal quality in his top notes. It was a typically Irish tenor voice—of the finest sort, and by far the most beautiful I ever had heard.

"The boy sang wonderfully, too, even then. It was evident to one uninitiated in the art of singing what manner of tenor he was; and the probability of his future status. The audience present at that Gaelic League concert sensed all that I have said, and received him with enthusiasm. But I doubt if any one was so completely overjoyed as I. I did not wait to hear the encore which the auditors demanded after 'The Irish Emigrant.' As fast as my legs would carry me, I rushed upstairs to Mr. Newman's office.

" 'If you would hear the greatest Irish tenor ever produced,' I gasped out, 'come quickly.' But Mr. Newman, with whom I had been associated for eighteen years, only smiled. 'I'm busy, Michael,' he replied, 'but when I've finished I'll try to get down.' He thought me over-enthusiastic, because McCormack was a fellow-countryman.

"Well, I returned to the auditorium to hear the rest of that Irish boy's songs. And I never doubted—not when John struggled against obstacles after he made London his headquarters —that he would eventually be accepted as not only the greatest Irish singer, but the greatest singer in the world."

CHAPTER VII

STUDIES IN ITALY

I was busy in a study in an enticingly secluded part of the McCormacks' Rocklea home, late on the night when John recounted Mr. Foley's announcement of the proposed benefit concert. About me, on a large table, were ranged letters, memoranda, and private documents belonging to the tenor to which he had given me access; a veritable mass of informative and interesting data —and many pages of the manuscript of this book. Few persons have been privileged to burrow into the material which lay about; it represented the accumulations of years, some of it almost as old as the Irish singer himself.

The night was cool, for it was before the hot period of our remarkable summer of Nineteen Hundred Eighteen, and a breeze touched with a salty aroma of the Sound came through the open windows into the room. An electric lamp, nearly hidden by a wide-spreading and drooping shade, shed its rays in a circle of generous size.

I sat smoking my pipe, rather meditatively, and finding a growing interest in each hitherto new, to me, fact as I dug it from some hiding-place, and recorded it where it belonged. It was past midnight, an hour when some minds are most active: the working time for the few just as it is sleeping time for the many.

A stiffness of body from long sitting over my work sent me to my feet and to the window where the curtains fluttered under the wind. It had died down since our earlier landing from the dory, but it still whipped the Sound waters until the surface was tipped with cappings that showed dead white under the light of the moon. The lawn was dark, but at the pierhead, beyond, a small space was illumined.

And then there crossed my gaze a moving fig-ure. I saw it first to my left, about a hundred feet from the house. But instead of proceeding in my direction the figure, which was unquestion-ably a man's, was headed for the pier. I saw it go on—past the south side of the lawn, to the beach and out upon the pier. In another moment the man would be in the spot where the moon's rays touched.

I watched, curiosity more than concern holding my attention, for the instant when the figure should break from darkness into comparative light. Ten seconds, five more passed. Then I saw. There was no mistaking the contour of that body, the flare of shoulders and the bared head. It was McCormack.

Wondering what took him up and out at that hour of night, for he is a sound sleeper, I left him to whatever object he might have had in view, and returned to my work. It was a matter of perhaps a quarter of an hour when I heard a footfall behind me, which brought me about to face the direction of the sound.

"Hello, John!" I greeted. "What keeps you up?"

"I saw your light, from outside," he responded, ignoring my question. He walked over to the table, picked up the pages of the manuscript and sitting down began to read. He did not look up or speak until he had finished; whereupon he laid the typed script aside to discuss certain parts of it.

I have never before written a book in collaboration, but should circumstances make such procedure wise again I shouldn't mind having as collaborator John McCormack. He has the writer's discernment and feeling, and an unerring sense of what belongs. Sitting there, he offered several suggestions: changes, at one point, of elimination, of addition at another and rephrasing of some quotations of his own that his exact words should be set down. We made them, on the spot; which seemed to give the tenor satisfaction. At any rate, he lighted a cigarette, inhaled and blew the smoke above his head.

"You don't mind, I hope—those suggestions. You see I'm rather particular about having everything just as it happened."

I told him his desire was likewise mine, that without such aid as he was giving we could not make the book the thing it was intended to be: an authorized version of the story of his life, his own tale which, so to speak, should be an official document.

He seemed pleased at that. Mrs. McCormack confided to me, the next day, that John had fussed continually ever since our work had begun; fussed as he does when he undertakes anything worth while, in his continually expressed belief

100

that whatever is worth doing at all is worth doing well.   And in the remaining weeks of our combined endeavor, weeks filled with almost daily consultation, McCormack displayed the same interest, the same concern for accuracy and consistency and an unflagging zeal to do the job well. Never once did he become irritable under my fusillade of questions; he would go over again any episode which needed clarifying, and in our revisions his patience never broke.

"I was thinking—outside, there—what a lot I have to be thankful for.   I like to wander around, that way, sometimes, to get off by myself and try to get an unbiased perspective.   It's a great help to keep one on the rails; a stabilizer of the best sort."

I agreed, as I often did when John fell into one of his communicative moods, by inclining my head.

"Funny," he observed, "but just a moment ago, down on the pier, I happened to recall the first time I heard Caruso.   It wasn't long before I left Dublin for Italy, and a short time after I had made my records for the Edison and Gramophone companies.   It was at Covent Garden, London; the opera, 'La Bohême.'   You can well

imagine my state of mind at reaching my seat in
that distinguished old institution. My heart
fluttered almost as a spinster's at the moment of
approaching proposal. I had read and heard so
much about this great artist that I could scarcely
wait for the curtain.

" 'La Bohême' was as much of a novelty as the
tenor, but it was he in whom my interest centred:
the type of his voice, his manner of using it and
his interpretative style. My ears and mind were
full of the man and I was as nervous as a horse at
the starting-post until Caruso, garbed as the
Bohemian *Rodolfo,* sang his opening phrases.

"I was not there in the rôle of cantankerous,
captious critic. Presumptuousness held no part
of me. But when I listened to the opening
phrases of Puccini's music, sung by that indescribably glorious voice as Caruso alone could
sing, my jaw dropped as though hung on a hinge.
Such smoothness and purity of tone, and such
quality; it was like a stream of liquid gold.

"And yet, one other person in Covent Garden
had a slightly different and, I thought, odd impression. Attracted by the same magnet as I,
J. C. Doyle, the baritone I spoke of and a fine
man and artist, and his brother Jim went to the

performance, dilating upon the capacities of one of the greatest, if not *the* greatest, of singers of all time. The tenor was well along in the first act, and nearing the Rocconto aria, when Jim Doyle, unaware that he was actually hearing Caruso at the moment, remarked to his brother: 'Well, if Caruso can sing any better than this boy, Caruso certainly can sing!'

"It was the best lesson, up to that moment, I had ever received and a stimulus which cannot be described. The sound of Caruso's voice that night lingered in my ears for months, and will doubtless linger there always. It will always be to me one of the memorable moments of my life. I looked up to him, as I do still, as a supremely gifted artist; unique, performing vocal feats no other tenor can, and standing apart from the rest, a model for all.

"I sang a number of concert engagements during Nineteen Hundred Four and Five; in Dublin and several other places, and for the usual small fees, varying from twenty to thirty shillings. But I was no aggrieved participant. Each appearance carried a definite significance and was something to be seriously regarded as a duty to my public and myself. I have been that way always, and shall continue to be. For no matter how seemingly inconsequential the task, it is worth doing in only a single way.

"At last came the night of my benefit concert: Mr. Foley had prepared for it with his accustomed businesslike thoroughness, neglecting his own interests and toiling with such zealousness and disregard of his own health that on the day of days he was confined to his bed, under his physician's care. Yet he could not be dissuaded from rising at six o'clock and, after vainly attempting to eat, going to the hall and into the box office to see personally that all moneys were accurately accounted for.

"I think we may term that unselfish devotion.

"The concert was considered a success. My patrons (and I deeply appreciate their willingness to help a young singing student get his desired education) appeared pleased and liked, especially, the songs I sang at the concert, which were 'In Her Simplicity,' the last act aria from 'Mignon,' 'The Snowy Breasted Pearl,' and Tosti's 'My Dreams.' These were the three programme numbers, but there were many encores.

"Well, the concert netted me ninety pounds;

104

and Mr. Foley and Lily, who had triumphed with me in the affair, and I held a mild celebration at the Foley home.

"My affairs were arranged: the good-byes to my parents and sisters and brother said, my belongings packed, and I was ready to depart southward. Then occurred a strange incident. Mr. Fair, living in Athone and a friend of father's, an amateur singer of limited capacities, but one who had studied extensively and was really well informed, though an indifferent performer himself, stopped me on the street.

" 'I understand you are going to Italy to study,' said he; 'who is to be your teacher?' I told him I had no idea. 'Well,' volunteered Mr. Fair, 'I spent some time over there; and I worked with ever so many so-called singing masters. Most of them are incapable; many are charlatans.' I received this information with trepidation. 'I did find, however,' declared the doctor positively, 'one man who knew his business. His name is Vincenzo Sabatini. He's an old man, past seventy now, yet he is the one you should go to— if he will consent to take you.'

"I left Dublin with a letter to Sabatini from Mr. Fair, and *en route* I rehearsed until letter-perfect the plea I should make to induce him to accept me as a pupil.

"Milan was reached at last; Milan with its thousands of singing hopefuls, boys and girls from all lands, vying with one another for the equipment which should yield them victory and its fruits. An ambitious lot, some of them excellently equipped for their desired tasks and others less fortunate, perhaps; but all of them doing their best according to their individual lights."

John got up, stretched his arms, and took a turn to the window and back.

"And when you arrived at Sabatini's studio," I observed, suggestively, "you found that you had—lost the letter of introduction?"

"That would have been more or less dramatic," agreed McCormack, "only it wasn't what happened. There was small chance, for I had the thing pinned to the inside pocket of my waistcoat; with a safety-pin, too. As I did not speak or understand Italian it was agreed that I should be identified by a handkerchief tied about one arm, and I stood on the station platform until I was seen and rescued.

"Yes," he remarked, reseating himself, "I had

106

the letter. And I held it in my hand when I went into the old *maestro's* studio, my legs somewhat wobbly from nervous anticipation of hearing a possible 'no.'

"I can see him even now," mused the tenor, "a wonderfully preserved man, physically, look-ing fifteen years younger than he was, with white hair, which was thin and was brushed straight back, and moustache, and eyebrows silvered, too, and a broad brow above wide-set eyes.

"Disturbed you, then?"

"Not in the way I had expected to be," replied John. "There was a quality about Sabatini of old-fashioned courtliness which softened his piercing gaze. He spoke almost no word of my language, but his wife was an Englishwoman— his accompanist and valued aide. It was she who had first greeted me, and she opened the letter from Mr. Fair as Sabatini advanced a few steps and greeted me with a formality that held no coldness. He was no poseur.

"I scrutinized him as he listened while his wife read the letter to him, and I was thus engaged when the *maestro* looked up.

" 'So you would become a singer,' queried Sabbatini; 'well, let us see if there is the chance.'

He retraced his steps to a chair near the piano, where Signora Sabatini sat waiting while I selected my music.

"I don't know why I experienced no sense of fear, standing before that critical voice-master and well aware that it was then or never. It was a moment of inexpressible anxiety. Yet my mind never was clearer nor my confidence more secure. I sang, spurred by the possible reward, with more fervor than was my wont. The test was completed in a few minutes; the time arrived which my boyish longing had lived over and over again during the days of unleashed hopes.

"Sabatini did not immediately speak, but he rose slowly from his seat as though cogitating something important and not to be prematurely divulged. Then he turned to his wife, and spoke rapidly to her in Italian—something at which she inclined her head, speaking Italian also as she did so.

" 'You have come to ask me if I will take you as a pupil—and that I will. But I cannot place your voice.' My heart felt a lump of lead at those portentous words. 'I cannot place your voice,' said the *maestro*, 'because God did that.'

"I vaguely recollect his saying other things, but I did not comprehend. His words kept revolving in my mind, like the turning of a wheel; and I kept seeing them chase after one another in that single phrase: 'I cannot place your voice, God did that.' "

We sat in the secluded study, John McCormack and I, for some minutes, in silence. He had painted his word-picture well; I could glimpse the youth of twenty, eager and buoyant, getting his verdict and being a bit stunned by it.

"I discovered, later, that Sabatini liked my voice and believed a career was assured. But he explained the elements involved: opportunity and what I suppose we might designate a 'break in the luck.'

"I cannot complain as to that. Luck or fortune, or Providence's beneficent dispensation has been rather near my elbow. And I *have* worked, and endured privations and disappointments. Without them the singer does not feel; not to the depths of his soul.

"Well," exclaimed the tenor, and he emerged abruptly and with some show of physical force as of having brusquely shed himself of some internal cloak of sentiment, "we arranged for lessons, Sabatini and I. One every day, excepting Sundays; the price twenty dollars a month. And on March 21st, 1905, we began.

"I found living quarters in Pension Betham Via Brera 5 at thirty dollars a month, including my meals. Once installed and my tuition under way I felt the world a bright and exceedingly good-natured place to live in. I began blithely, almost, a song in my heart as continually as it was on my lips.

"Details of a singing student's routine make commonplace reading. Mine was no different course from that of any other aspirant for singing honors; from those, I should say, who were serious and had to make time and money count. For me there were no periods of idleness or questionable pleasures. There is but a single expression which fits what I did: I 'plugged.'

"Two objects engaged the chief attention of Sabatini in our work: the acquiring of a *mezza-voce*, which I did not have by nature, and the freeing of my high tones. The voice was not what is called a 'long' voice (by which I mean plenty of compass, from bottom to top) and the top notes were in my throat; but to get them out with freedom, so that a high A or B-flat had

110

.the same relative quality as the lower part of the voice, required constant, painstaking teaching on Sabatini's part and practice on my own. The *mezza-voce* (singing with half the volume of the full voice, or with less than half) was a slow process; often I grew discouraged over it.

"My *maestro* spent no time teaching me the operas. The rôles of every opera now in my repertoire (I have twenty-five) I learned by myself. When they were musically committed to memory Sabatini 'passed' them, as we say in singing parlance, and offered suggestions as to their interpretation. But my endeavors, as may be apparent, so far as Sabatini is concerned, lay in the direction of acquiring an evenness of the vocal scale; of making the voice smooth in every note, and in gaining ease of production and certainty—in short, a technique which in time would become so perfect mechanically as to allow me to forget technique, while I sang, and devote my attention exclusively to the interpretation of the music and of the text. For such singing, I contend, is what constitutes the art and permits the artist to convey his message with sincerity to his hearers.

"I remained in Milan, during that first stay,

from March, Nineteen Hundred Five, to May—
just two months. In that time I studied Italian
assiduously, giving hours each day to it and
mingling freely with Italians in practising the
speech. My Latin and Greek knowledge was of
inestimable help and besides I had the lingual
facility, so much so that in six weeks from my
arrival in Milan I understood everything in Italian which was said, and spoke with reasonable
fluency.

"Sabatini discontinued his teaching before
warm weather arrived, and as I knew no pronounced advancement could be made during his
absence, I elected to return to Ireland and come
back to Italy the following fall. So I wrote
home that I should soon depart, and before June
arrived I was again in Dublin—and devoting
myself to Miss Lily Foley."

CHAPTER VIII

THE RETURN TO ITALY

"During that summer of 1905," said McCormack, "I gained some understanding of how fortunate I was in having the pledge of Lily Foley to become Mrs. John McCormack. I spent part of those four months in Dublin and part with my family in Athlone. And I was happy. My conjecture as to the future was probably a stimulating force, and the few concert engagements which came to me helped. Nor will I forget the strength I felt in the unspeakably unselfish friendship of Patrick Foley —my second father.

"Time does not pass as swiftly to the young as to the old. It lingered, throughout those months in Nineteen Hundred Five, and although I was loath to leave those I loved I felt the tug of duty; of having much to accomplish, and of the path of that accomplishment leading toward

113

Italy. There I found myself, in October; twenty-one, and eager.

"My dear old Sabatini had returned to his studio—it was a romantic address, Via Victor Hugo, Number Four—the day before I reached Milan. I found him there, after I had settled down at the same Pension Betham, Number Five Via Brera, and had hurried to greet him. Having got a start in the spring, I trod the streets of Milan with a feeling of belonging there, in a way. The buildings and byways were familiar, even some of the people I met as I passed along; and I spoke the language.

"I had been to mass that morning, and my hopes were soaring. Health and optimism were mine—and the faith of the Irish Catholic. In that mood of good-will towards men I reached Sabatini's studio, to be greeted, first, by Signora Sabatini. She was calm, as was her custom, but glad to see me. I could see that in her fine eyes, and feel it in the warm clasp of her artistic fingers.

"But it was a more demonstrative reception which the *maestro* gave me; one typical of those of his nationality who entertain affection for another. He came from one side of his studio in

114

the direction of the doorway, his thin, white hair brushed back from his brow and those piercing eyes of his denoting an unmistakable gleam.

" 'Giovanni,' he exclaimed, and I thought I detected the suggestion of a quaver in his voice, *'caro mio.'* Then the dear man kissed me on both cheeks. But he was no happier to welcome me than I was to see him again, and to feel his vigorous hand-clasp which held for me a wealth of meaning.

"He pushed me forcibly into a chair, plying me with questions in a veritable stream of Italian which came too fast to permit immediate answering. But his paramount interest was in my voice. He had been, once, to Liverpool and more often than I could count had averred that it had taken him three years in the soft air of his beloved Italy to get the fog and chill of that Liverpool atmosphere from his throat.

" 'Giovanni,' he would say, 'how is it that you are of England, yet with that voice?' And my reply, invariably, would in substance be, 'But, *maestro,* England is not Ireland nor Ireland England.' Whereat he always shook his head, in a slow side to side movement as if unable to comprehend how a little matter in distance could make such a difference.

"On this particular October morning Sabatini was a physical and mental dynamo. He shortly had me standing at my lesson, with his wife at the piano. He was a source of wonderment to me, at all times, and that three-quarters of an hour disclosed the same facility of that seventy-four-year-old man at detecting vocal flaws and the same astuteness in applying corrective measures which, I presume, he had possessed twenty years before. I likewise shall never forget how he sang for me 'Salve Dimore,' from 'Faust,' with an evenness of scale which was a revelation."

It was on a muggy July morning or Nineteen Hundred Eighteen, in New York City, that the tenor related to me the facts incorporated in the opening pages of this chapter. Business had brought him from the luxurious coolness of Rocklea to the broiling and humid heat of America's metropolis at the height of summer, and Nature, man and beast suffered. We sat at a table in the grill of one of John's clubs. He showed the effects of his previous weeks of physical training and diet, of normal living and a tranquil mind, which leave their unmistakable marks.

" 'Aida' was the first opera I heard in Italy," announced the tenor. His vision was not for immediate and nearby things; he was looking far backwards, and from the upturned quirk of his mouth contemplating pleasant things. "De Macchi was the tenor, Boninsegna sang *Aida* and, I think, Stracciari had the rôle of *Amonasro*."

His pause, after these words, was such that I ventured a question. "Was the performance a good one?"

"Very," he replied. "It had the fire and life which Verdi believed 'Aida' required. 'Il Barbiere di Siviglia' was the second operatic work I listened to in Milan; in La Scala. De Luca, now one of the first baritones at the New York Metropolitan, Barrientos, its coloratura soprano, and Pini-Corsi, a former Metropolitan buffo-basso now dead, also were in the cast. The tenor was Fernindo De Lucia, a glorious artist. I have heard and seen few finer presentations of this opera, which offers a wealth of vocal opportunity to the principals who are given that opportunity by a composer who did not rob them of it through covering their parts with unnecessarily heavy orchestration—the Frankenstein of modern operas and the most potent cause of vocal wrecks the opera singer of this generation has to face."

"And Sabatini? He felt, in this respect, as you feel?"

"Assuredly," said McCormack. "Modern opera was a thing he detested, because of its impossible demands upon the voice, above all else. He had reasons, and good ones, you may believe. For he rightly contended that the human singing voice cannot be driven, in the singer's effort to be heard, against a mass of orchestral tone without damage to the vocal instrument."

The tenor was interrupted here by a fellow club-member insistent upon a brief visit and a discussion on the war and other topics of the moment. John drifted from music and into these non-related subjects with interest, and showed his grasp of each to be that of an educated, thoughtful citizen, broad enough to consider matters outside his own particular sphere of professional effort.

"There was so much in Milan of artistic and historic interest," resumed McCormack, "that I never lacked for an occupation of benefit to me.

Music, of course, came first, yet I counted literature and the fine arts as accompanying essentials,
and I seized every chance to extend my acquaintance with them all.

"The picture gallery of Brera, directly opposite where I lived, was one of the spots where I
spent much time.   The building was erected, in
1651, as a Jesuit college and continued as that
until the year of American independence.   At
that time it was installed, and has since continued, as the seat of the Accademia di Belle Arti;
and within the gallery may be found the re-
nowned 'Sposalizio' of Raphael, pictures and
frescoes by Ferrari, Luini and Bramantino as
well as a library of over three hundred thousand
volumes.   There is much else besides: thousands
of rare coins and a splendid observatory, and
art works by those masters Paolo Veronese,
Moroni, Bellini, Bonifazio, Paris Bordone, Cima
da Conegliano and others of their time.

"It was in the Brera Gallery that my instinc-
tive taste for good pictures had its early cultiva-
tion.   The interpretation of a song is but the
rearing of a piece of musical architecture; and
no slight help is to be found in the study of good

119

canvases, wherein the eye recognizes, among other outstanding elements, line and color and form.

"I was fond, too, of looking at the statue of Leonardo da Vinci, which stands in the Piazza della Scala within a stone's toss of the Teatro della Scala—that famous opera-house which the world knows best as La Scala. Nor could I keep away from the nearby Galleria Vittorio Emanuele, that magnificent arcade in the form of a Latin cross with its octagonal centre which is topped, at a height of one hundred sixty feet, with a glass cupola.

"The parks and streets were my inanimate friends, and I would wander for hours at a time through them—learning a lesson or relaxing in the artistic stimulus which they somehow seemed to reflect.

"I endeavored conscientiously to waste no time. I counted well the value of a day's hours, and they were never quite enough. I cannot remember that Italy was a playground for me, unless I estimate my studies as that. I enjoyed them enough, it is true, and they consumed my waking moments rather completely. But with student celebrations I had no acquaintance, for

the sufficient reasons of lacking money and super-
fluous time. My musical hay had to be made
while the sun shone, and there was no guarantee
that it might not suddenly set. It threatened to
do that, by the way, during the early winter of
that 1905–1906 season, and would have done so
but for the generosity of my staunch friend
Bishop Clancy, of Summerhill College.

"Friends," said John, "are among the best
things of life. To make and keep them has been
one of the things I have never ceased to be grateful for, because my present position is in considerable measure due to their loyalty and responsiveness to various personal needs. I am
convinced of that. I've not turned to many of
these friends, it is true, but when I did none of
them refused what I sought.

"It was that way with Bishop Clancy. My
money had run very low, and I began to worry.
There was no way that I knew to earn any, in
Milan, with such resources as were mine. I hesitated long before writing Bishop Clancy; it does
not come easy to me to ask for assistance, even
such assistance as I feel confident I may repay
at a given time.

"But, after days of reflection on the matter, I

decided; and I then composed a letter to the Bishop, explaining my need for fifty pounds—if I were to be able to remain in Milan—and asking him to lend me that amount, if it were convenient. I was almost sorry when I let the letter to Bishop Clancy slip from my fingers into the post-box. What if he were to refuse? My youthful mind held a swarm of conjectures, and I fretted until I got my answer, which, when I held it unopened in my shaking fingers, I scarcely dared read."

"Yet you had faith?"

"Yes," answered John, "but I was tormented with a questioning of having done the right thing. I need not have worried. That letter from Bishop Clancy was a solace, a strengthener that lifted me up and made my religion a more majestic thing to me than ever.

"The Bishop wrote that he was glad I had asked that favor. It gave him, he said, a great comfort to be able to show his affection for me, and his confidence in my future. He hadn't by him at the time, the full fifty pounds; only twenty-five, which he enclosed. But he would send the remainder, he promised, in three months. And this he did."

Bishop Curley, John's boyhood friend, told

me something of this incident. The tenor had said in his letter that he would return the loan in three years; and in three years, to the month, he kept his word. Also, he had a beautiful chalice (made with Irish amethysts and other gems) which he presented to Bishop Clancy. The Bishop died in 1912, which took from John McCormack a real friend, but that same chalice (which Bishop Clancy left in his will to Summerhill College, McCormack's alma mater) is used each day in the mass and a special *memento* always is said for the donor.

"With my mind at ease," continued McCormack, "I progressed at a rapid rate. Each day an accompanist came to me, and in exchange for one franc an hour played through those operas I was learning for my repertoire. It is not expensive, in Italy, to become a musician if one will toil. A set purpose and some natural ability appear the prerequisites. By this time I read at sight rather well, and I was always a good student. So the repertoire grew.

"Sabatini's patient toil with me seemed also to be a productive affair. He never tired. He would scold me, often, when I was timid in giving a top note with the same freedom as a lower one,

and then he would call to me, his eyes snapping:
'Avanti, Giovanni, *avanti!'* But he never tired.
For he was more, merely, than *maestro;* he was
my friend.

"I used to revel in those walks of ours, which
now and again took us to the Galleria—headquarters for musical-conductors, singers, arrived
and otherwise, and musical agents—where Sabatini would be met with salutations on all sides.
He would touch up my Italian, and in his quaint
and courtly fashion command his Giovanni to
give him *his* lesson in English. And then, after
our stroll, we would often end at Sabatini's
home at the dinner hour, my *maestro* gently in-
sisting that I should remain to eat with him and
his wife. I always was glad to stop, for those
were treasure hours—which can never be recalled.

"And one December day, arriving at the studio
for my lesson, Sabatini eyed me covertly from
over the hand that pulled at his thin, silvery
moustache. I sensed that he was up to something; his whole manner was that of a grown-up
child who has something of importance to im-
part to one he is fond of. He had evidently
planned just how he should tell me: first, to

pique my interest and, thereafter, compel me to guess a dozen things, and finally 'give it up.'

"He is . . . dead, now—dear soul! And, I know, gone to his deserved reward. But I can see him, as plainly as though it happened yesterday, standing near the window in his studio, playing with his moustache and eyeing me like a mischievous schoolboy.

" 'Giovanni!' he cried. 'There is news. Something I must tell to you.' Then a purposeful pause. 'I wonder, now; had I better?' as though addressing himself. I was eager, but to please him I pretended to be half frantic with suspense and besought him to speak out. Then, as I have already related, he insisted that I guess, which I of course did, while he watched me with evident delight at withholding the news which he would announce when I was bursting with anxiety.

"Finally, according to the prescribed course I would follow, I announced my inability to correctly read his mind. Elated, he made his announcement, much as though promulgating some order of state.

"And the news he held for me was the opportunity for an *audition* (which was equivalent to an engagement) to sing in seven opera performances in the Teatro Chiabrera, at Savona, a small town near Genoa. A baritone named Felici, a friend of Sabatini, had arranged for the engagement, but it carried no fee. All I could expect to get from it were such experience and glory as it might yield."

CHAPTER IX

CONCLUDING STUDIES IN ITALY

Our seats in the chair car of the late afternoon express train were in the extreme rear, isolated from the nearest passengers, which permitted us to talk uninterruptedly and without fear of annoying others. Stamford was the first stop and there we knew that Wilkinson would be waiting, with the motor-car.

"Don't say it's hot," growled John, noting I was about to speak.

"Why not sing it, then, if it annoys you to talk?"

"Just for that I *won't* sing, and I will talk . . . about singing, when I made that opera début at Savona. The *audition* went satisfactorily, and Felici closed matters with the theatre impresario. So I went to the boarding-house where I should stop while rehearsing and singing my seven performances.

"The plan called for my singing five times in

Mascagni's 'L'Amico Fritz' and twice in an opera by Dupont called 'La Cabrera.' Preparations went without any serious trouble, and the night at length came for the opening performance. 'L'Amico Fritz' had been selected by the impresario and those of us who were to appear were anxious. A crowded audience was assured and when the curtain rose we saw that it was on hand, ready to applaud or condemn according as it was pleased or not.

"I was certain enough of my singing, but the acting part of my rôle was on my mind. In those days I did not appreciate what repose of body means, or the use of a gesture in a natural way when it is necessary to convey something to an assemblage.

"So I kept my arms busily employed througnout the opera, one set of gestures in particular causing Felici to remark after the performance: 'Why, Giovanni, did you spread out both arms as though making some present to the people; always the arms, like the railroad man's signal.' It was good advice which Felici gave and I heeded it. But what I think is more interesting is one other episode, of a different order.

"I sang with sufficient assurance and every-

John McCormack as Fritz in Act III of L'Amico Fritz *at the
Teatro Chiabrera, Savona, January 1906.*

The Teatro Chiabrera, Savona, in a photograph taken in 1885.

thing seemed to me to be going well until I approached a point in the opera in which I knew my audience would want from a certain top note plenty of noise. I hadn't figured it out before the performance, but as the place drew nearer I decided suddenly, as we should say nowadays, to 'camouflage' that particular tone. It was the big aria for tenor which has a top B-flat. I hadn't a good B-flat then, and when the moment came to let it go I walked to the footlights, opened my mouth and in look and attitude did my best to give an imitation of a tenor ripping out a ringing high note—though I purposely gave forth no sound.

"As true as I'm sitting here I got a round of applause."

"How do you account for it?" I wanted to know.

"Nothing but the audience's imagination," replied John. "The people *thought* that through the orchestral *forte* they were hearing what they wanted to hear, and were satisfied. But wait . . . until I tell the sequel.

"The following night I thought, when the moment for the high B-flat approached, 'I'll let them have it this time with the voice.' I did, and—would you believe it?—it didn't get over, at all. The reason is that they actually heard the tone, which hadn't the fibre and ring their imaginations had allowed them to fancy was there the preceding night."

It was a delicate question, yet it had a bearing upon John's career, so I ventured to ask: "You had a . . . success?"

"I shouldn't call it that," he answered, and with no show of irritation whatsoever. "It was, of course, nothing like what the Italians term a fiasco. Still, if medals had been awarded I should not have found my chest completely covered with them. I believe it would be within the full truth to say that I was mildly 'accepted.'

"The Italian public, however, never became enthusiastic over me. Some time later—I'll tell the facts at the proper place—when I came down from England, an artist, to sing a brief season at the San Carlo, in Naples, I caused no furore. But some day, when the War is over, I am going back to Italy to sing in opera. I think I'll be ready then for them, and I hope they'll be ready for me."

I surmised that McCormack would drift into

recounting his concluding Milan student days before our train passed Greenwich. He had fallen into another of those reflective silences of his as we rushed through Larchmont; it held into Mamaroneck; showed a trace of awakening as the station signs of Harrison blurred before my eyes, and with Rye fading behind John stirred in his seat.

"Destroying letters," he remarked, "is sometimes a pity."

"Some kinds of letters," I agreed.

"Mine were that kind," replied the tenor, a pensive touch in that full-toned speaking voice of his. "I used to write, in detail, to my fiancée of my Milan experiences: my thoughts and labors, everything, I believe, which happened to me in which she would be interested. And in some way, shortly before our marriage, they were destroyed. I've often wished I had them now.

"However—" McCormack is somewhat philosophical, and he turned abruptly from this subject to a pleasanter one—"Sabatini welcomed me back from Savona and wanted to know my version as to all that had happened. I had to tell him of each occurrence, down to the most insignificant one, and, that finished, to recapitulate the important points, with care for completeness and precision.

"It must have been a natural feeling, Sabatini had only a few pupils, then. He was an old man, as I have said. And severe. He had respect for the truth only, and no facility (nor inclination in that direction, either) for subterfuge. Things he didn't mean he could not say, or act. He was a plain man—simple and honest. It pleases me to think that his sympathies were more largely for me than any other pupil he had. Probably he considered I was most in need of them. He sat in his arm-chair as I talked on, nodding occasionally and clasping and unclasping his lean fingers.

" 'For the beginning, Giovanni, it is well—I think.' I saw that he was endeavoring to dissipate any misgivings I entertained as to the lack of real success. 'The start, he go slow; and bye and bye he pick up.' That was typical of the *maestro*. To build slowly, with a view to permanency, was his creed and he held to it with the tenacity of one of half his years.

"After the Savona début, which was in December of Nineteen Five, I progressed rapidly.

Those appearances put something into my singing which had not theretofore been present: a degree of confidence in self that allowed a broader style, a greater freedom and brought its consequent artistic growth.

"It was some two months later that my second opportunity arrived to sing in opera, this time under conditions that were to bring me money. Contracts were signed for ten performances of 'Faust,' for a fee of two hundred francs, in Santa Crōce, a little town near Florence. But it was an expensive affair, in spite of what I got, for one hundred and sixty francs went to the railway company which took me from Milan to my destination and back. But I had my appearances, under the name of Giovanni Foli (Italianizing my name, and my future father-in-law's, as I had also done for the Savona engagement) and an experience that has induced laughter whenever I have since recalled the incident.

"The soprano was an attractive young woman, who was accompanied by her mother. I had found time to wander about Santa Crōce, and as my bump of location is well developed I learned the direction of those spots about the theatre, and the boarding-house where we stopped. Listen, now, to this; it's the one adventure of the kind in my experience.

"We had finished a rehearsal. As I came outside the theatre I met the soprano and her mother, evidently confused as to the way to the boarding-house and hesitating to walk that way unescorted. A vehicle—one of the closed sort one finds in that part of Italy—drove along the street at that moment, and I hailed it and invited the two ladies to accompany me in it to the place, which was presided over by the impresario's wife, whom I shall never forget as a remarkable cook.

"I did not like the looks of the driver. Sour-visaged, he was, with shaggy brows; a brigandish looking fellow, who might have graduated from the country into a village, or, possibly, have been on vacation. I put the soprano and her mother into the vehicle, and followed them.

"There was conversation about the rehearsal and we drove on. But when we came to a certain spot I observed the driver turned to his left instead of going to the right, which I remembered was the way to our home. I had not missed, either, I might add, a few moments before the turn, seeing a man climb up and on to the back of our carriage. I was instantly suspicious, for it was growing dark and the driver's reply to my order to go the other way brought a surly response.

" 'The hotel's to the right, not the direction you're taking,' I said. I leaned out of the carriage window, and glared at the fellow. And looking rearwards I caught a glimpse of the suspicious passenger perched on our back axle.

" 'No, signor,' retorted our driver, 'the hotel is the way I am going. Just a different route.'

" 'Well, you go the way I tell you, or—' "

"Well," I said, a trifle impatiently perhaps, "go on. Don't stop in the middle of it. I suppose you drew your trusty pistol."

John grinned. "You guessed it. I did,—a nickel-plated thirty-two-calibre peanut shooter."

"You, a tenor, packing a gun?" I was astonished; but I saw that McCormack was not exaggerating. He was in dead earnest.

"A foolish kid-notion," he admitted, "but it worked. I always carried the thing about; and when I shoved it outside the window and issued orders the driver wheeled as I desired—and I noticed the man behind drop off and disappear in the dusk.

"But I was shaking all over. If those brigands— and I've no doubt they were that—

had put up a fight I should probably have been whipped."

"February and March slipped by and April brought the flowers of spring and that balminess of air which makes Milan a place of joy at that time of year. I was disturbed for the immediate future, for again my funds were below the mark of safety. But vocally I seemed to be on solid earth.

"My high tones at last were coming with freedom and had the quality corresponding to those in the lower part of the voice. And that elusive, to me, *mezza-voce* seemed well-nigh conquered. Musically I was well along and the repertoire one of respectable proportions. In a year my advancement had been rather remarkable; so, at any rate, it appeared, and others besides Sabatini spoke of this—which came back to me by roundabout courses.

"What it had usually taken others much longer to acquire had been given me quickly. Yet an operatic career (so far as Italy might be introduced into it) did not loom upon the immediate horizon with any significant glow."

John lapsed into silence again, looked out of the window, and back at me. "Stamford," he said. We picked up our hats and walked forward and out to the car platform as the train drew into the station and stopped. The machine was purring along the Boston Post Road before McCormack returned to his subject.

"Somewhere," he remarked, "there was started a story that Sabatini demanded his tuition in advance. That's an error. He never, at any time during my study with him, mentioned in that connection the word 'money' to me. And it was some time after I left Milan, in May, Nineteen Six, that I was able to hand him the forty dollars I owed him for those last two months when I was on my way from London to sing at the San Carlo, in Naples.

"When I went to him with my financial troubles he smiled in his fatherly way, saying: 'You shall not worry, Giovanni, about that small sum. One day, when it is convenient, you will send him to me.' He regarded me as a son; and I well remember his greeting a day when I arrived in Milan from London, March, 1909, an arrival on a train which also carried Sabatini's own son into the station.

"We came down the station platform, very near together, with young Sabatini slightly in advance. His father shook hands with him, nothing more. Then he walked on, to me, and kissed me on both cheeks.

"He understood me," explained McCormack. "That, unquestionably, was one of the causes of his moulding my voice as he did, and of guiding me in my interpretations of the opera rôles I learned. He would say to me: *'Crescendo* here, Giovanni, to secure the effect we want'; or 'Some more emphasis to that phrase'; or 'Do not hurry it.' He knew the finishing touches required. Yet he was insistent that I put into each interpretation the individuality of my own conception. He liked the artist to 'give and take' in his own way, here and there, as seemed to him necessary.

"I left Sabatini, on the morning I started back to Ireland, standing at the door of his studio and waving me a farewell. It marked the conclusion of my formal studies with him, not the end of our friendship, for he lived eight years longer, long enough to allow me to be able to send him more pupils than he could find time to accept."

The machine stopped at the McCormack door and we got out and went into the house.

CHAPTER X

A storm broke before the dinner hour passed; an old-fashioned storm with lightning and crackling thunder-peals that reverberated from ear-splitting sonority into *decrescendi* that carry them off, fainter and fainter, into vast distance. The rain fell fast, and whipped by the gusts against the window-panes made eerie sounds. Inside Rocklea we were snug enough. Over the coffee the fury of the elements heightened, if anything, that feeling of content which comes to a healthy person after having dined well.

Cyril McCormack was leaning in the hollow of his mother's arm, and half against the chair, talking to her in an affectionately manly way. Gwenny sat in her father's lap, her cheek against his, one hand fondling his neck; but her drooping lids forecast the sand-man's coming. The rest of us—Miss Foley, Edwin Schneider (one of the

139

family, almost) and I—sat variously about, in good humor.

Wanting to smoke, and write a bit, I disappeared after a time in the direction of that remote study referred to in an earlier chapter. From the higher windows a better view of the Sound was to be had. I peered, as well as the driving rain would allow, to see what the waters were doing, but nothing more than veils of spray from waves dashing against the pier was my reward.

So I went to the desk and work.

It was a night either for early retiring or late sitting-up and the former evidently must have been the majority verdict in the McCormack family; for I had not been busy half an hour before John strolled in to announce himself the sole survivor, and talkatively inclined.

I invited him to one of his own chairs and pushed back from the desk to face him.

"If I were a painter," began the tenor, "such a storm would send me with tubes and brush to my easel. I shouldn't have to see it in detail, either. What the darkness reveals would be enough. My imagination could do the rest."

"Then it suggests something to you?" I asked.

John acquiesced. "Those first days in Dublin, when I arrived there from Italy after the death of my second father, Patrick Foley. Some great prop seemed all at once to have been removed from the world, which loomed vaguely larger and more threatening to my youthful mind. A sort of cold solemnity seemed upon everything, as though the world itself were a personality that looked with disinterested questioning upon me, as if to say: 'And what, pray, will you do now?' It was very much that way; and this night is a reminder.

"I feel, as you know," said the tenor, "rather deeply. During those days that dragged on after my return I could not set myself to anything. Something seemed to have been removed from my being. I slept badly and had no appetite and could not concentrate. Over the whole of me was an uncontrollable desire to fold up and lie down.

"Of course, that sort of thing could not be permitted to go on indefinitely. The fact revealed itself one morning as I arose. So I summoned a resolute manner, squelched as well as I was able the dejection within me and went out of the house in quest of work. If effort would count,

I argued, I should have no self-accusation; and the following week was one of sufficient activity, so far as I was concerned.

"In the evenings I saw Miss Foley, my fiancée, and together we would review the sum of the day's accomplishments. She had, besides her own qualities of appeal to me, her father's astuteness of mind. I think we began to see how necessary each was to the other. For myself, I was endeavoring constantly to escape answering in my own mind an internally voiced question which I never allowed to be fully put. But I knew, without practising self-deception, what it was. I wanted to make Miss Foley Mrs. McCormack.

"But there was the important matter of earning capacity to be faced.

"It was when I was in one of these moods that I met Tom Bissette, Miss Foley's brother-in-law, and confided my trouble to him. I asked what he thought about my reflection upon the wisdom of marriage at such a time.

" 'The best thing for you both,' he promptly replied. 'So far as I can see nothing can be gained by waiting. There may be hardship for awhile, but what's that to a man of courage? I have confidence in you, Mac,' he averred; 'you will make a career, and money. And if you want to marry Lily, go ahead.'

"Can you fancy what a tonic such advice was to me?" asked John, but he allowed me no reply. He went right on. "I hurried to Miss Foley by the shortest route, and told her I thought we shouldn't delay our wedding any longer. She listened smilingly, while I argued on. I daresay I was agitated. When I at length paused for breath, and to survey her reception of my presumably unexpected announcement, she calmly rejoined: 'I think so too, John.'

"After that our sole thought was of the wedding, and to hasten it. I wrote the family, in Athlone, and received the approbation of my father and mother with assurances that they would be with us on the appointed date, if at all possible.

"At last my heart's desire was to be realized. Singing took a back seat during those preparatory days for the ceremony—except for the desultory phrases I sang for the joy of the approaching happiest hour of my life. Lily brightened, too, and bloomed.

"The Foley family was prominent in Dublin,

and the announcement of her coming marriage to me on July second, Nineteen Six, was not without its community interest. And on that day, at 7 o'clock in the morning, Lily Foley and I were united in the Marlborough Street Cathedral, in Dublin, and left for London at 8:30 the same morning.

"We should have enjoyed a lengthy honeymoon, but—we decided it out of fashion. So we contented ourselves with a trip to London, where we prowled delightedly about, two happy youngsters with an abiding faith in things.

"But the McCormack exchequer was by no means in a corpulent state, and it was not long before I realized that something must be done to keep the wolf from the garage."

"You mean the one where you kept your Rolls-Royce?"

"Yes," said John with a grin. "Well, I was seized with a bright idea. When I had made my twenty-five records of songs for the Gramophone Company you will recall that the contract stipulated I should not be asked to do over any record which chanced to be slightly imperfect. Remembering this, it occurred to me to go to the Gramophone people and suggest doing over any,

or every, record. I was, of course, a better artist
than when these songs had been sung, and I believed that some advertising of my return from
Italy would stimulate their sale."

"Not a bad idea," I commented.

"Humph!" said McCormack. "You think
so?"

"Didn't the Gramophone manager?"

"He did not. What do you suppose he said?
That any records I might make would be useless
to him.

"But," remarked John, with the flicker of a
smile about his mouth, "that company has since
paid me—let me see—yes, it has paid me in
royalties, for records I afterward made, one hundred and fifty thousand dollars. My secondary
proposition, when Mrs. McCormack and I were in
London, at the end of our honeymoon, was to
sing ten records for ten pounds apiece. They
might have acquired sole possession of them at
that price, and have had no obligation to pay me
a dollar of royalties.

"Of course, at the time, the refusal was a blow.
Yet it did not propel me into the state of dejection which many might assume would have followed. I have the artist nature, but none of the

tendency towards abrupt discouragement which that nature is presumed to have in the face of obstacles.

"My faith never really wavered, and a natural optimism buoyed me. And Mrs. McCormack was a brave little soul, a true wife who stood up bravely under all adversity with never a word of complaint.

"So I made the rounds of concert agency offices, getting a few insignificant engagements which paid little. More, much more, than I could earn we were spending for actual living expenses; and the small sum I had had when we were married was nearly gone."

I should like, here, to interject what Michael Keane told me of those McCormack struggles during my talk with him in his New York office.

"Shortly after McCormack came to London, upon finishing his studies in Italy, he made a contract with a London agent. The boy was inexperienced in the ways of business, and being generous himself he did not question the equity of any contract which might be drawn for him to sign. But this agent did not succeed in getting him any really serious engagements.

"Some idea of the character of this contract may be gathered from the fact that it was for the duration of McCormack's life. Fancy such an arrangement. Of course it couldn't last. Yet the cancellation of that document cost the tenor, years afterward, ten thousand dollars."

Mr. Keane had additional information of McCormack's experiences during those London days, all of which will be duly set down in the proper places.

"It was at this time that chance brought me, again, into communication with the Moody-Manners Opera Company," resumed McCormack. "At the request of Charles Manners I sang an *audition* for him, and he was pleased. 'If you could only act as well as you sing,' he mused, 'I'd give you twenty pounds a week.' This brought a retort such as I had made, in an almost similar way, before—that if I could *act* it would be Covent Garden I would seek, instead of a position with his company.

"London having shown slight signs of immediately warming to me," remarked McCormack, "we thought Italy might offer some operatic chance. A consultation in the John McCormack family ensued, and the board of directors—con-

147

sisting of Mrs. McCormack and myself—voted unanimously to make the journey to Milan, and, if necessary, to any other cities where possible engagements might be lurking."

Here the tenor got up, to go to the window. The rain still beat fiercely against the glass, driven by the wind which we could hear howling like a soul in anguish. I followed, to get the kinks out of my legs. A single flash of lightning made bright for a moment the terraced lawn and the leaping waters of the Sound.

"I had no more chance in Italy," remarked the tenor, "than a man would have trying to swim in that surf. I sang *audition* after *audition;* and opera-house managers listened, and passed me on. But *auditions* are not a fair criterion and my nerves never allowed me to do myself justice by them.

"We hadn't been long back in our small quarters in London before Fortune permitted herself to smile, just a little, upon us. I was desperate, willing enough to take anything which would pay at all. Through an agent I secured an engagement to sing at Queen's Hotel, in Leicester Square—for a guinea. It was not cabaret, as it has been said to be, but the appearance was inconsequential and meant nothing more than the five dollars I received.

"Other engagements, at different hotels, were offered me and gladly accepted. All the while I studied at home, and practised rigidly and sought to preserve a tranquil mind and an unwavering heart. But it wasn't easy. I began, during those dark days, to ask myself if I had not been ungenerous in asking the woman I loved to share with me those troublous times; it was difficult enough for a man.

"Then, one morning, an agent informed me he had arranged for me to appear as assisting artist to Camille Clifford, the original Gibson girl, and though the fee was only one guinea I jumped, as one will say, at the chance. That engagement led to others of the same kind, each one yielding approximately the same compensation and very little honor.

"Nevertheless, I would not have missed for a great deal the experience these appearances as assisting artist taught. I was, at any rate, becoming more at ease before an audience and practising in public the things which I had learned

in the studio and which, really, are never fixed in
a singer's equipment until they have been utilized
over and over again before many listeners, presumably critical.

"One of these singers whom I assisted, auring
that part of Nineteen Six, was Edna May. I
know that she is generally regarded as a comic
opera star—or was, in her period of success—
whose beauty and charm constituted her chief attributes of appeal. At the same time, I found
her voice an excellent one and her ability as a
singer distinctly above the average.

"It was a struggle, especially during those hot
August days that leave one physically limp at
their close and scarcely in the mood to be cheery
and bright, a struggle that went on during the
fall and winter, into the next spring. But Mrs.
McCormack and I kept up, nevertheless. Together we would plan for the future with as much
fortitude—and confidence, too—as though the
ultimate outcome were assured.

" 'You are destined to win, John,' Mrs. Mc-
Cormack would reiterate, and I believed that she
spoke the truth.

"How close she was to it we neither of us then
knew. I think it was the consciousness of our

doing all that we could do that kept our faith staunch. But better days were not far distant, and in March, 1907, there emerged from the glowering sky a ray of promise."

CHAPTER XI

McCormack had been standing at the study window during the closing part of his description of those trying London days. There seemed, in the storm outside, something which held and fascinated him; a similarity, perhaps, in the rain and wind and lightning, with intermittent thunder-claps, to the forces which opposed him when he and his girl-wife faced together the privations which the young seem best able to endure.

"I had met in the course of my London travels," said John, "a professor of singing in the Royal College of Music—Albert Vesetti. He had been accompanist to Adelina Patti, and on several occasions he had heard me sing and liked my voice. There were others, too, whom I formed acquaintance with, Charles Marshall, composer of 'I Hear You Calling,' who had played for me at small concerts, being one of these. But Vesetti had influence, and after one

152

of my most satisfactory appearances he offered to write a letter of introduction for me to Willie Boosey, who was an executive in the music publishing house of Chappell and Company, and another letter to Arthur Boosey, of Boosey and Company. These men were first cousins, but that did not prevent their being business rivals. It was a gracious act, and I accepted the letters with every appreciation of the motive prompting it.

"Somehow, however, I was evidently not intended at that particular time, to meet Willie Boosey. I sent word in by a clerk that I had a letter from Vesetti, and was informed that Mr. Boosey would see me in a few minutes, and would I wait. I did. For over an hour I sat patiently, until patience became worn to the bone.

"I thereupon—though precisely why I am unable to fathom—went from Chappell's to Arthur Boosey. But instead of waiting there, as I had done in the first instance, I sent my letter up to Arthur Boosey and left the place. So when I was sought to be taken to this gentleman I was nowhere about.

"This circumstance appeared to amuse Arthur Boosey, for at his next meeting with Vesetti he remarked: 'That was a strange young man you sent to me. He never even waited to learn whether I could see him. Have him call round again.'

"Now Arthur Boosey was in control of the Boosey Ballad Concerts, which formed an important part of London's musical offerings, and Vesetti had told me that if I appeared successfully in one of them my opportunities might be many and profitable. He was amused at Arthur Boosey's account of my call, and appeared to understand that I had not remained, after delivering his introductory letter, for fear of annoying the distinguished Boosey.

" 'Never mind,' consoled Vesetti, 'go again; and this time stay until you meet him.'

"I found Arthur Boosey a kindly man, with an understanding of human nature and a sympathy for struggling young singers—providing they displayed potentialities. His faith in Vesetti's judgment was confirmed, after he had heard me sing, and inviting me to return to his office we sat down to talk business.

" 'How would you like to sing at my next ballad concert?' he asked, after our introductory talk. You can guess my reply. 'Will three guineas be enough?' I replied, 'Yes, plenty.' Whereupon the arrangements were concluded, and I departed to prepare for the most auspicious London appearance which had thus far offered.

"Mrs. McCormack was excited when I brought her the news. 'It will make you,' she declared. So I got ready for the concert, working the *'Questa 'o Quella'* aria from 'Rigoletto,' and the other works I had chosen as nearly perfect in those respects I desired. Samuel Liddle, who was the official Boosey Ballad Concerts accompanist, and who had played for me when I sang Stephen Adams's 'Nirvana' for Arthur Boosey, gave me a suggestion, at this time, which turned out amazingly well.

" 'What you ought to do, Mac,' he advised, 'is to find some new ballad that just suits you, and introduce it at the first concert.'

" 'Fine,' I replied, 'if I could find the ballad.'

"At this Liddle dug out a piece of manuscript from his desk, went over to the piano and began to play it. The song was called 'A Farewell,' and had been set by Liddle himself to words by Charles Kingsley. I saw that it had possibilities, and after I had tried it over—which I did then and there—I found that it suited my voice so well that I decided, immediately, to use it at my ballad concert début.

To many readers of this book an English ballad concert is an institution whose functions are understood; but to those unfamiliar with the Boosey Ballad Concerts it must be explained that more than one singer rose or fell through them. They were held in Queen's Hall (until a few years ago, when circumstances that need not be related here caused their transfer to Albert Hall), on Saturday afternoons, and were attended by the smartest of London folk as well as by the masses. Musicians of position always attended, because there often appeared some distinguished pianist or violinist—in addition to the half-dozen or more singers who carried the main part of a programme.

It was not unusual for the London Symphony Society patrons to purchase seats for a symphony concert at Queen's Hall box-office, and at the same time obtain tickets for the approaching ballad concert. Established artists always found admirers there to greet them, and these connoisseurs—amateur and professional—inclined invariably a listening ear for the newcomer, and a critical ear it was.

156

"I will not intimate that all my eggs were in one basket," observed McCormack. "But . . . I knew what it would mean if I created any impression short of the exceptional. 'Getting by,' as we say, would never do. It had to be something of an emphatic nature; the accomplishment of enough to set talking those whose opinions carried weight.

"I arrived early at my dressing-room," continued the tenor, "in a state of calm. It was a form of nervousness I like, for it presages just the proper degree of apprehensiveness to balance the confidence necessary to do one's best. I had done my worrying at home: at night, when I should have slept, during my hours of practice preparation and in my talks with Mrs. McCormack. So my feeling, as I waited my turn, had in it nothing which an interpretative artist need fear.

"There was a large audience that Friday afternoon, the seats being quite filled. I was fifth on the list of singers, a favorable position, and my introductory aria, *'Questa 'o Quella.'* The moment to go out came at last, and with Samuel Liddle, the official accompanist, I appeared before my most important assemblage."

157

John stopped walking and removed his hands from his pockets. He selected a cigarette from a tray filled with them, and resumed his tramping between desk and window. But he did not light up. Twirling the cigarette between thumb and forefinger of one hand he continued his story.

"For a space of time infinitesimally small my heart sank. Nearly all musicians who appear before the public, and speakers, too, experience such a feeling, at some time, I am sure. It is the quick surge of doubt; of possible failure to meet the issue squarely. Yet I would not term it fear. Just a natural apprehension—that comes and departs almost in the flicker of the eye.

"I was myself, my calm self, almost instantly. And as I looked into the faces before me I thought: 'Well, here is my chance, and I shall make the most of it.' Then Liddle began the accompaniment.

"Before the song was finished I recognized from the audience that I was not failing. The voice was responsive and smooth, I had control of my resources and felt that my enunciation could be clearly understood. I could see little signs which auditors invariably indulge in whenever favorably impressed; and this encouraged me to let myself go more freely.

"One quickly catches the temper of an assemblage after a song has been sung. There is a difference between applause, spontaneously given because the givers have been moved, and the perfunctory clapping of hands which caps a mediocre effort. I left the stage, after profuse acknowledgement, with my nerve-centres tingling. I seemed to float, rather than to walk, to the stage exit. And following me came the sound of many palms beating against one another.

"Several persons were congregated about the place back stage where I stepped out of sight of the audience. I recall hearing, as from some distance, congratulatory words, and of receiving a hearty slap, from some one, on my back. The remainder of that afternoon remains in my memory as a sort of intoxicating daze.

"Mrs. McCormack, who had gone to Dublin, where Cyril was born shortly after my ballad concert début, sent me a telegram; and after I had read it I could only think of my faith rewarded; of answered prayers . . . and of an overpowering sense of gratitude.

"In the morning I looked out of our window into the street below with exultation. It was no premature anticipation of immediate rewards or of suddenly acquired fame; nothing of such nature. But at last there seemed a semblance of something tangible, to which I might attach myself with an assurance of reasonable hopes. Succinctly put: it was a successfully executed first step.

"But if I rejoiced for Mrs. McCormack and for myself I felt thankful that my good friends who recommended me, and Arthur Boosey who provided me my chance, had not had their confidence misplaced. In this buoyant vein I called on Mr. Boosey. Without hesitation, yet with no fulsome words, he informed me that I had exceeded expectations. 'If you do as well at the second concert no one will be sorry.' It was like him, to put it in that way; no rousing of false hopes that might be dissipated at the next test, just wholesome encouragement which is what the young singer on the brink of progress requires."

McCormack had rather worked himself up in relating this début. I did not wonder at it. He lived that afternoon over again, right there in the secluded Rocklea study while the storm blared outside—a weird accompaniment to the tale.

"And the second Boosey Concert, how did that go?"

"Even better, if anything, than the first. You see, I had more confidence; I really had. It was more of the genuine order. The sort I possessed at the first concert was more or less false, which was commanded by what will I had to come and stay with me for that particular afternoon.

"I am told that there had been some talk among musicians, and lovers of music, about the singing of a young Irish tenor at the last Boosey Ballad Concert, that he had proved a surprise, and was to sing on the next programme. Of course, among people who follow musical affairs an interest to hear me ensued. You know how it is; a personal desire to investigate for one's self, to determine how much of truth there may be in assertions of the reputed capacities of a new artist.

"I did not, of course, know that my second appearance was to be memorable in my life and to enlist the subsequent confidence and support of a man influential in large affairs in London.

Little things so often have a marked bearing upon our destinies, and here was an instance with respect to my own.

"The man I refer to—he is dead, now, to the sorrow of innumerable thousands—was Sir John Murray Scott. He was secretary to the late Sir Richard Wallace, son of the Marquis of Herford, whose art collection was one of the most complete ever in the possession of a single individual. Sir John had been practically reared by Sir Richard Wallace, whose wife, Lady Wallace, regarded Sir John almost as her own son. And it is true that after the death of her husband she summoned Sir John and told him it was her wish that the famous art collection be conveyed to him. It was like Sir John to refuse. He explained that, though he was a man of means, it would be difficult for him to pay the inheritance tax on the art collection. But apart from this, he insisted that the time had come for these art works to be made available to the people, and he therefore suggested that it be tendered the British Museum.

"Sir John," continued McCormack, "was himself an admirable pianist. His musical

*John McCormack and one Maestro Disconzi (otherwise un-
identified), Savona, February 1906.*

John McCormack as he appeared shortly after his return from Italy in 1906.

knowledge was extensive and he possessed to a remarkable degree the critical faculty. No less exacting a music reviewer than Jimmy Davidson, critic for the London *Times*, respected Sir John's judgment to an extent that caused him, frequently, to ask his friend to attend a notable concert and write the critique.

"At that second Boosey Ballad Concert Sir John heard me sing for the first time. And I appeared to have qualities of voice and feeling and style which enlisted his respect, as I was later to discover. To have gained an admirer in a man of the standing and knowledge of Sir John would have been compensation enough for one appearance, but that Friday afternoon did another thing for me.

"It so happened that the *Telegraph's* music critic delegated the covering of that concert to a gifted writer on the staff, Robert Maguire. And 'Bob' Maguire, as he was affectionately called, was a man of culture. Without having been trained in the technique of music, Maguire had the faculty of unerring judgment, even though incapable of discerning the whys and wherefores on which his judgment was based. I only know that his opinions in matters musical commanded respect among the many who were fortunate in having his acquaintance, and that he wrote entertainingly and often with brilliant style. Moreover, he had a fine baritone voice and sang well.

"Bob heard me at the second Boosey concert; and in the *Telegraph* of the next day there appeared, in his article, mention of a new tenor, an Irishman named John McCormack, whose future held superlative promise. 'It would be unfair,' wrote Maguire, in substance, 'to compare this inexperienced singer with Caruso, yet his voice has much of the quality of that greatest of all tenors.'

"When I read that article," said John, "I no longer doubted. It seemed a mere matter of time; a series of progressive steps onward, until I should finally be accepted as an artist and accorded the engagements and emoluments which an artist commands. From that day I may say that the turning point in my career arrived. I never was unfortunate enough to drop backward. There came disappointments, trials and obstacles to overcome; but the drudgery and heart-aches were past.

"Some time afterward, when we moved into

another section of London, I made a delightful discovery—my next door neighbor, a man whom until then I had never seen, was Bob Maguire; and we became intimate friends."

CHAPTER XII

LONDON RECOGNIZES MC CORMACK

Noroton, Connecticut, lies in a beautiful country. Skirting a part of Long Island Sound, it drops back through sweeps of hills, green and wooded, that form a landscape varying to the eye. It is uncommonly beautiful after rain, which freshens; and the morning following our extended vigil the countryside burst with beauty.

I was up and dressed early. A morning walk, in that section, is no opportunity to be neglected. I descended from my room, treading quietly down the staircase lest I arouse others who had not done with their sleep.

So intent was I with caution that I did not observe, until I was on the bottom landing, a figure bent over the stick-rack in the hall. As the figure straightened up I recognized the shoulders, broad as a walking-beam, and the rest of John McCormack's sturdy frame. He turned, and seeing me, sniffed in surprise and opened the outer door.

"Running out for some fresh air?"

I confessed the accusation and my gratification that I should have aid in the exploration.

"Well, then, you'll have to walk. No loafing, or you walk alone."

I said nothing in reply. I needed my breath, for the tenor struck a pace, and held to it, that would have made Dan O'Leary cast an envious eye. For several miles John had no words for me. He was cheery enough, and companionable in a silence we both understood. But the present concerned nature and a brisk walk and the deep inhaling of health-giving pure air.

"Tired?" demanded McCormack.

I lied a little in a denial.

John looked down at me—I'm shorter than he, and some pounds lighter—and grinned. "I weighed before starting," he confided. "I'm dropping steadily, under my training." I replied that he looked it, as he did. Not much above the two hundred mark, his lines were athletic and showed a man of thirty-four conditioning fast.

"What did you think of that story I told you last night?"

I answered that he had stopped at an interesting point at which I was not unwilling he should resume. John grunted at this, strode on for a couple of hundred yards farther, and picked up his narrative.

"I don't suppose any one ever will know the joy I got from the letters my father and mother sent me when they heard of my singing at the second Boosey Concert. You would have thought they were happier than I. Well, possibly they were; for I know something, myself, of parental love. It's a wonderful thing. A man's never completely a man, nor a woman a woman, until children come. With them the world takes on a different look. It puts something into the perspective which isn't otherwise there. So the letters from mother and father made my own gladness the greater because of theirs.

"Vincent O'Brien rather chortled a bit, too. You see, he took a justifiable pride in his tenor discovery, and Sabatini, my good *maestro*, who wrote that Giovanni was only getting started and reminded me of numerous counselings he had given me in the past.

"Mrs. McCormack, naturally, also wrote, from Dublin. It thrilled me to read her words and know that her patience was not to be in vain.

"One meets many people in music life, and I have been no exception to this. Sometimes these meetings are uncommonly productive, and lead to strange happenings. I almost think they are the guidings of Destiny's hand. I had such an experience two days after the second Ballad Concert, when Miss Eva Gauthier, a Canadian soprano then studying in London, called me by 'phone and asked if I would like to go with her, the following evening, to call on Sir John Murray Scott. I of course knew who Sir John was; who, in London, didn't? Yet I was loath to accept Miss Gauthier's invitation without one from Sir John himself. So I explained to Miss Gauthier. She communicated with him . . . which she could with propriety do, because he was a close friend of Sir Wilfrid Laurier, Canada's premier, whose protégée Miss Gauthier was.

"Sir John responded immediately, saying: 'If he is the young tenor I heard at the Boosey concert bring him with you. I admire his voice and should like to meet him.'

"We went and that marked the beginning of a friendship that lasted until Sir John's death. I've always called him my fairy-godfather, because of his kindnesses. He was a huge man physically, and just as large in brain and heart. He played a piano for us that evening, with a touch more velvety and singing than many a distinguished pianist I have heard. I recall his saying that the test for a pianoforte artist was an ability to play the slow movement of Beethoven's 'Moonlight' Sonata; just as the mark of a singer's skill rose or fell according to the *cantilena* displayed. I sang several songs that evening for Sir John, whose presence had an indescribably stimulating effect upon me.

"The news of my Boosey successes traveled fast. I received engagements for a number of concerts, and they paid fairly well and sent me steadily along the path I desired. Offers of various kinds came also and some I was glad to consider.

"Arthur Boosey, convinced now of my usefulness to him, summoned me. 'I am, as you know, finishing with the ballad concerts for the season, but next year I can use you for each of the seven. And if the fee is satisfactory we will draw the contract now.' That was the start of our long-held relations, which resulted in a life contract—which is one of my prized possessions

170

—to sing at any Boosey Ballad Concert I may designate at the highest appearance fee ever paid.

"After having waited and worked so long for recognition it was good to taste it. I was like a Marathon runner who drinks thirstily of water after his punishing journey; but I tried to evade the danger of complacency. Long before, a friend, Mrs. Denny Lane, had warned me of the proverb: 'Non progredi, est regredi,' and I heeded that. In art one never stands still; there must be movement, either forward or back, and I wished to advance.

"About this time Willie Boosey sent for me. I of course went at once to see him and was taken into his office where he shook hands with me cordially and asked me to be seated. He did not endeavor to disguise the issue, his conversation—after he had congratulated me on my ballad concert success—turning at once to his own series.

" 'You are an artist,' he said, 'and the public likes you. I want you to sing at my concerts and am willing to pay you your own price.'

"I thanked him, and answered, 'I am sorry, Mr. Boosey, but you haven't money enough in your establishment to induce me to appear on your programmes. Arthur Boosey gave me my chance when I needed it, and I shall remain with him.'

"Willie Boosey sat there looking at me for some time before making answer; I'll always respect what he said. 'Thanks, McCormack,' he replied, 'I'm glad to know one singer who understands gratitude.' I left Willie Boosey more than ever sure that the straight course is the best, in respects other than keeping one's conscience at peace.

"Spring was near at hand, and just before it broke in that year, Nineteen Seven, came my first invitation to sing at a symphony concert. The artist who had been engaged fell ill suddenly, and word of the opening reached my new-found friend, Sir John Murray Scott, chairman of the Sunday Concert Society, who immediately nominated me for the vacancy. I was gratified when Henry J. Wood, conductor of the London Symphony, asked me if I would appear because a year before, when William Ludwig had presented me to Sir Henry, he had not encouraged me.

"The concert was one of those held on Sunday afternoons and was largely attended. The

172

rehearsal had been accomplished, I felt, to the satisfaction of the conductor, and I was less apprehensive after it; for Wood held rigid ideas musically and I wished particularly to have my musicianship satisfy him. My object was to please sufficiently to justify being engaged to sing at one of the Friday afternoon concerts."

"And were you?"

"Yes; the first symphony appearance roused the best in me. And on the Good Friday programme I appeared as soloist. But I think that Sir John Murray Scott was chiefly responsible for the re-engagement. He believed the success merited encouragement and he counted my symphony début as that. The second appearance rather fortified my confidence. I was not so conceited as to regard a moderate triumph as providing laurels to be rested on; but the public and the press, and some musician friends, told me that I was ready for serious singing under large auspices, and I believed them.

"But in the midst of these bits of good fortune came another, and greater one. For on the 26th of March, Nineteen Seven, in Dublin, Cyril was born. I got word, by telegraph, and can't you just imagine my feelings? I wanted to shout the good news from the housetops. I can safely say I never felt more genuinely proud in my life; in fact I felt as every young father feels at the safe arrival of his first-born. I had hoped our first-born would be a son, and the news seemed further evidence that I was being smiled on. Music disappeared from my mind, for the time being, and I hurried to Dublin and remained until Mrs. McCormack and Cyril were well enough to allow me to return without worrying about them.

"Every week seemed to strengthen the friendship between Sir John Murray Scott and me. He was good enough to invite me often to his home, and there I benefited far more even than I was then able to comprehend. For Sir John's outlook upon life was broad, and he imparted to those privileged to come in contact with him an appreciation of what such a perspective meant. I know in my own case that he stimulated the finer qualities and eventually enabled me to understand that to become a great singing artist— in the full sense—one must be more, merely, than singer and musician.

"Some time before these days (to retrace our steps a bit), Gordon Cleather had suggested

John McCormack in Faust, *Dublin, May 1907.*

John McCormack and Sir John Murray Scott, a photograph taken in London about the time of McCormack's 1907 Covent Garden debut.

my seeing George Edwardes, manager of the London Gaiety and Daly's Theatre, who was then planning to present 'The Waltz Dream,' which has a fine part for tenor and takes a tenor to sing it. But Mr. Edwardes was out of town, and the acting manager—J. A. E. Malone— whom everyone called 'Alphabet' Malone, was 'chesty' under his temporary authority.

"He consented to hear me sing, which struck me as a bit of humor because, while I was in the midst of the aria (I think the 'Flower Song,' from 'Carmen'), I saw that he was utterly unable to make anything out of it. Nevertheless, he was not unwilling, at that, to pass an opinion and offer me a position in the chorus at ten dollars a week. 'But, Malone,' Cleather said, 'you surely can use McCormack as understudy to your first tenor.' Malone, however, held no such notion. 'Take it or leave it,' he said. I couldn't well take a position in the chorus, so I 'left it.'

"I related this experience, one evening, to Sir John Murray Scott, when calling at his house, and he laughed. 'One of these days,' he said, 'that will make a good story.' Whether it does, there is a sequel, which I will tell a little farther on, that *did* make a good story, and brought to Mr. Edwardes's manager a rebuke for having failed, at the time, to communicate with him concerning me.

"My voice, as warm weather approached, became more responsive and my ambitions increased. Covent Garden was a spot on which I had always had a secret eye, and every time I heard an opera there I yearned, a little more than the time before, for the day which would find me singing on that historic stage; more than once, on such an occasion, having said to Mrs. McCormack that I'd give anything, sometime, to have her see me up there.

"However, I kept my ambition to myself; for presumptuousness is one element I dislike. Still, the inner suggestion continued to make itself felt, so I was brought one evening to Cleofonte Campanini, who was the Covent Garden first-conductor. He was courteous enough, and agreed to hear me. 'Bring something up to my rehearsal room,' he suggested, 'and we'll see how it goes.'

"I did, as soon as I could get my music; and I sang through for him, from start to close, the tenor part in 'Cavalleria Rusticana.' 'Hm,' said Campanini when I had sung the last note, '*bella voce,* but I think you are not ready yet—for Covent Garden.' "

"I was under the impression," I interjected, "that Campanini was responsible for your Covent Garden engagement, and also for your having been brought over to the Manhattan, in New York."

"For the latter, yes; for Covent Garden, no." Then he went on. "In order that the procedure, and the difficulties one encounters before full-fledged consideration is to be had from those controlling Covent Gardent, I will explain how the authority was divided.

"There was—and still is—a board of directors, with a chairman, which exercised a supervising control over the policy and administration. This board, similar to that of the New York Metropolitan Opera House, had a personnel of wealthy and prominent men; gentlemen who figured in important affairs of finance, the arts, politics and society. 'Harry' V. Higgins was chairman of the board, and to him the heads of the various departments (I believe we may call them that) reported and from him took their counsel.

"The operating side of Covent Garden ran in

a dual way.   There was the business end, and the artistic.   Neil Forsyth, who later became one of my dear friends, was business manager of Covent Garden, and he had an assistant and numerous aides.   Percy Pitt served as a sort of adviser in the choice of repertoire, conductors and artists, and occasionally elected to conduct a performance.   He was, in a way, the link between the artistic and business parts of the organization; the man upon whose judgment and recommendations Mr. Higgins and his co-directors of the board largely relied.

"An unknown singer, seeking consideration of Covent Garden authorities, often failed to secure their attention. Some assistant conductor would be delegated to hear the candidate, to determine whether it was worth while for Mr. Pitt to hear him, or to have Mr. Pitt and several of the conductors assemble in a sort of pretentious *audition*.

"The second time I tried for Covent Garden the *audition* took place in Bechstein Hall, where Percy Pitt and several others heard me; but fortune did not then smile on me.

" 'Twas rather blue to get this setback on top of Campanini's verdict.   Among other things he and Pitt feared was that my voice was not robust enough for opera—particularly that given in Covent Garden. Yet I was not willing to consider the matter settled. It was discouraging, I admit; still a hope continued to beat within me."

For a few hundred yards McCormack and I trudged along the cement road leading towards his summer home, he thinking, doubtless, of that earlier summer when his efforts had enlisted so little response.

"But," said McCormack, increasing his stride after glancing at his watch and noting that we should have to hurry to reach Rocklea at the breakfast hour, "something important happened soon after. Sir John apparently had held the Covent Garden idea, just as I had, though he had also kept it to himself. He broached the matter one late afternoon, while I was having tea with him, and informed me he had arranged that I should sing for Percy Pitt and his associates, in a few days, in Covent Garden.

"Pitt was a splendid musician, he had been for many years accompanist at Arthur Boosey's Ballad Concerts, and his word was relied on implicitly by 'Harry' Higgins, and the other directors of Covent Garden. Once more, for the third time, I got ready for an *audition,* and the importance of this one rather told on my nerves. It isn't easy, you may believe, to undertake a musical recovery after having previously failed to impress. Then, I was not unaware that if Pitt approved me Campanini might interfere. But it was all in a lifetime, and I summoned courage and went to Covent Garden.

"The director was sitting nonchalantly in an orchestra-chair with others who were to hear me gathered about. Pitt greeted me and wasted no time in asking me to proceed.

"To the stage I went, somewhat apprehensive of the outcome, yet not over-nervous. Campanini's and Pitt's words kept returning to my mind. These thoughts, and my own determination to make as much as I could of this opportunity, conflicted; but I let them fight it out, gradually steadied myself and signalling the accompanist that I was ready I faced my critical auditors.

" *'Che Gelida Manina'* went fairly well. When I had finished I requested the accompanist to begin the 'Carmen Flower Song.' You see, I was anxious to do enough to give Pitt as

180

complete an idea as one can obtain through a single hearing of a singer of the extent of my voice and style. Once well into the aria I lost myself, almost completely, to externals, and in this second number I felt that I was achieving a creditable mark.

"The 'Flower Song' is not easy for the singer. Though often badly done in opera, it is a composition wherein the artist may disclose qualities of superiority—in the smoothness of tone, *cantilena*, warmth of style and dramatic vigor. Well done it always commands admiration, and the singer who thus interprets it gains admiration, too.

"I finished the high B-flat, and the closing phrase that comes immediately after, with a peculiar sensation. It is odd," mused John, "how one gets a premonition sometimes. I've said that I'm rather psychic. I appeared to be that day. I could almost have anticipated what the verdict would be, and as I put away the opera scores in my music-portfolio I was prepared for a favorable decision.

"It wasn't easy to assume a calm manner as I approached Pitt and his associates, who were seated in the body of the auditorium. But I stood, waiting for Pitt's words, with my heart pounding violently.

Pitt told me they would advise me of the directors' decision, and I went away. Later that day a 'phone message called me to Covent Garden.

" 'We have decided,' he said, 'to engage you —if fifteen pounds a week will be sufficient.'

"I didn't tell him so, but I would have sung for nothing. I only answered, 'I thank you, very much. If I once get into Covent Garden you will never get me out.'

"I didn't mean it to sound boastful; I was in no such mood. I only believed, in those conditions which prevailed in this wonderful opera house, that I could satisfy, and continue to do so for a long time. Pitt grasped my meaning, I'm sure, for he smiled at my words, and informed me that he would have the contract prepared for me to sign, and asked me to return the following day."

We passed through the gate at Rocklea, and on up the graveled walk to the house, just as the faint sounding of the gong announcing breakfast reached our ears.

CHAPTER XIII

LONDON OPENS ITS ARMS

John felt like fishing that morning. After his swim and a frolic with his Belgian police dog, Nellie, he announced to Mrs. McCormack that the mood was on him. "Big fellows," declared John, "which give one a tussle."

Cyril and Gwen shared their father's fishing desires and scurried off to get into their rubber-boots preparatory to the jaunt to the beach to dig the requisite clams for bait.

But Mrs. McCormack had Red Cross duties to perform and they could not wait. So she and her sister, Miss Foley, left us to our luck, which turned out to be rather good.

Wilkinson got the dory ready, and by that time Gwen and Cyril appeared, carrying between them a large pail generously filled with the lure for our finny game.

"It's odd," mused John, as he stood at the wheel of the *Rocklea*, "what the possession of that

183

Covent Garden contract did for me. It was recognition, after repeated efforts to gain it, and my confidence in myself became surer. For two days I was so filled with the joy of possession of the long-coveted document that I wasn't able to do much save to think about it. You see, I was impressionable, and rather young, which explains my state of mind."

Back of us, in the dory, Cyril and Gwen were singing; in unison, their soprano voices rising higher and higher. John stopped talking, and half turned, to listen. "They scarcely ever stop," he remarked, which was the truth. From personal knowledge I am aware that they sing at least five hours in every twenty-four; and every sort of music which the voice may give forth. This morning they engaged in competition to see which could sustain the longer phrase, and each would fill the lungs to the limit and hold on to the tone as though life depended on the test. Then Gwen, whose voice is agile, loosed scales and turns and trills until the air resounded with her warbling. And Cyril, scorning that character of vocal feat, gave himself (in the midst of his sister's singing) to altitudinous notes. It was an Ellen Beach Yaw effect.

"I never stop them," explained John; nor do I blame him. For their voices are sympathetic and true. Nor should it occasion surprise if, one day, Gwendolyn McCormack developed into a distinguished coloratura soprano, perhaps another Galli-Curci.

When I spoke of this to John he imparted to me this particular piece of information.

"You are absolutely correct about Gwen's coloratura soprano tendencies. When Mme. Galli-Curci first heard her—she was singing much as you just heard her sing—that great artist said to me: 'It would not in the least surprise me if Gwenny one day became a second Galli-Curci. (What a wonderful artist and charming body she is!)

"She really meant what she said. Mme. Galli-Curci does not go out of her way, for courtesy's sake, to say nice things—especially if they might fall into the category of exaggeration. Nor is it remarkable that Gwen and Cyril should sing as they do (apart from their having what I believe anyone will recognize as exceptional natural voices), because they have heard the best music, always, about the house. Their taste has therefore been unconsciously formed for musical masterpieces. The morning Mme. Galli-Curci heard them singing the Bach double-concerto she was actually astonished. Yet there is nothing about their having sung that composition which occasions surprise among those of us in the family, though I'll admit it is uncommon. Still, they had heard it so often from the Victor phonograph record as played by Kreisler and Zimbalist that it had sunk deep into their memories. And I want to say here, that I consider the educational value of what is being done by the Victor Talking Machine Company to be without comparison. What wouldn't I give to have records of Mario and the other great artists of early days as the Victor Company could make them!

The tenor forsook the subject of his children's musical and vocal qualifications, after those last words. Shortly afterward he got back again to Covent Garden.

"I made my début there in October, on the fifteenth, Nineteen Hundred Seven. It is a fact that I have sung there each successive season since, up to Nineteen Fourteen, when the war broke out. And I have a contract calling for the next season Covent Garden gives—which I hope will open with a gala performance in honor of the Allies' victory and which I pray, for the sake of humanity, will be soon. To complete the record it is pertinent, no doubt, to state that my remuneration has increased rather considerably.

"There is an old saying that 'it never rains but it pours,' which is applicable to that particular summer. Before I got away to go to Mrs. McCormack and Cyril in Dublin, and to visit my father and mother and sisters and brother, in Athlone, negotiations were commenced to appear in the tour of Harrison Concerts, an important series given throughout England and Scotland, and the contract signed (at a good figure) before I left London.

"But with all this good fortune, which seemed heaping into my lap, I seemed to cleave more than ever to my old friends. I've been that way, and shall not change. Sammy Liddle, one of the finest accompanists living, saw much of me, when he sat wading through manuscript music in the little room of his in Arthur Boosey's place. I spent considerable time with him every day, that year and in others that followed. Going through much new music—even though a deal of it was admittedly bad music—did me

187

no harm. Sammy would play, and I would hum through those manuscripts; and occasionally we would discover a promising ballad, which would be published and have its sale. Many of these I, of course, subsequently sang at a Boosey Concert.

"I recollect one day the manuscripts were all very bad. Nothing amongst those which we ran through either of us could consider. One after another they were tossed aside, impossible. 'Hopeless,' said Sammy, making a wry face as he looked up at me. 'Oh, for just one fairly respectable piece of music!' That gave me a thought.

" 'Here, Sammy,' I remarked, taking a folded piece of manuscript from my pocket, 'is something we might try; play it.' He put the paper on the music rack, straightened the folds and as he played I sang the words and music.

" 'Not a bad idea,' admitted Sammy, 'and I rather like that *pianissimo* high A-natural at the end.' We repeated the song, and once more Liddle had an encouraging word to say for it. Arthur Boosey, who had listened, remarked, 'I don't think much of it.' 'Well,' I informed him, 'Charlie Marshall wrote the music and John

Bardsley took it to Willie Boosey, who couldn't see enough in the song to accept it. But if you recommend it for publication I'll sing it at the first ballad concert in the fall.' That settled the matter, because Boosey would publish anything I thought well enough of to sing publicly and the song was prepared for the audiences. And I did sing it, several weeks later.

"The name of that song is 'I Hear You Calling Me,' and next to 'The Holy City' it has sold more copies than any other piece of music ever printed."

John steered the *Rocklea* past the New York Police Department yacht, which lay at anchor about a mile and a half off Rocklea, and a short distance beyond where one of the several fishing-grounds thereabouts lay. We dropped the anchor and got out our poles. But Cyril had forgotten to bring enough sinkers, and there was a panic. How would we get our hooks to the bottom? Wilkinson and Cyril—who has a mechanical turn and is forever puttering about machinery—got their inventive minds busy, and Gwen finally found herself using a drop line with a wrench for a sinker.

"We sought other quarters in the fall," John

189

went on later as we were homeward bound, "when Mrs. McCormack, Baby Cyril and I reached London. Six months had brought a change in our financial status; we had some butter, then, for our bread and an occasional piece of cake. It was a relief, although I find an odd pleasure in reflecting upon the hardships of my student and early professional career. There were many happy days in them.

"The main business, you may be sure, was preparing for the opera début. There could be no half-way measures here; Covent Garden audiences knew the best, were accustomed to it and countenanced no other. Allowances, I judged, would be made for a newcomer of twenty-three; still he would have to attain a definite standard, in voice and art—to succeed. Which I meant, if it lay within me, to do."

John threw over the wheel hard a-port, and the *Rocklea* circled a stake marking the shallow channel and went off into deeper water.

"There were numerous rehearsals, and every one was kindness itself. I'll not forget that, because those first rehearsals mean so much to a young artist. The opera for my début was 'Cavalleria Rusticana,' in which I knew the notes and words backwards. Every bit of action and stage business I had memorized until, I think, I could have done the entire rôle in a trance. I wanted it that way, for in an emergency the memory, thoroughly charged, will often act mechanically and carry one through a danger-spot to safety.

"The night of nights—and it was all that— came at last. It was a fine night, and clear, which I took as a favorable omen. I had a light supper at half-past three, at Sir John Murray Scott's, and he sent me to the theatre in his brougham. Six o'clock found me in my dressing-room at Covent Garden. 'Cavalleria Rusticana' preceded the second part of the double-bill which consisted, as it usually does when the Mascagni work is performed, of 'I Pagliacci.' So I was made up and ready for the stage before the tenor arrived who was to appear in the latter opera.

"He was not sympathetic; self-sufficient and with no kind word for a beginner. And of all the principals cast that night he, alone, said nothing to stiffen my spine. But one of the artists helped enough to make up for his surliness; a courteous chap, with the milk of human kindness in his heart. It is strange what little things one remembers! I was feeling badly. I saw him poking his head in at my doorway, at my invitation to enter, after his knock.

" 'My name is Sammarco,' said the stranger, 'and I have come to wish you good luck.' He said some other things, too, but the words wishing me luck stuck in my memory. Good old Sammarco—and he isn't so old, either—he's as fine a man as he is artist. And ever the friend.

"He went away then, and the unsympathetic tenor (we shared the same dressing-room) came back to get ready for his work. So I went outside, for the curtain was not far off."

"And were you nervous?" I asked.

"I was so nervous," replied McCormack, "that I ceased to be nervous. I guess the nerves, for that evening, were thoroughly burned out. In the wings I met Borghild Bryhn, who was to sing *Santuzza*, and Angelo Scandiani, the baritone. Also *Maestro* Panizza, the conductor. The time was close and . . . I was ready.

"How thankful I was, standing there, for my brief operatic experience in Italy; the Savona and Santa Crŏce appearances. At least I knew how to move on the stage, and I kept repeating over and over the warning of Sabatini's baritone friend, Felici, about my semaphorian arms. I shouldn't appear ridiculous, that was sure; and if my voice responded—well, I'd take my chances.

"Anyway, I should have a chance to warm up before going out to face the thousands there in front; the men and women who were to say 'yes' or 'no' to my maiden effort. The serenade, which *Turridu* sings behind the curtain before it is raised, would give me that chance. And presently it came. I got the signal, the harpist began the introduction and I set myself."

John stopped at that climacteric point to maneuver the dory into its berth between two rowboats moored just to one side of the float, which gave us small entering space. I watched him standing before the wheel, his legs well spread and firm in his white flannel trousers and two massive arms showing above the wheel. He looked the fighter, and a clean one, who doesn't quit under fire.

Wilkinson made the *Rocklea* fast, and we clambered ashore. On the way up—Cyril and Gwen were hurrying ahead—McCormack finished the story.

"For a second, possibly only half a second,"

he confessed, "I thought I'd die. I stood looking at the harpist, with my mouth as parched as
though I'd been footing it through a desert.
Then to myself I said, 'Old boy, you've *got* to!'

"It was while I was singing the serenade that
Mrs. McCormack, Miss Foley and the others of
the party entered the box. Mrs. McCormack
told me, long afterwards, that it was an ordeal
she could scarcely endure.

"The rest of it was easy enough, as débuts go.
I guess I'd suffered until there was nothing left
in me to suffer. For the serenade to *Lola* went
fairly well—so the people and management
thought, and the music critics, who wrote about
the performance for the papers of next day. I
had steadied before having sung a dozen measures of the serenade, so that when I made my entrance I was as cold as ice. Nor do I exaggerate; I mean just that . . . as cold as ice.

"But the tribute which I thought most about,
and the one that I can never feel enough gratitude for, was the actions of my singer-colleagues
who attended that performance. To my personal knowledge, many of them sacrificed paying engagements—besides buying places for the

opera—which had been accepted for that same evening.

"A sort of free-masonry among many of the singers existed, then, in London, and these 'pals' of mine—they were that, in the best sense of that term—were generous enough to forget any pecuniary advantages to themselves to show their good will toward me, and to want to be in Covent Garden when I was making the début.

"No less a person than Neil Forsyth, business manager of Covent Garden, said to me: 'Mc-Cormack you did splendidly and what a wonderful reception you got! One would have thought you were an actor-manager!'

"Everything, that night, seemed magnified. I saw with a clarity of vision which, I presume, was due to the highly sensitized condition of my nerves; and my hearing was the same. I anticipated all that was to come: every musical phrase and word, long before its proper moment, and every action the rôle demands and each gesture.

"That's about all. In less than an hour and a quarter it was all over. They told me, in my dressing-room, that I had won. I was rather tired; but happy. I cleaned the grease paint from my face and got into my street clothes, and with Mrs. McCormack and Miss Foley went home. And that night I slept."

CHAPTER XIV

THE ARTIST DEVELOPS

Business matters having called me to New York I did not see McCormack again for several days. It was an afternoon, in late July, when I descended from an express train at Stamford station; the third day of Nineteen Eighteen's first hot spell on the upper Atlantic seaboard. I chartered a "flivver" and away we darted, toward Noroton and Rocklea, some eight miles off.

John was seated, alone, on the veranda when I arrived, looking cool and unperturbed in tennis garb. "So there you are!" he said, by way of greeting. "What made you pick out this particular day to come out?" he demanded. "I don't feel like working."

"I'm sorry, John," I replied, "but there's much copy to be gone over before we mail it to the publisher. But if you're feeling lazy suppose I run back to town."

"You'll do nothing of the kind," he rejoined,

with that note in his voice which one always hears there when he fears he may unintentionally have hurt another's feelings. One must travel far to find a softer heart than John McCormack's —or any so generous.

"All right," he commanded, with assumed gruffness, "get out the manuscript." This I did, and he was soon deep in the reading of it, lying back in a huge porch-chair, the picture of a student at work. From time to time, with his pencil, he made corrections: changing whole sentences, rearranging others, adding here a word and, there, striking one out. At other points he suggested the introduction of new material, which I noted on paper. Oh, yes! John McCormack is more than singer. He wasn't made Doctor of Literature by Holy Cross College, in Nineteen Seventeen, on the strength of his voice alone.

Two hours of this and the task was finished. And by that time John was in the mood for more work.

"We left off, the other night, at the Covent Garden début—didn't we?" He lapsed into silence for a few moments, then continued.

"It's a wonderful feeling that success brings,

when you've worked for it. And rather gratifying to be able to read about it, in the newspapers. That's what I did, the morning after I 'débuted' at Covent Garden. The critics were most kind. They shared the view that I had 'arrived,' and expressed an interest in what my future efforts should bring forth.

"Do you grasp that? It's the secret of an artist's forward movement towards the ultimate goal: 'So far so good, but what of the morrow?' One cannot rest, no matter how fine the achievement. Good, better, best—and after that 'best' something still more, that's beyond. There is no stopping-place in art. For the more one does the more people expect. There is no rest for whoever is conscientious; if the critics and public become momentarily satisfied the artist should not be. So we go on, occasionally content, but never for more than the briefest possible time.

"And when one reaches the top rung in the ladder the task to remain there is harder, much, than the climb. The slightest jostle destroys the balance. No! The life of a singer, if he (or she) is admitted into the sacred portals, is not easy—though some folks mistakenly fancy that it is. You've got to live up to what the people feel you are as an artist.

"Mrs. McCormack and I read carefully the reviews of my previous evening's performance and then discussed our own opinions. We invariably do that. Praise is pleasant to hear or read, but it never helps one to progress. Criticism does that; the kind of criticism I call constructive—which builds up, and never tears down. After breakfast I went out for a walk, and to reflect.

"As I have just said, getting to a desired artistic place is difficult enough, but it is staying there that is the rub. And I had felt that once accepted by a Covent Garden audience I could retain, for as long as I maintained my skill, the good will of each audience. This was the matter of chiefest concern, just then. The second and third and fourth appearances would decide. I therefore gave myself to their consideration.

"My second Covent Garden rôle was *The Duke*, in 'Rigoletto,' which was to be performed with a cast including Luisa Tetrazzini, then the rage of London, as *Gilda*, and Sammarco in the character of *Rigoletto*. This work of Verdi's, which demands that the tenor be able truly to sing, was different from Mascagni's. I had heard Mme. Tetrazzini for the first time in my life only a few weeks before (it was her first Covent Garden season) and the opportunity which brought me as her associate in the leading tenor rôle of an opera was enough to stir me, if nothing else had. Her kindness to me cannot be overestimated, and several times that night she would encourage me with a word or two, just as Sammarco did, when he was near. I was warmly applauded after the *Duke's* famous aria, *La Donna é Mobile,* and my portion of the quartette, which had to be repeated, elicited favorable comment. Tetrazzini sang superbly, and Sammarco's *Rigoletto* (which I consider magnificent), was almost incomparable.

"I was far less nervous throughout this performance than during the 'Cavalleria Rusticana.' Its music was my sort of music, peculiarly suited to my voice and methods, and my acceptance brought me greater satisfaction than anything else I had done. It seemed, too, to remove the last vestige of lurking doubt within me. I might vary in the quality of my endeavors, but I was certain, at last, of my capacities. The future lay with me, wholly.

"Self-confidence (by which I do not mean egotism) I had now acquired, and I found myself facing each audience with greater assurance and acquitting myself with an increased freedom. So when the third opera I was asked to sing that season—'Don Giovanni'—arrived I was perfectly secure. The rôle was *Don Ottavio*. Of all composers Mozart made greatest demands for pure singing upon the artist, but what a joy it is to sing him! He cannot evade the issue, and woe betide the one who has no *cantilena* or elegance of style. Mario Sammarco, the baritone who had befriended me at my début, was cast for the *Giovanni* (a rôle in which I have always been sorry that New York never got a chance to hear him), Lolla Miranda was the *Zerlina*, and Fely Litvinna had been chosen for *Donna Anna*. The third opera out of the way, I breathed with comparative ease once more and said a silent prayer of thanksgiving.

"Cyril was growing fast and Mrs. McCormack looked a girl of eighteen. She made a home for us and gave me something worth working for. Do you wonder that I was able to sing? I was in a jubilant mood constantly, at work or at play, and the weeks leaped on, bringing fresh experi-

John McCormack in 1909, a photograph inscribed to Dr. Kielty, the president of Summerhill College, Sligo Ireland.

John and Lily McCormack

ences and carrying my name throughout the land.

"My operatic work was, naturally, the most important, but I had plenty to do besides. The Arthur Boosey Ballad Concerts began again in the fall of Nineteen Seven and in each of these I sang, with steady appreciation of the audiences. Other concert engagements came to me, also, and at length the visits, on the Harrison programmes, to Birmingham, Leeds, Glasgow, Manchester, and other cities. I have often wondered why some cities in Ireland were not included in the tour.

"It was some time thereabouts, that the sequel occurred to my experience with 'Alphabet' Malone, of Daly's Theatre. George Edwardes was in tenor difficulties again, and bemoaning the scarcity of one who could both sing and act when my friend, Gordon Cleather, who had taken me to Malone, some months before, happened in.

" 'If I could only get the man I want,' sighed Edwardes.

" 'Too bad,' sympathized Cleather. 'I brought you just the chap, but Malone couldn't see him.'

"Whereupon Edwardes, instantly alert, replied: 'Get him for me.'

" 'Sorry,' answered my friend languidly, 'but he's singing with Tetrazzini in 'Rigoletto' at Covent Garden to-night.'

"It was not long after that incident that I met George Edwardes, with whom I finally became intimately acquainted. Speaking one day of the amusing refusal of Malone to engage me Edwardes verified Cleather's story and said: 'Had I heard you at that time, John, I'd have been willing to sign a ten-years' contract with you.'

"Perhaps it is just as well that we didn't meet. It may have been another of Destiny's moves to guide me in the direction I was intended to go. For had I appeared at Daly's my entire career might have veered off in another direction.

"I was going along rather fast during that season. I studied with all diligence and omitted nothing which might strengthen my resources. There is everything in getting a good start, and I resolved, while people were talking about me, to profit by all that offered. My youth, and my sudden rise from obscurity into Covent Garden and concert popularity in a few months, were topics of conversation. There were pessimists, who hinted that I might not last, but their smallness did no harm.

"My fairy-godfather, Sir John Murray Scott, was happy over what had come to me. 'There are bigger things ahead for you, my boy,' he would say to me, 'so neglect nothing; prepare for them.' His influence helped me incalculably, and the example he himself set. It meant something just to be near him and hear him talk, not alone on music, which he thoroughly knew in all its branches and history, but on the kindred arts and on politics, science, philosophy, finance and travel. He was what I would call a well-informed man, one well-traveled, who remembered.

"It was no commonplace task to satisfy such a man, and I was content only when I felt that I was near to, if not completely, satisfying him. Sir John believed in shooting at a high-hung star, and drilled into me that idea. But for all his task-mastership he wielded no iron hand. His way was to lead rather than to drive; and it was also his way, after patient observation of a protégé, to drop him if he showed an unwillingness to respond. That was all. He 'sized' a man, to use a colloquialism, lightning fast and gave him a fair chance—but no more than that. And the gentleman, unvaryingly; it was inborn.

"So, you see, I had my advantages."

Two small dogs drew near: one a sable-coated Pekinese of aristocratic mien, the other white and woolly with a waggish air. I should call him a John T. McCutcheon dog, for he was that sort; he answered to the name Towser. Go-Go, the Peke, stopped a few feet short of McCormack and disdainfully sniffed the air.

"A queer pup," confided John, "whose friends are mostly of the kitchen. But Towser, here, is a pal." And the woolly pup wagged his roguish tail at this, and emitted a short bark. They were off, directly, to their play, and the tenor went on with his talk.

"The Harrison concerts were interesting that year," he said, "and broadened my acquaintance with audiences. It allowed me to see something of other cities and the experience helped. Incidentally, my repertoire grew steadily and my musical knowledge, for besides studying I lost no opportunity to hear as much good music as I could, especially that for the orchestra. And another thing: I fussed a little at the piano. For I realized that some day I should need musicianship—which few singers appear to feel they care to acquire.

"Naturally, I met many people . . . in all walks of life. I liked that for I suppose I am what Americans call 'a mixer.' Apart from the interest one finds in new acquaintances a friend or two occasionally grows from them; and, then, it sharpens the wits. Yes, the study of human nature is an absorbing thing.

"When spring came, in Nineteen Eight, I began to want a home we should own, one wherein Mrs. McCormack and I might feel a sense of proprietorship. It was right, too, that we take our place of residence in a community befitting my enhanced position and amongst those whom I now met with some frequency.

"We found, at last, the very place that suited us. It was in Hampstead, where the fresh air was just what Cyril needed, and with plenty of foliage about. And when Gwen was born, July 21, 1908 (like Cyril, in Dublin), we had a home of our own, and I considered myself a fortunate man."

CHAPTER XV

"To him that hath" (or as McCormack's brother-in-law, Tom Bissette, would say, "Much wants more") never was more fully exemplified than in the case of John McCormack. One success appeared to beget another, and the tenor's following increased steadily and his friendships and acquaintances, too.

The fall of Nineteen Eight found him busier than ever, with an abundance of concerts and his second Covent Garden season looming near. John was twenty-four, an accepted artist with a widening road showing ahead.

Still, he had yet a singing honor which, strangely enough, had not offered. Vocally and musically one of the most admirably equipped of any tenor singing oratorio, he had never appeared in a festival. It was one of those unexplainable circumstances which he has confessed his inability to fathom.

208

"There was enough, however, in other channels to occupy me as fully as my time allowed. So I gave the matter no concern. Yet that part of my career is peculiarly blank. Gervaise Elwes, one of the few intellectual tenors in the oratorio field, and the finest interpreter of that difficult music which Sir Edward Elgar wrote in 'The Dream of Gerontius' for tenor, was one of the foremost artists at that time. Another was John Coates, with a splendid oratorio style.

"I began my Nineteen-Eight and Nine season with a voice that was gaining in power and, people said, in quality. I was invariably careful to keep within the limits of my voice, for I always have felt that no tone is proper to sing that carries a power which mars its quality. In other words, when, to secure power, the natural beauty of the tone suffers that tone is not right. I have tried to keep to that rule, and when a friend once asked me why I did not give 'more voice' (he was a singer) I replied that I would be singing for years after he had finished his career. My words have since proved correct.

"No, there is nothing in the so-called 'big' tone. To make a noise for sake of inducing applause is not singing, and certainly far removed from artistry. I could cite numerous instances, were I so minded, to demonstrate my contention. Something held in reserve should be the undeviating custom of every singer, not alone because it imparts to the voice the most agreeable quality possible, but likewise for the longevity of the instrument.

"The shouter may cause a tremendous fuss among certain adherents of the high note long held, but what is the ultimate cost? A ruined voice often, years before its usefulness should have waned. Nor are young singers the only ones who should respect this indisputable fact. We have instances, of annual occurrence, of singers—especially those of the opera—who have more natural voice than knowledge of its correct use who fade within a few seasons, and fall miserably.

"I was fortunate in discovering all this at the outset of my career. Sabatini preached this vocal gospel. Sir John Murray Scott also emphasized it. Other valued counselors agreed that such a course was the wise one. So I adhered to my custom, and to-day my voice is, I think, better than ever, and should continue to improve until the day I decide I shall retire—

which, by the way, I shall do while I am at the top of my powers, in voice as well as in my interpretative resources.

"My second Covent Garden season witnessed strides in the desired direction. I had added to my repertoire, and was called on to appear in the three rôles I had first learned, and several more besides. At the close of my fourth year I had sung *Turiddu, The Duke, Don Ottavio* and the principal tenor rôles in 'La Bohême,' 'Madama Butterfly,' 'La Tosca,' 'La Traviata,' 'Lucia di Lammermoor,' 'Lakmè,' 'Faust,' 'Romeo and Juliet' and 'The Pearl Fishers.'

"One does not gain freedom of stage routine in a few performances. The easy actor, in opera, is not too often encountered. It is a difficult matter—which many do not know because their intimacy with the opera singing is limited—to provide an adequate dramatic impersonation of a rôle while singing it. And the cause is due largely to the lack of what I will call synchronization between music and text; the pauses in the connective of phrases which destroy the possibility of logical dramatic continuity and frequently place an artist in passivity when the action should not be arrested.

211

"To surmount such obstacles—which is less difficult in some operas than in others—requires long and arduous training before the public, and a talent to combine acting with singing. 'Operatic' gestures do not, as the expert knows, constitute dramatic action, and never will. To mould characterization of a rôle with its musical side is an art, a many-sided one, and has few masters. I strove to acquire it, but it came slowly—especially in that second year, when music had, of course, to be the main thing.

"But I got on."

"I began meeting, more and more, beginning with the season of Nineteen Eight and Nine, people who were personalities. It was then that I was presented to the late King Edward and Queen Alexandra, all the other members of the Royal Family and (then and later) met numerous sovereigns of other countries, princes and princesses, persons of the nobility and diplomatic corps and army and navy attachés.

"I have never, for some cause, experienced for great folk any particular sense of awe; and while I welcomed my opportunity it did not set my head awhirl. They were sovereigns for whom I entertained respect; the Queen, espe-

cially, being a personage I had long wanted to
meet.   And it's odd, too, how that desire appeared to have some basis—in what was subsequently realized.   For it was to be my good fortune to see the womanly side of Queen Alexandra, and to discover some of those qualities which
have endeared her to her people.

"She was, as most of us know, quite hard of
hearing.   Yet she did not (at least at that time)
make use of mechanical devices which accentu-
ate a weakened hearing sense.   I recall being
presented to Queen Alexandra in the drawing-
room of the town house of Lady de Grey, March-
ioness of Ripon, one afternoon in the winter of
Nineteen Eight.   I remember, as though it happened only yesterday, the entire affair, which was
one of the many for which Lady de Grey was
noted and which no other hostess in London
equalled.

"With her attendants-in-waiting, Queen Alexandra received me; seated, and with a smile.
One hears the word 'graciousness' sometimes applied to a manner, but too often misapplied.
Here, however, was an instance where it perfectly fitted, for the Queen was gracious in the
fullest degree; the aristocrat personified.   And

yet by no word or gesture or mannerism did she seek to impress upon one her rank and position. I think it was that 'to-the-manner-born' air, rightfully hers, which she so gently wore which drew me to her. She could not be other than the gentlewoman she was, God bless her!

"By inclination I am democratic. It is, to my way of thinking, what one is and does that truly counts. But I admire simplicity in those in high places; and the bigger one is the simpler that person should be. Queen Alexandra was such a woman, and it became her.

"When it came my turn I sang as I had seldom sung, up to that time. The song was 'I Hear You Calling Me.' Of course I was curious to hear what she would say, and how. It would be something complimentary—that much I knew—but I was scarcely prepared for her particular words.

" 'I go often to Albert Hall, and even when the band plays *double-forte*, I scarcely hear,' she said, with a smile that struck me as wistful, though uncomplaining. 'But . . . I heard perfectly even that last *pianissimo* tone of yours.'

"It was almost pathetic, and my eyes grew misty. Yet I managed to tell her how grateful I was at being able to sing so that she could hear

—everything. Just think of having to miss hearing all the beautiful music there is to hear because of such a physical misfortune. If I were to have to choose between deafness and loss of sight (please God it may never be either) I should rather be blind.

"It was a distinguished assemblage at that musicale of Lady de Grey's; large and composed of men and women who were leaders, in every walk of life that counted. They all were most attentive, too, when an artist was performing. Maggie Teyte, the soprano, and Gilibert, whose death a few years ago took away a true man as well as a great artist, and I provided the music on that occasion. Gilibert was incomparable in his interpretation of songs, and everyone knows Miss Teyte's skill.

"That experience has always remained vividly in my memory.

"There were others, at about that time," he continued, "and they had their interesting features. Some were out of the ordinary. All the while the weeks slipped by, and one evening, at Covent Garden, Mario Sammarco came to me.

" 'Giovanni,' he said, 'what you do in March?' It was a pregnant question, and I asked my bari-

215

tone friend what he meant by it. He explained that if I chose I might have an engagement to sing at the spring opera season to be given at the San Carlo, in Naples.

"I was keen to go. Italy still remained an unproved field for my abilities, and at that stage of my development I believed that if ever Italians would accept me this would be the time. The honorarium was satisfactory—one thousand francs a performance—so I accepted Sammarco's offer.

"On the way Mrs. McCormack and I stopped off at Milan, to see my old *maestro*, Sabatini. We were both overjoyed at meeting again, and Sabatini made a great fuss over Mrs. McCormack. After matters had quieted I took out my bill-fold: 'Let me see,' I said, 'two hundred francs (forty dollars), that was the amount for the last two months of tuition, wasn't it, *maestro?*'

"And what do you think Sabatini asked? . . . He wanted to know if I could conveniently spare it.

"With his next breath he began berating me for sending him so many pupils. For, as it had happened, my tone-production had elicited in-

216

quiries as to who my master had been, and when I recommended Sabatini—and I *did* recommend him, you may be sure—students flocked to his place. Incidentally, while we are on this matter, I once had the novel experience of being pointed to by a celebrated English teacher of voice as a perfect specimen of 'how best to sing.' 'I did not show him,' said this man, 'but the way he sings is the right way.'

"Before he would talk on the many matters of common interest to us both," laughed John, "Sabatini insisted I should have a lesson. 'The bad habits,' he said insinuatingly, 'I will see if you have formed them.' And for half an hour he stripped my voice bare.

"Then he appeared satisfied. That I had gone on in the way he hoped I might go gave him inexpressible delight. One or two things he did not approve, and frankly said so. But when he had finished with me I gathered fresh confidence in myself; for the dangerous period in my vocal career had been safely passed, and I believed that a continuance of those same methods would guard my tone-production in the future.

"Madame Sabatini came into the studio

then, to play while I sang operatic arias the *maestro* insisted he must hear. He let me finish each one; then we would discuss it: Sabatini suggesting changes which I instantly recognized would add to their interpretative value. We had several hours of this, and I finished a wiser singer and a better one.

"It is that way," explained the tenor, "that the artist is made. And the greatest, even at their zenith, have always some things to learn. For myself, I am never quite satisfied. My artistic desire is invariably just beyond my reach; and no public applause or written critical opinion can compensate for what, in my heart, I know to be short of my goal. I know I can never reach the ideal I have set myself.

"However," he exclaimed, "that is straying from the issue.

"Mrs. McCormack and I reached Naples in good time, and went to the Excelsior Hotel, and from our windows had a clear view of Mt. Vesuvius. I was fit, yet misgivings that I should not duplicate my Covent Garden success disturbed my quietude. I knew what Italians like in a tenor voice, and the kind of singing by which they measure an artist."

"You didn't, as I recall."

"Your memory serves you well," responded John. "There was no furore; no 'bis' calls or cries of 'bravo!' *The Duke* in 'Rigoletto' was the first rôle I sang. The impresario said I could not have done it better; a finished performance, he called it, in every respect. And I got applause, oh, yes, I got that—from those who recognized singing when they heard it. What I didn't get was an ovation, which was the thing I had desired, above all else.

"But there is something I must tell you about," he observed. "It was unique; the only experience of its kind in my career—the hiring of a claque and subsidizing of music critics."

"You did that?"

"I did . . . and it cost me, for that San Carlo engagement, twelve hundred and fifty francs."

"Two hundred and fifty dollars! Why did you do it?"

"Persuasion—that it was the customary thing to do, and that refusal to follow precedent would injure my chances. I wanted success. I wanted a fair chance to win it; and I also felt justified in using all the factors which other sing-

219

ers—tenor singers—had. I wished no undue advantage; but I did wish an even break. Having that I knew I should have to be satisfied (so far as Italy was concerned) with my deserts.

"It was the first time, and likewise the last, that I availed myself of what many opera singers regard as a 'privilege.' The hirelings comprising the claque probably did their work. And the newspapers spoke well of my singing. But I was displeased with the transaction—'disgusted' is, probably, the better word. For the system is insincere, to put it in the mildest term."

McCormack touched upon a subject, when he brought up the claque, which has been widely discussed (in America, especially) for many years. New York, more than any other city, has felt its influence and opera patrons have voiced their protests openly and with vehemence. During the last few seasons, newspapers have had objections to make to this unfortunate system which, as McCormack correctly says, is a menace to both artists and public.

"But apart from the undesirable methods of some of these paid-to-make-applause agents, the very existence of such applause is an insult to an intelligent audience, and invariably an annoy-

John McCormack as the Duke of Mantua in Act III of Rigo-
letto. *This photograph, dated May 26, 1909 is inscribed by
McCormack to his "dear friend and colleague" Francesco
Daddi, a tenor who sang with him in performances of* La
Boheme *and* Lucia di Lammermoor *at the Manhattan Opera
House. Daddi created the part of Beppe in the world premiere
of* Pagliacci *in Milan in 1892.*

John and Lily McCormack, with Cyril and Gwen, San Francisco, 1912.

ance which should prompt any far-sighted impresario to stop it at once. And any singer who hires a claque is either misled, quite ignorant of the unfortunate position thereby caused, or else so engrossed with ego as to be blind to the evil consequences.

"The state of never knowing when one is doing well or ill, which is immediately created when a singer has a claque 'out in front,' should prompt the singer who believes in the claque to consider the matter. The competent and sincere singer needs no claque. The average audience is able to ascertain for itself the estimate of an artist. Nor should anyone hold any delusion about fooling several thousand persons by injecting a brand of made-to-order applause in the hope of having it sound spontaneous.

"Any claquer will unhesitatingly state that he can instantly 'spot' the claque at work; not only its precise location in an auditorium, but each location and how many claquers comprise each group. Audiences, who have now had experience enough with this sort of thing, have also become expert in detecting this false applause.

"So, if we analyze it, the claque is very evidently useless, in addition to being a nuisance, and defeats its purpose by drawing to the artist paying for it condemnation for employing such practice rather than the admiration which is desired.

"Finally, if an artist be serious and honest with himself, he will surely prefer to take his chances. With an acknowledged position his recognition is reasonably certain. And should the exception now and again occur why descend to the petty procedure of hiring a few rough-visaged persons with large hands to make a noise? Suppose, once in a season, the applause of an audience does not completely satisfy? What difference does it make, so long as the singer's artistic soul is pleased?"

With everything McCormack has said I agree. So do thousands of others. And in the course of time the claque—in America, anyway—will be a thing of the past.

"I wouldn't have missed the San Carlo engagement—for what it brought—for more than I can name. Before returning to London I had conferred upon me one of the great honors of my career; an honor bestowed personally by Pope Pius X, which I shall recount directly.

"I felt tired when the San Carlo engagement came to an end, in April of Nineteen Hundred Nine. I had sung, besides the opening opera, in 'Traviata' and 'Rigoletto,' and appeared on the same stage with some excellent singers and my artistic resources were the better because of the experience.

"It was early April when Mrs. McCormack and I departed for Rome—with our friends, Mary Anderson, her husband, 'Tony' Navarro, and the two Misses Scott, sisters of Sir John, and his brother Walter, who made up our party."

223

CHAPTER XVI

POPE PIUS X CONFERS A BLESSING

The children—Cyril and Gwenny—had gone to bed. Though eight-thirty o'clock in the evening (according to the hour of daylight-saving plan then in vogue) it was sixty minutes earlier, by the sun; and that planet still hovered in the sky. A breeze blew up from the Sound to where Mrs. McCormack and I sat on the veranda.

Miss Foley was busy elsewhere; John had matters of consequence which had called him to his writing-desk, and so Mrs. McCormack and I waited until the others should join us.

I was pleased that it was so, for Mrs. Mc-Cormack—usually silent as to her husband's achievements—was disposed to speak about them.

"I should like, almost better than anything I know," she said, "to have the public appreciate how earnest John is." She glanced over at me, and smiled—almost longingly. So far as one

224

might infer, Mrs. McCormack had everything her heart wished: a devoted husband, two children, the consciousness of honors well won, health for all near to her, and the goods of the world in abundance. It would have been a perfectly natural assumption to regard John's position as made; his earnestness with respect to his art something to be taken for granted. Yet that wish—it interested one.

"What makes you question such a thing? Have you forgotten his Boston Symphony appearances? His Beethoven? And the programmes at Boston? Even his average programmes; take any one of them, with their lightest ballads . . . which mean so much to hundreds of thousands!" For I am not at one with some, who have failed, as yet, to probe the function of the simple song, and what it does for the majority.

Mrs. McCormack brightened, I thought, at this, and nodded her head.

"I've forgotten none of those things," she replied; "perhaps it is an over-conscientiousness about John, which I always have. He has it, too. Possibly it's contagious." She laughed merrily at this. "But—everyone *should* know"

225

(she was very positive on this point) "that *John* is thinking, striving constantly, for his audiences. And that he bends his life to what he believes they want and expect of him. Many people do know; which makes me anxious that it should be unanimous."

I explained that unanimity, in art, was an unattainable thing, to which she agreed. And this wish, it seems to me, is one which should be emphasized. No person knows John McCormack as Mrs. McCormack knows him, so that what she says about her husband's earnestness should be passed along, from one to another, and reiterated until the whole world knows.

"He has three things in life," continued Mrs. McCormack, in an unexpected burst of confidence: "His family, his Catholic faith, and his art. To each one his allegiance is complete; John never does a thing by halves. So, for the benefit of those who go to hear him sing and who derive comfort from his singing, I should be happy to have them know what I know.

"I have no doubt that it was meant that he should perform the public service which he is performing. That is the reason, and the only one, why I let him go on his long tours—when I, and the children, feel the need of him here at home. It is the reason, too, why I dread the day when he must curtail the fatiguing journeys, and the work, and the preparation which wears him in mind and body. You comprehend, don't you, how anxious I am that, doing this work, the sincerity back of it should be felt by every single soul?"

John could not very well have told me that. So I was glad that Mrs. McCormack had spoken, in just that quiet way of hers—the expressed hope of a wife who has stood shoulder to shoulder with her husband from the beginning of his career, and gone on up with him to the top.

The screen-door slammed just then, and John came outside.

"A little ride in the *Cyril*" (the McCormack power-boat) "would be a cooling excursion, don't you think?" he demanded. We thought so, and Miss Foley, appearing at that moment, did, too. So we walked to the pier, got aboard and were soon scooting out into the Sound.

It was late when we got back, with a full moon and many stars in the sky. Not a night for sleep, if one were talkatively inclined and a listener were near. So when Mrs. McCormack and Miss

227

Foley left us John and I sat by ourselves on the veranda, no sounds save the locusts' calls falling upon our ears. I kept my eye on the glow of John's cigarette; it was growing duller, a sign that his mind was becoming active. After a time he began.

"It was 9 o'clock on Holy Thursday morning of one of those perfect Italian spring days," said the tenor, in a lowered tone, "that we set out from our hotel in Rome to the Vatican. In this center of learning, the home of Italy's aristocrats and the gravitating place of diplomats the world over, we passed along: Mrs. McCormack, Mary Anderson, the Misses Scott, Mr. Scott, 'Tony' Navarro and I—a group of pilgrims wending our way to that glorious edifice wherein the Princes of the Church assemble and plan for Christianity's good. And, as custom decreed, we men wore full evening dress, the women in black, with veils.

"I had thought often of such a journey; from the schooldays in Athlone on through the various phases of my life, in its hours of trials and joys. There was the intense blue of an Italian sky overhead, a blue which almost gave to the atmosphere a transparency to the eye, and from the buildings as we passed along there were cast now and again across our path varying shadows.

"The day, had we picked it, could not have been more suitable to the occasion. For majesty stalked everywhere, while all about us there seemed to breathe 'Peace on Earth, Good Will toward Men.' I had never seen the Vatican. But from photographs I recognized it, quickly enough, as we approached.

"Our visit, of course, had been made known to the Holy Father, in a propitious way. Intercession in our behalf had come from distinguished dignitaries: Monsignor Fraser, President of the Scotch College, and Monsignor Bisletti. And that knowledge buoyed me, though I entered the portals with the others with trepidation and a feeling of numbness about my legs that made them dully heavy. For here I was, at last, at the fountainhead of the Church; a solitary soul, and diffident, yet eager to push on and clutching faintly at a hope I felt to be slipping, now that I drew near.

"It was the one moment in all my life, until now, that awe seized and held me. The majesty of the Church and all it represents pervaded the interior of the outer room where we all stood.

Others must have noticed, for directly the major-domo came over to us with an air of friendly intercession and asked what he might do.

"Miss Anderson and her husband, who knew the Holy Father, spoke to the major-domo, who, after showing us to seats, departed to a large doorway beyond—a doorway leading into the sacred chamber wherein the Holy Father, Pope Pius X, then was.

"I cannot refrain from attributing what occurred to that unwavering Irish Catholic Faith to which I hold, and which has been my solace in many a weary hour, for sitting there I said three silent 'Hail Marys' to the Mother of Mt. Carmel, my patroness, and wished that it might be my honor and privilege to kneel before Pope Pius X and receive his blessing in his private room. And strangely, too, Mrs. McCormack, at that same moment, held similar thoughts in her mind. And then . . ."

I sat very quiet.

". . . Monsignor Semper, private secretary to Pope Pius X, came through the door I sat fixedly watching, and straight over to where we sat. I could not have moved, had my life depended upon it, to rise at that moment. I was able only to sit erect and stare, aware all the time of his nearing approach, until he stood above me, smiling.

" 'The Holy Father,' he said in a rich voice, 'will be pleased to receive you, Mr. McCormack, and your friends.'

"For the life of me I could not restrain the subconscious feeling of my own insignificance as, following the secretary, I went with our party through the doorway and inside that room. Some little distance away, on his daïs, he sat; all in white, the visual sanctification of what he represented: His Highness, Pope Pius X.

"Never had I seen such a beautiful face. It was oval, but though seamed with fine lines and a bit drawn through the illness from which he was then grievously suffering, in every feature one saw reflected the kindness of a great soul. His hair was very white and very long, and brushed straight back so that it touched, at its farthest ends, his collar. On the back of his head was his little *succhetto* and about his neck a gold chain and a cross.

"I have said that he was all in white, and so he was. And his robes were a sort of wool, edged with white moire silk, and about his waist he

231

wore a wide sash similarly trimmed.   He seemed
to me, and I have always so thought of him since,
as the saintly and simple white father of Christen-
dom.   The Holy Father sat there as his secretary
led us towards him, quite erect and looking out
of eyes that were almost too bright.   I think his
power of will had much to do with keeping him
out of his bed.

"He greeted Mary Anderson and 'Tony' Navarro, first, then the rest of us, as we knelt before
him in a semi-circle.

" 'Oh,' he said, in a low but wonderfully musical voice, 'and so this is our tenor.'   Miss Anderson had spoken my name, swiftly, and then
stepped to one side.   I stood there, mute for the
moment, unable, it appeared, to do more than
to feast my eyes upon that beautiful face, which
held me (only one word adequately expresses it)
enthralled.

"Then, with the rarest of smiles, the Holy
Father extended his hand to me—a hand white
almost to transparency, with the veins showing
blue along its back.   I took it, with the tips of
my fingers, kissed it and the ring of St. Peter on
his finger.

"And as I knelt there, emotions racing through

my Irish blood such as it is beyond my powers to even attempt to describe, Pope Pius X blessed me."

I was not surprised when John ceased speech then. The last part of his description had been voiced somewhat haltingly; lengthy pauses between words, as though he saw himself living over again that experience. The tenor's head, too, had fallen slightly forward, so that his chin rested close to his chest. Now he sat there, in that attitude, intensely quiet and with no sign of life other than the breathing which moved his big shoulders.

"I rose," he finally said, "unutterably happy. I remembered nothing clearly after that; only of moving with the others and reaching the outer room, where we had waited.

"The Holy Father followed soon afterward. And I saw him stop, on his way to the general audience, in each of four rooms that partly surround his own, to speak to different people who were waiting for him, and to bestow upon them his blessing as head of the greatest of churches, and the beloved of three hundred millions of faithful souls.

"I am emotional, and I could no longer retain my self-control. I wept . . . and was unable to proceed, for nearly half an hour.

"We did not leave the Vatican, then, either; for there were the art treasures to be viewed and other things of historic appeal to us. I could not hurry; each canvas and the *objets d'art* held something more to me than artistic value. Even those of less splendid mastery than others were hallowed, to my eyes.

"So we finally came away.

"It was nearly noon when we walked down the Vatican steps. But I did not bring myself back to the modern world until evening. Mrs. McCormack can tell you; she felt as I did."

CHAPTER XVII

The tide was in at seven that morning, and I went across Rocklea lawn towards the pier for a before-breakfast swim. I was on the string-piece before I caught sight of a head, a couple of hundred yards out in the Sound, and heard a hail—John McCormack's, unmistakably, even at that distance.

I dove and stroked my way towards the tenor, who was amusing himself in small-boy fashion: treading, duck-diving, cavorting about with an assortment of swimming strokes and varying all this by occasionally interjecting an imitation of a sea-lion's roar—which makes a noise if you catch the water just right with the lips.

"Nine pounds under top-weight, this morning," announced John gleefully; "ten minutes more of this, then breakfast and on to the gymnasium. Whereupon the tenor allowed himself to sink beneath the water, and I sprinted off to escape the ducking I knew threatened.

235

John reappeared presently, with a grin of disappointment spread on his tanned face. "You moved," he charged goodnaturedly, after which we gave ourselves to the swim.

Breakfast over I went to the study while John drove to the gymnasium of tortures for two hours of hand-ball and gruelling physical effort that terminated in kneading that I am told feels like being run over by a steam-roller.

It was two o'clock before the McCormack schedule brought him to me and our purpose of those days.

"The single memento of that visit to the Vatican," he remarked, "was a medallion of St. Cecelia, which Pope Pius X had blessed. I've carried it ever since." And zealously, it would appear, for it is on his person during every waking hour and never does he make a professional appearance without that medallion carried in his pocket, at the end of his watch-chain.

"It had been a glorious trip, to Italy, but home is always home and Mrs. McCormack and I were not sorry when we were in our Hampstead abode once more. The Covent Garden Grand season was near, and I set to work to prepare for my part in it.

"The winter had been an eventful one," he went on, and as the desire for reminiscence seemed strong I was glad to have him indulge it. Thus far he had said little about the celebrities he had met at the London homes he had visited. With his thoughts traveling in the direction of those experiences I concluded he would recall some interesting incidents to relate.

"For so young a man," said John, "I was fortunate. My artist colleagues were all my seniors. To be included with them in the invitations to notable homes was something to appreciate. For every such occasion enlarged my list of acquaintances. Occasionally it yielded me a steadfast friend.

"Lady de Grey's place—Combe Court, it was called, at Kingston-on-Thames—always held attractions. Only the most successful artists were asked to participate in the musicales, and I was not unmindful of the honor when such an invitation was extended to me. At first finding myself in the midst of so many distinguished personages (as they were pointed out to me, one after another), I felt abashed. It was my introduction to members of the royal family, and of the peerage, and to personalities I knew about but never had beheld at close range. So my diffidence, I daresay, was natural enough. There has to be a beginning, with every one.

"But during those first seasons at Covent Garden the experience widened; nearly every one was considerate of me, and I profited by these opportunities to mingle with men and women who were of some account in the world. Fine minds there were, too, among them; and not many who were so engrossed with themselves as to be inconsiderate.

"A magnificent type of man was Prince Francis, of Teck, brother to Queen Mary,—magnificent, physically; nearly six feet-three, with the patrician's features, formed like an Apollo and with the gentlest nature and most democratic ways. You felt him the thoroughbred the moment he came near. He radiated strength and authority, in the way one will who is born to it.

"I recall, often, his offhand manner of speech to me at various meetings in different London homes. On one occasion, referring to some important topic of the hour, he remarked: 'Doesn't it make your Irish blood boil, McCormack? It does mine.' "

The tenor stretched himself in his chair, patted

one of the dogs who nosed his arm, and emitted a short laugh.

"What's the row?" I demanded.

"I was thinking of an experience I once had, singing for the late King Edward. It was at the United States Ambassadorial residence, then occupied by Whitelaw Reid. Lillian Nordica and I were the singers at that musicale; I'll always have that experience to put me in good humor when I feel the need for it.

"Mme. Nordica sang first, and mighty well; she was an artist. But when she rejoined me, just outside the music-room, she was convulsed. She was some moments in controlling her mirth, the cause of which I was impatient to learn.

" 'Never mind, John,' she said, 'you'll discover for yourself, soon enough. 'Twould be a pity to spoil it.'

"I left her, with a curious feeling, and entered the music-room and walked over to the piano. King Edward and a group of men stood together, near one window. Though I fancied they had seen me come in and prepare for my first number none gave me the slightest attention; they couldn't do so, out of deference to his Majesty, who continued talking in a very loud tone.

239

"I waited; but the talking still continued. I should have stood there, silent, for a long time had not the accompanist prompted me to proceed.

" 'But the King?' I queried.

" 'Will stop his talk when you begin singing . . . possibly.'

"So I started. And straight through to the end I sang that song, which never made the least impression on King Edward. He maintained his conversation, in a very loud voice; and when I had finished he was still talking. He is dead, now, and I don't wish to appear disrespectful; yet I cannot refrain from remarking upon the difference between his attitude towards an artist and that of Queen Alexandra.

"Those were wonderful days, though," said the tenor, with a smile. They developed many friendships, which have lasted. Mary Anderson was one.

"I can see her, now, that first afternoon when she recited to me, entire, Shakespeare's address to the players. Think of that privilege! I did not immediately grasp what the composition was, nor what it meant to be her exclusive auditor. But as she went on and on, with her superb eloquence and power, I caught the spirit and began to appreciate. She was in smiles, at the end; for she had seen how moved I had been.

" Such experiences leave upon a nature like mine something of an impress. I did not get over the effects of that reading of Mary Anderson's for weeks. At intervals, and in the most unexpected places, phrases of that address would return to me—heard, almost, as if that superb artist herself had appeared suddenly before me and declaimed them.

"She is what we hear mentioned, often, as a womanly-woman. The better one gets to know her the more this is revealed. She has mentality and all the sensitiveness of the artist, with the most lovable ways imaginable. And wonderful eyes—that's the word: 'wonderful.' Tony Navarro is a fortunate man; and I am proud to count him my friend. Yes—they are an exceptional couple.

"There were few of the notable London homes which I was not lucky enough to enter at these musicales I describe. The Duchess of Marlborough's, the Duchess of Manchester's, the Duke of Portland's, the Aga Khan's and numerous others—embassies of the different countries among them.   The Dowager Empress of Russia, Queen Alexandra's sister, was one of the illustrious personages I was honored in meeting; and the King of Portugal . . . and hosts of others.

"There was one affair which continued, throughout an evening, with most of the guests (to say nothing of the artists) in smiles.   It was given by the Aga Khan of India—a sort of Pope, I believe, in his country.   There was scarcely a minute during the soirée that he did not walk to and fro, in a pair of shoes that squeaked with each step he took like small animals protesting in a cage.

"But that was all in the day's work.   What meant far more to me were the hours spent with my good friends: Sir John Murray Scott, and his charming sisters; Neil Forsyth, General Manager of Covent Garden (poor chap, he was accidentally drowned, in Nineteen Fourteen), Mary Anderson and Tony Navarro.

"Theirs was an influence which any man might have been glad to feel and profit by.   I've no doubt each one helped me immeasurably during that period of my life, and career, to steer a straight course.   They say that a man is known by his associates; he progresses, or retrogresses, according to the quality of those associates. So you may see what advantages were mine. For when a man goes out into the world it remains for him to attract—quite as much as to choose, for choice, alone, will not always suffice—the right sort of friends. Up to that point it is the influence of the parents which counts; his upbringing. Thereafter, it is with the man . . . or woman.

"However—I'll not philosophize further.

"That spring of Nineteen Hundred Nine was auspicious. Covent Garden was preparing for a gala performance to be given in honor of President Fallieres of France, and I was among those chosen to participate. It was a distinguished occasion, and the attendance composed of the nobility, members of the various foreign diplomatic corps, army and navy officers and attachés and other persons of importance in London. I shall later describe the second Covent Garden gala performance in which I took part, given two years later in honor of the coronation of King George V.

"Mrs. McCormack left for Dublin soon after this gala performance; and on the 21st of July, I received news of the arrival of a baby girl, no less a person than your young friend Gwendolyn herself."

The words were barely uttered when Gwen appeared, sprang into her father's lap and smiling across at me proceeded to impress John McCormack with the fact that he was her particular and personal property.

CHAPTER XVIII

HAMMERSTEIN, CAMPANINI AND AMERICA

There is a short man of whom newspaper men have been wont freely to write who threw his shadow across the path of John McCormack in the spring of Nineteen Hundred Nine. He wore a moustache and a pointed beard then, as now, and mostly upon his head a top hat famed for its caricaturing by cartoonists, whose facile pencils tilted it at rakish angles over a rotund face distinguished, chiefly, by the humor lighted by two very bright eyes.

America might name him from this description alone. But lest others, who know him less intimately than New Yorkers, be impatient to learn just who is meant we will supply the information: Oscar Hammerstein.

Hammerstein, the astute; Hammerstein, the resourceful; Hammerstein, than whom no cleverer impresario ever signed a contract, or fed an opera-going public upon the best to be had.

245

JOHN McCORMACK

A fighter, who made the enemies a good fighter will; a familiar figure in the courts of law, but to those he liked and to those who gave him their loyalty, a staunch friend.

"The greatest tragedy that ever befell musical New York," declared McCormack with conviction, "was when the Manhattan Opera House closed its doors in Nineteen Hundred Ten." Countless others feel the same way in that matter. There was only one Oscar; there never can be another.

Cleofonte Campanini had gradually come to discover qualities in the singing of John McCormack that roused his admiration. Like other uncommon men, Campanini was not afraid to change his mind. The young Irish tenor had developed since he had reached Covent Garden, and in him Campanini (who was Hammerstein's first-conductor and musical advisor) began to discern a candidate for possible honors across the seas. He spoke to Oscar of McCormack, at the close of the Manhattan's 1908–1909 season—on the verge of departing for Covent Garden to assume his conductorship duties there beginning with the gala performance in honor of President Fallieres which has been described.

John McCormack as Mario Cavaradossi in Act III of Tosca.

John McCormack as Edgardo in Lucia di Lammermoor.

"Hear him, at all events," counseled Campanini, and sailed.

"I was not unprepared, when I met Hammerstein," said John. "Campanini had told me, 'The Manhattan would just suit your voice, and I want you. But before we sign let us wait for Oscar. He will arrive soon.'"

Gwen McCormack clambered down from her father's knees and John watched her scamper off with the dogs, on some errand of joyous youth.

"I was drawn at once towards Hammerstein," admitted the tenor. "He was a 'different' sort of impresario. He'd heard me before we met— at a Covent Garden performance—and had formed his opinion.

"Some time later I was told of a remark he had made concerning me.

" 'With that voice,' said Oscar, 'and his Irish name—what a career he could have in concerts.'

"That's what I call scoring a bull's-eye. He had vision, Oscar Hammerstein. I doubt if he stopped to analyze. He just sensed a thing, in that instantaneous way of his; and generally he was right. And I should like to say that no keener judge of an artist lives than Oscar Hammerstein. He's unerring.

247

"I was introduced to him by Campanini, at Covent Garden after a rehearsal. He wore his famous top hat, and from his mouth protruded one of his almost equally famous cigars—doubtless one of his own hand-manufacture, a practice he indulged in even when the distracting business of running an opera house occupied most of the twenty-four hours of each of his days.

"Hammerstein had an ingratiating personality. Magnetic, he was, and straightforward. And I shall never cease to be grateful to him for the opportunities he so freely gave me. 'Well, Mike,' he would say, 'what do you think; can you do it? Yes? All right, go ahead.' So brief a conversation as this would settle the question of a new rôle, and fill me with confidence to sing a dozen.

"We didn't spend much time over negotiations. Campanini offered me a three years' contract, (which was already drawn and only awaited Oscar's signature) with a salary of seven hundred dollars a week for the first season, eight hundred a week for the second, and twelve hundred and fifty for the third season. And I accepted the offer."

A haze had begun to vaporize things, creeping with imperceptible stealth as John had talked so that, in my attentiveness to the tale, I had taken no notice. My host was settled comfortably in a wicker easy-chair, his face pillowed against one fist, his eyes seeing nothing immediately thereabouts. I let my gaze traverse from the now-hidden waters of the Sound, impatient for the resumption of conversation.

"Substantial fees had been my lot that season," said John. "In those desirable London homes I received, for my singing, considerably more than the fifty guineas which those incomparable artists Mario and Grisi had received together for such services—and I saw, with my own eyes, a cheque for one of these concerts. Then there was the concert which I was instrumental in giving, for the benefit of the survivors of the Messina disaster—held in Albert Hall—which netted seven hundred pounds. Representatives of all the diplomatic corps were present, and the orchestra (at the special request of Queen Alexandra) played Elgar's 'Pomp and Circumstance.'

"The acceptance of Hammerstein's American operatic offer was, as I explained to him, dependent upon my being able to arrange with the Harrison concert management for the cancellation of appearances then prepared for me for the approaching autumn. I was glad when I was informed that this could be done. It left the way clear, and I began to speculate upon the future.

"That first visit to the United States, five years before, had left an unfortunate impression. My treatment was not a thing easy to forget. But, I argued, 'The St. Louis Fair isn't New York, and matters probably will take a different turn.'

"Sir John Murray Scott agreed that the Hammerstein contract was one to accept. His counsel always was sound. Even in those early Covent Garden days he had reminded me: 'Caruso has a Caruso style, Mario had a Mario style—do you cultivate a McCormack style. Do not imitate another, no matter how great he may be nor how much he may do that appeals to your tastes. Be original, and with your resources you will become a personality yourself.'

"Now, in my mental perturbation, I found solace in the assurances of Sir John. Listening to him talk I found apprehensiveness waning; and other friends, in their views of the proposed

American engagement, coincided with Sir John.

"I took, at that period, to evening strolls near my Hampstead home, and during one of them stopped a stranger to ask him for a match. It was a trivial enough incident, which I soon forgot. I had no suspicion, even, that the stranger knew who I was; but it seems that he did. For three years later, during a summer visit to Hampstead I received this letter."

The tenor handed me the communication, unsigned as to name, and bearing the date July 23, 1912. It was so unusual that I suggested that it be incorporated, in facsimile, in this book.

"There was much to do before the date of departure for New York," explained McCormack. "I had numerous friends to take farewells of, realizing that they could not safely be delayed until last moments. And there was the gathering together of such things as one would require. In the midst of the London part of that task I received a request from the Odeon Phonograph Company to confer with their executives.

"They wanted me to make some records, at terms thoroughly satisfactory, and I signed a contract. About this time, also the gentleman of the Gramophone Company—the one who had told me three years before that I was worth nothing to him—made overtures. But I was in no hurry, or need at the time for funds, so I put him off. Other offers, of record-making, I likewise sidetracked. Then I went to Dublin.

"Gwen was chubby and healthy, Cyril had grown into a sturdy youngster of two and Mrs. McCormack was unspeakably happy. For a week we let nothing interfere with our visit. I became, altogether, a man of family; willing to forget songs and singing in those closest to me. It was a week, also, of gradual mental readjustment; of calls from friends, who discovered (as friends will, intuitive-fashion) that I had returned, and who came to talk and gather the latest news from London.

"Then followed my trip to Athlone.

"I never go there—to this day—that the sight of familiar spots does not bring tears to my eyes. I had played football here, and there had a fight with one of my rivals, while in various places (as I walked along toward the McCormack home) some incident of my youth reenacted itself—to my momentary pleasure or sorrow.

252

"Scores of people stopped me, wrung my hand till it tingled, and demanded, in those few moments I was then able to spare, accounts of what had befallen me since I had last been home. There's nothing like such home-coming greetings—from Tom, Dick and Harry; the old crowd, which has known you since you were a kid and is just as happy in your success as you are yourself.

"But I got on, after such interruptions, and at length went through the gate and up to the front door. Mother grabbed me first, then my sisters. Father and Jim came in at noon-time, for lunch, and we held a pow-wow, which ended with my telling all the details of the Hammerstein engagement.

"But those times came to an end—all too suddenly.

"Embarking-time arrived. With Mrs. McCormack, I went aboard the steamship, on October fifteenth, Nineteen Hundred Nine, in Queenstown. And on that day, our friends waving to us from the dock, we sailed away—westward. I felt my throat catch as the shore faded, becoming at last a mere fringe on the horizon.

" 'What,' I asked myself, 'is in store for me?'

JOHN McCORMACK

"That night, in solitude, I paced the deck of the great liner. Stars rose in the clear sky and a brisk wind whipped disquietude from my thoughts and brought tranquillity. Thus heartened I went below, to my cabin and rest."

CHAPTER XIX

"Enterprise," assured McCormack to me one cool day which succeeded those of oven-like heat which sent July, 1918, on its backward way, "will always be associated, for me, with those tireless and keen-scented men of the daily press. They are marvels of energy, as well as of inquisitiveness, and with faculties of divination I never could solve. With their corkscrew methods they extract from one's mind more than he suspects lies there, and next he knows he reads it in print.

"The trip to New York from Queenstown was uneventful. The usual ship-concerts, in which I appeared; the daily deck-walks, the lolling in chairs, meals, a bit of gossip and sleep. One day was but a repetition of another that preceded: the routine of life at sea aboard a modern liner, and that infinite space which met the eye when one looked away from her. To me there is something sublimely majestic about the ocean; a suggestion of mysterious power. But it did

255

not exert itself during our five-days' run. We had good weather and a propitious voyage. I recall no musician of distinction among my fellow passengers, other than Gustav Mahler—who kept much to himself.

"Coming up New York bay those same scenes I had first beheld five years before reappeared. Their mental effect, however, was different. I was to an extent sophisticated; less the green lad from the Emerald Isle with teeth uncut. Shortly came the ships-news reporters, with their investigating minds.

"Treading American soil again I felt a thrill. My physical objective was reached, another link in the chain of my career about to be forged. Into a cab—this time a taxi—I put Mrs. McCormack, and the driver whirled us off, towards the Hoffman House, at Broadway and Twenty-fifth Street, where our quarters were in waiting.

"I fell quickly into the way of things, for I am an adaptable animal. For a few days Mrs. McCormack and I suffered the pangs of homesickness in their severe stage. But they gradually disappeared. The marvelous energy of the people one met in the streets, which had not so impressed me at my first American visit, was rather startling. There were times when this physical violence, this rushing of persons past one with set mouths and staring eyes, was unnerving. They epitomized the exhaustless aggressiveness of the nation; a horde of humans competing ruthlessly with one another, seeking their goals which they seemed bent on having or dying in the attempt. I dare not think what might have happened had it been my fate to clash with them in their mad scramble for the attainable. I was glad that my course lay in quieter places, though the struggle there, if less outwardly violent, is nevertheless a fight.

"I suppose," mused the tenor, "it is largely as our feelings incline. Still, I cannot repress, every time I find myself in a business-bent New York crowd, that sudden feeling of pity for those I see buffeting past. For in every group there is one failure; some man or woman struggling vainly against odds—unable to win, yet plodding doggedly on."

With his description of all this John had grown restless. I noticed his big hands clench until the muscles of his forearms flexed in huge ridges. His mouth, too, had a firmer line, and those smiling Irish eyes narrowed. I was not surprised.

McCormack cannot see others suffer without experiencing suffering himself. He's strong and rough enough, with the rough and strong; who can take as well as give, when hard knocks come. But underneath, if you look, you will find a sensitive heart—that beats for the oppressed, for the sad and the weak.

No one, deserving help, ever goes for it in vain to John McCormack. It is natural for him to lend others a hand. And if you would probe the real McCormack you must be near him when he reads some letter from a little old lady something like the following, written in New York in 1915.

"Dear Mr. McCormack:

"As I am a little old woman with hair as white as snow, and you, thank Heaven! are a very young man, it seems to me that, at the ending of your season here, I might try to express my heartfelt appreciation of your recitals in New York. I have joyfully attended them all—have asked appreciative friends to go with me and I have sent many who have gratefully told me of their delight. For us all, in a greater or less degree, this has been a winter heavily shadowed by sorrow and anxiety for others. I have found my greater pleasure at your concerts; on Sunday afternoon

I shall listen to the last note that you sing, with a delight that I find in your every song, but with the keenest regret that we must wait so long before we can hear you again.

"All along my life—abroad and in this country—I have heard the greatest singers of many lands sing in their prime, many of them ballads and songs that you give us. But, for myself, they have never been as flawless and satisfying. With the beautiful voice is the perfect reading —the right value and clear enunciation of each word and new values given to many words. For instance, I have never heard a singer give to the word 'repose' that sense of peaceful rest, deeply desired, that you give to this word. In her youth I heard Patti give to the word 'alone' a depth and pathos, unusual in her singing—a sense of utter loss and desolation that I can still distinctly recall.

"I could select many words whose value has been enriched and deepened, as you have sung them. If anyone should say to me: 'I should like to read simply and appealingly, giving a sense of beauty and richness of the English language—to whom shall I turn?' I should say: 'Go to every concert that Mr. McCormack gives —you can't hope to sing as he does but you can learn from him to read as you desire.'

"If you had no singing voice left,—and far indeed may that evil day be!—I should still go to hear you read your songs and for that alone I believe you would still gather throngs. As for the singing itself, I will say that you could sing the shoes off my feet and I'd never know they were gone (I've a strain of Irish blood, you see).

"If I were a young woman I could not send you this letter. It is one of the few compensations of age, that one can say and do as one pleases. But with all the enthusiasm of early youth, I could not have the deep enjoyment of your singing that I have at this late hour, when I know fully the cares and sorrows and losses that life can bring.

"Young, with perfect health, with a rich endowment in so many directions and with your dear ones around you to give you peace and joy and rest, you know of sorrowful things only through the sure intuitions given to an artist's soul—may you and yours never learn of them in any other way!

"Believing that all generous natures rejoice in giving pleasure through their gifts, I feel sure that you will understand my wish to express my deep appreciation and hearty thanks, as I have tried to do here, for what has been one of the greatest joys of my life. Someone said to me yesterday—'I hope that his marvelous success may not turn Mr. McCormack's head.' I said: 'It never will if he is really great. Mr. Edwin

Booth whose success came in his early youth,
said to me not long before his death: 'I have
never known what it was to end an evening's
work at all satisfied with myself. No public applause or praise of friends could change my own
view. My standard was always beyond my
reach; I could always see where I failed to reach
it.'

"All the truly great people I have known have
expressed this feeling in one way or another. So
I feel that it is only the very small, poorly endowed, natures that can be at all harmed by praise
of their work, whatever that work may be.

"I have written with an easy conscience, for
I do not expect any word in reply to my letter.
I could not be so selfish and so cruel as to add
that task for a tired man, tired indeed you must
be, as your long, full season ends. No, this is
just a wee voice in the chorus of voices that have
told you just the same things in far better words
than I can find—it makes no faintest demand
upon you in any way. Next season I hope,
through my friend Mrs. William McAdoo, to have
the pleasure of an introduction to Mrs. McCormack, of whom I have heard the pleasantest
things, and yourself.

"For that good time I shall wait—with an old
woman's heartiest thanks and blessings for the
songs that have brightened her life, and for the

singer—and with all best Easter wishes for Mrs. McCormack, the children and yourself,

> "I remain,
>> "Gratefully yours,
> "_____"

It would destroy the sense of fitness to give the name of the lady who wrote John McCormack, from the depths of her heart. But there is one thing I can say—she received a reply, penned, I am sure, by a hand that was not altogether steady and guided by a pair of eyes not free from moments of blurred vision. And that little lady is now one of the good friends of the tenor and his wife.

For that human understanding, which is so large a part of McCormack's nature, is one of the principal elements which have made him the singer he is; which had carried him, even on the eve of his Manhattan Opera House début, far along in his ability to touch his hearers and to move them with the emotions he felt.

I intimated, some pages back, that John does not flinch under punishment. It was well for him, on Wednesday, November 10, 1909, that he belonged to no timorous kin and lacked no faith in himself. For nearly three weeks the

John McCormack as Alfredo in La Traviata.

John McCormack as Tonio in The Daughter of the Regiment.

tenor's voice had refused to become adjusted to the climatic conditions of New York. Rest and throat-specialists brought no improvement to the roughened membranes surrounding that golden voice-box. John's début-morning dawned with his voice still below par, and in no condition for the oncoming demands.

But he had been announced, he was a fighter —and he wouldn't quit.

Until an hour before curtain-time the responsiveness of John's voice was uncertain. It was only natural that he should have walked the floor of his hotel chamber a large part of that day; and that he should have turned, in his hour of need, to prayer. He did both, and submitted to the ministrations of his physican, Dr. Dupont. "But not once," asserts Mrs. McCormack, "did his faith waver. 'I'll go on,' he would repeat, from time to time, 'and get through all right.'"

Those of us who were present at the Manhattan, that evening, remember how he got through. With Tetrazzini and Sammarco, and with Anselmi conducting, John McCormack made his American operatic début as *Alfredo* in "Traviata." And without stint that large and discriminating audience "rose to him" (as some of the critics averred) and accepted him as a tenor they wished to hear.

In better voice, since then, he has given a better account of himself. But experts did not disagree as to the purity of those lyric tones, the delightful freedom of their delivery and the unaffected style with which Verdi's music was sung. From that November night of Nineteen Hundred Nine there was no doubt as to the future in this country of John McCormack. Whether there were any in the Manhattan audience with the vision of Oscar Hammerstein, when he foresaw McCormack's concert possibilities, I do not know. What I do recall is that he passed his test, and entered into those precincts sought by many but gained by the few.

CHAPTER XX

"For me," said McCormack when next the mood was upon him to go on with his narrative, "a first performance is no conclusive test. An accident may mar it, some lucky circumstance swing it higher than it deserves. The second and the third appearances are what truly count, for then the people know, and the artist may determine for himself, how far he is likely to go and the possible sum total of his accomplishment. To 'repeat,' if I may use the phrase, is the measure by which we are estimated and which finally classifies us in the niche where we belong.

"I lay next morning, in my bed, thinking deeply of what the succeeding days should bring forth. On the following Monday I was cast for *Edgardo*, in 'Lucia,' and later in that week I knew I should be called on to do *Tonio* in 'The Daughter of the Regiment.' I already had read the newspaper reviews, which were eminently fair. Several were emphatic in their predictions for me;

265

and, so far as I could gather, my début was a matter for congratulation—as I soon found out.

"The 'phone bell rang and answering it I heard Oscar's voice on the wire.

" 'You should be in good voice this morning, Mike,' he announced, 'the press is for you.'

" 'Mike!' By that name Hammerstein always called me, after that, and he still does. I rather liked it, for it always rang, when he used it, with a touch of sincere cordiality.

"I tubbed, dressed and after breakfast felt physically better than I had since I had arrived in New York. The period of greatest apprehensiveness was past. There seemed no good reason why I should not continue with the success I had begun, and I determined to do my best to this end. The throat, when Dr. Dupont came to examine it, showed no ill effects from having sung the previous night. That comforted me, and when I left the hotel for a stroll I doubt if I would willingly have changed places with anyone—had such a thing been possible."

"And the 'Lucia' and 'Regiment' performances—they satisfied you?"

"I am never satisfied. Flaws are always apparent, in whatever I may do. But the rôles in

266

those two operas . . . you should know how I sang them; you were there."

He had sung them well—that's a matter of record. His voice, too, was in a more normal state and he gave it more freely. John's confidence in the outcome also appeared to have stiffened. He no longer doubted, even slightly. Public acceptance had been swift; he could safely conclude that he would go far. With that consciousness—which he confesses he then felt—he sang with increased authority, and as the season wore on McCormack gained in adherents and in the mastery of his art.

But for me, John McCormack's *metier* has ever been the song. He is the singer *per se;* and in singing one has quite enough to do without concerning himself with externals, as is more or less compulsory in opera. For I remember no great opera artist, excelling in the dramatic side, who was correspondingly satisfactory as a singer. Jean de Reszke is a possible exception, yet he was more the singer than the actor. Fernando de Lucia, whom McCormack admired devotedly, proved that one night most conclusively. He sang *Don Jose* in "Carmen" shortly after Jean de Reszke had appeared in that rôle, and forever after de Reszke's *Don Jose* was a milk and watery affair in acting comparison.

So I was interested in McCormack's first concert appearance, which took place in the Manhattan Opera House one November Sunday evening. Unhampered by the trappings and shams of that hybrid art-form—the opera—the tenor was most gloriously at ease. Even then his diction was a thing of joy for those who appreciate that much of the superiority of the voice, to all other instruments, is its capacity for speech. McCormack gave us the text that night; clearly, so that every syllable could be understood. And people went away from the concert talking about it. "I never passed a more enjoyable season than that first and only one at the Manhattan," said McCormack, dreamily. "I was not long in discovering the financial whirlpool which was threatening to engulf Hammerstein, and it seemed a shocking and unfair thing. For he was a great man. And he deserved to succeed. Yet, with all the weight that he alone carried, he maintained a marvelous poise. With me, he was always serene. I know of his fits of temper, and some of the causes—which were enough to have tried Job. Still, he invariably greeted me with that contagious smile. We of the Manhattan were like a happy family, and there were some great artists in it. Nellie Melba, whose beautiful singing still may be taken as a criterion by far younger artists of to-day; Mary Garden, unique artist, if ever there was one, who is as incomparable in those rôles exclusively hers as she was ten years ago; Luisa Tetrazzini, whose brilliant voice was something to remember, as is her thoughtful kindness to me when I needed it; Mario Sammarco, friend always and one of the great artists of his time; Maurice Renaud, one of the most finished baritones France has produced; Charles Gilibert, the inimitable, gentle soul that he was; Giovanni Zenatello, whose heroic tenor voice continues to move his audiences; Mariette Mazarin, whose *Elektra* remains in my memory as one of the herculean vocal feats possible to a dramatic soprano; Jeanne Gerville-Reache and Clothilde Bressler-Gianoli, two mezzo-sopranos whose equals one seldom finds; Lina Cavalieri, Hector Dufranne, Charles Dalmores, and others.

"But that list tells part of the Hammerstein story—and is proof enough of what he did for musical New York. Then there were the operas that he gave—though not all of them, of course, in that single year I was a member of his company. Just think! 'Pelleas et Melisande,' 'Thais,' 'Louise,' 'Le Jongleur de Notre Dame,' 'Elektra,'—to mention a few of the absolute novelties—and the revivals he made!

"I've heard him called 'resourceful Oscar,' " said McCormack, reflectively, "and that he was. And a thorn, always, in the side of the Metropolitan Opera Company's flesh—though just why he was so construed I never could comprehend. For he was a stimulant to that management; forever keeping a competitor alert, as he should be kept—which is good for opera.

"That competition, by the way, was a public delight. There were no idle moments, for any of us—at either institution. We were spurred on to our best beyond the spurring usual in most opera houses. There was the consciousness of close personal scrutiny, of keenest criticism of our efforts—and that was the artistic advantage of every one of us.

"There have been stories, as I know, that Hammerstein was weeks behind with his artists' salaries. I have always doubted those tales. From such evidence as came before me they did not hold water. For myself I can say that what

270

Andrew and Hannah McCormack, John and Lily McCormack with their son Cyril (?) at the McCormack family home, number 5 Goldsmith Terrace, Athlone. This photograph was taken perhaps just before McCormack's 1909 Manhattan Opera House engagement.

John McCormack in 1910.

was due me always came promptly, and not a day late. Even when the finances became pinched Oscar never asked me to wait, or complained at the heavy drain which his pay-roll wrought. I could see how worried he was, but, while he was discouraged, he continued a fighter to the end.

"He crumpled a bit, towards the end of the season. He confessed to me, then, that he was probably through. 'But you will be taken care of, Mike; tenors such as you are are rare.'"

I know, incidentally, that by that remark Oscar Hammerstein meant more than the voice when he said "such tenors as you are are rare." He said so to me, often. "McCormack's got a tenor voice, but there the tenor part of him ends. He's a man."

An incident tending to indicate such to be the case was John's comment upon his first interview in America. "Sylvester Rawling, music editor of the New York *Evening World*, was the first newspaperman to whom I talked extensively for publication," said the tenor. "He sent word up to my hotel rooms that he would like to see me. I had an engagement for tea, at the Waldorf Astoria, and hadn't time to invite him to stop for what he wanted. 'But,' I said to Rawling, 'I'll be glad to have you come along; perhaps we can chat on the way over there.' He was so considerate in the matter, and wrote such an interesting story, that I never can forget."

John poured forth the story of this chapter one cloudy afternoon, as he stood leaning against the rail of his Rocklea pier. He seemed downcast, during that portion relating to the decline of Hammerstein. Now and again he would shake his head sadly before proceeding farther. But eventually he got back, once more, to the sequence of events.

"With New York comfortably started," confided John, "I began to look toward my first appearances in other cities. The Manhattan took its weekly jaunts to Philadelphia, as you remember, and Hammerstein had told me I should soon have my chance at the Quakers. 'They'll either be for or against you,' he said, 'they are no halfway sort over there.'

"I marveled at the opera house, when I first saw its depth. Oscar had built it (he could never keep out of real estate, or inventing tobacco-machinery) during his third New York season and Philadelphia then had a suitably modern place for its operatic occasions. It was named the Metropolitan and was a huge affair.

"We traveled from New York to Philadelphia and return by special train—excepting those who remained over, after a hard performance, to rest comfortably in a hotel. Those trips were jolly affairs: one chair car being reserved for the principal artists, the conductor and members of the executive staff. Hammerstein always went along, for he believed in the theory of personal supervision.

" 'When I'm there, Mike,' he would say, 'I can step lively if anything goes wrong.' So he was generally on the ground, receiving reports, keeping his stars in a congenial mood and serving as he alone could as diplomat extraordinary.

"My Philadelphia début was accomplished without mishap; the performance moving smoothly under Sturani's conductorship, and my fellow artists contributing their full share. I was becoming, I might say, somewhat at home and those earlier fears of American annoyances had disappeared. I considered myself launched in the new country, and a fixture with that particular organization.

"But the bubble of trouble hovered near,

almost ready to break, and I discovered its presence not long after the New Year. That was an interesting experience, by the way—the celebration of my first New Year's Eve in the United States. I was not to sing in an opera performance that night, which left Mrs. McCormack and me free to accept an invitation to be the guests of friends, our objective being a popular hotel.

"It meant rather more to me than the mere ushering in of a new year, as the old one passed on. If others about us in that room were out for jollification I held a deeper feeling. For me the glamor of that enlivening display was more than an assemblage of men and women celebrating an annual event. It reflected, as I surveyed the scene, the exquisite feminine toilettes, the fortunes in displayed jewels, and the merrymaking, something symbolic of my career to come. I chose, at least, to consider it so—and I gave myself unreservedly to an open-eyed dream of onward travel in my profession, building, I confess, a few modest castles out of air. Our host interrupted me, every little while, to point out some personage; but the identifying process over I would drift back to that pleasurable occupation in which most people indulge."

The *Cyril,* with the remainder of the McCormack family aboard, tooted a warning at that moment, and John checked his narrative and turned to wave a welcoming hand. We waited until Wilkinson had landed the power-boat against the float and helped the passengers ashore. Cyril and Gwen stopped their singing long enough to voice, in their treble duet, the experiences of that swift trip, and with that were off on a run for the house, Mrs. McCormack and Miss Foley following at a more leisurely pace.

"It seems only yesterday," mused John, watching the retreating figures of his children, "that I was striving to get a foothold in this country. Only when I look at them, and recall that they were only babies, then, do I realize how time flies. After all, Longfellow appreciated what it meant when he wrote that wonderful line, 'Life is but a day's journey from the cradle to the grave.'

"It was in January," said the tenor, rousing himself, "that I was engaged for my first Chicago appearance. Max Rabinoff, an impresario who has since been identified with conspicuous ventures—the Pavlowa ballet tournees and the two American tours of the Boston-National Grand Opera Company—was the active manager of a series of concerts then being given in the Chicago Auditorium. Many distinguished artists, vocalists and instrumentalists, were appearing at these affairs, and the Chicago Philharmonic Orchestra.

"The possibilities of the United States now impressed me as more important than any I had had; for I had been assured: 'If New York approves you, McCormack, that means the rest of the country.' Philadelphia's endorsement having been obtained, I was anxious to test my resources before both Chicago and Boston audiences; and if they approved, I reasoned, I might feel assured.

"But that Chicago appearance was not wholly satisfactory. The audience was not a large one, and the many empty seats in that vast space proved disconcerting. I had fancied the duplication—in size—of assemblages such as I had faced in New York and Philadelphia, and the disappointment took the edge off my anticipations. Still, I figured, as I stood there on the Auditorium stage, I must gain their approval. So I sang with all that was in me, one of the most satisfying achievements (personally) since I had reached America. I shall always be grateful to that audience. It responded in recognizing what I did. The people appeared to understand. Now, when I sing in Chicago, there are never seats enough to accommodate those who are considerate enough to want to hear me sing.

"The New York season at the Manhattan wore on. Each night that I appeared I would stop, at the first entrance on the left of the stage, to talk with Oscar Hammerstein. He always sat there, throughout every performance, the keenest observer of all; making mental notes which he afterwards turned to account.

"He had a rare mind, too, and a wit that was lightning-like in action. It was his sense of humor, I often think, that enabled him to continue during that fateful Nineteen Nine and Ten season, when he foresaw the end. I was walking with him, back stage, one night during an intermission. The set was undergoing a change, and wings were being rushed to their places, drops raised and lowered, and properties carried to various spots. Oscar, as was his custom, was smoking—though I believe it was not in strict accordance with a city ordinance. The fireman detailed to watch that part of the house passed us.

"He looked at Hammerstein, then at his burning cigar, and fixed the impresario with an accusing look. 'Never mind,' returned Oscar with that ingratiating smile of his, 'it's a fireproof cigar.'

"Scores of such stories are told of him; he was a unique man.

"I feel prejudiced in his favor because, as I have said, of his willingness always to give an artist a chance. I had never sung in 'Bohême' with the Manhattan, and had long wanted to do so. But for some reason the opportunity had never offered. One morning Hammerstein met me at the opera-house.

" 'Do you know "Bohême" well enough to go on in it in Philadelphia to-morrow night?'

"I replied, without hesitation (though I was not thoroughly 'up' on the last act), 'Yes.'

" 'All right, then, get ready to sing it.'

"I went to that fine conductor, Guiseppe Sturani, and confessed my predicament. 'I know the notes,' I explained, 'but I am rusty and shall need your help to give me the cues.'

" 'Don't worry, my boy,' replied Sturani, 'just

keep your eye on me during that last act; you don't have to fuss about the acting, *Mimi's* doing the dying; watch, and I'll give you every entrance.' Good old Sturani, he never failed me once.

"During the visit to Philadelphia," the tenor went on, "a banquet was given for me which I thoroughly enjoyed. The arrangements were made by Mr. Michael Doyle and among those present was the lieutenant-governor of Pennsylvania, representing the governor, while Archbishop Ryan was represented by his assistant bishop. The orchestra of the opera-house paid me the great compliment of coming over, and, under the direction of *Maestro* Sturani, playing several numbers at the banquet.

"After the New York and Philadelphia seasons Oscar sent us for a week to Boston where I sang three performances with Tetrazzini. Here, too, a banquet was given me—at the Algonquin Club, by some prominent citizens, the mayor making the address of welcome."

CHAPTER XXI

A CHANGE OF AMERICAN BASE

"I went aboard the Queenstown-bound liner, on an early April day, in Nineteen Ten, with a tug of doubt at my heart. The formal sale of the Manhattan Opera House artists-contracts and belongings to the Metropolitan had not been consummated, yet I knew that my Manhattan days were at an end. Hammerstein had already sailed for Europe; a despondent figure, as he shook hands with me in farewell, his eyes heavy with the fatigue of worry.

"From a selfish viewpoint, I need have had no apprehension. The public and the press had received me with every consideration. I had sung my first opera rôle in Boston—*Edgardo* in 'Lucia,' with Tetrazzini and Sammarco—on March twenty-ninth. The Boston Theatre was too small for the audience that tried to get in; and there was a repetition of this at 'The Daughter of the Regiment' performance two evenings later, and the presentation of 'Traviata' on April second.

"My reputation—I say it in all modesty—had begun to swing out over the country, thanks to the interest of the newspapers and magazines. Their 'features,' as they are called, and the interviews, so widely circulated, had their effect. The American press is a marvelous institution: able, fearless (not right, invariably, of course, for it is only human in its liability to err), aggressive and tireless in its efforts to progress. If it is not one hundred per cent. perfect—which nothing in life is—the exceptions to approximate efficiency such as I mention are relatively few. And to the press of America, daily, weekly and monthly, my debt is large. In my humble way, I may have served as useful 'copy'; I realize that had I not been that the editors would not have troubled. Nevertheless, without such publicity as they gratuitously conferred, my reputation would have been slower in the making. The word of mouth route is effective, but not so swift a process for the dissemination of fact as the printed phrase of generous distribution.

"But I never employed a press agent. Not

that I do not entertain respect for the profession and an admiration for its members' imaginative facility which will never cease. It was, perhaps, only a whim to decline such services as were proffered; or, mayhap, a subconscious warning to leave the thing to the editors and reporters and special writers themselves. For, if the truth be laid bare, I have always believed that the American spirit is prone to seek that which keeps to itself, while at the same time it shows a consistent tendency to push aside that which urges consideration in a forward way.

"If you merit space in news or feature columns you may rest assured that editorial discernment will land you there. If one doesn't belong— well, clever and persistent publicity agents will often secure a bit of that valuable space. But in such circumstances the subject is a marked man, or woman. And gradually, in the course of time, the stories of 'Jones' or 'Smith' fall from under editorial eyes into the handiest wastebasket."

We had wandered from the pier to the beach, and John seated himself there, on a large rock, and picking up stones tossed them absently into the water. The sun was dropping nearer the

282

horizon line and a freshening breeze began whipping the surface of the Sound into gently churning waves.

"It was such a day as this," said John, "that I landed at Fishguard after the Manhattan season, with Mrs. McCormack, and very eager, too, to get ashore to Cyril and Gwen, and our waiting friends. For it was next door to home, you know, and we had been absent for six months. I'm nearly an American citizen, now, and I feel that I belong here. But there's something about the land a man is born in that grips and holds him fast—as it should. I never catch sight of Ireland's shoreline that my breathing doesn't quicken and my heart pound a little faster—every time. And when my time comes to die, I hope it may be in that country where my first cry was given and that what is left of me, in an earthly way, may rest in Irish soil.

"Mrs. McCormack and I went as quickly as we could to our Hampstead home. Cyril and Gwen were waiting for us. The journey from Fishguard had been too slow, and the rasping of air-brakes for the stops were no sedatives to our impatience.

"But it was good, at length, to be in our own

283

place with those near us from whom we had been so long separated. Miss Mary Scott, Sir John's sister, was soon on the telephone to welcome us and learn the latest news since she had last heard. In all these years we have had no friend more true than Miss Scott; none whose friendship held all one likes to contemplate friendship to be.

"To this day, though circumstances prevent the frequent personal meetings we should like, she never fails to send us a letter by each boat carrying mail. When we are at Hampstead she calls us every morning over the telephone.

"And during the Covent Garden days I always saw her before a performance. In the early afternoon Sir John would send one of his carriages for me, and I would be driven to his home. There, in his study, along about three o'clock, a servant would bring a basket containing oysters, a perfectly broiled steak and other edibles—with a little bottle of chablis.

"These thoughtful courtesies, which help to make life, had a heartening effect I will not endeavor to describe. They were resumed upon our return home that spring, and after a brief rest I began my Covent Garden season. On the days when I did not appear in opera Miss Scott and I would often sing duets. She had a sympathetic soprano, and her sister played accompaniments well. Occasionally her brother Walter, who owns the Rode Stradivarius violin, would join us, playing the obligatos.

"I well remember, also, the facility of Sir John Murray Scott's elder sister, Miss Alicia, as a composer. She knew the voice and its possibilities, and her songs were always 'singable'; with no impossible intervals or straining for effects. One of the best she wrote was 'Within the Garden of My Heart,' which I sang at the Boosey Ballad Concerts and made a record for with the Victor Talking Machine Company."

The news of the transfer, to the Metropolitan, of all the Manhattan operatic effects, including the contracts with the artists, was conveyed to McCormack through the daily press. He was most amazed when he read the cabled account. He had never heard of singers being bought and sold like so much cattle; it seemed almost a return to the slavery days.

His annoyance had moderated, however, when he received a cablegram from Andreas Dippel, the first general manager of the Chicago-Philadelphia Grand Opera Company (which consisted of the nucleus of the old Manhattan) stating that his company wished to avail itself of McCormack's services for the approaching season.

"I tried to take as much rest as was possible, that summer," said the tenor. "But I gave two concerts in Dublin, where I am glad to say the people welcomed me enthusiastically; for Dublin is an intensely musical city.

"The Dublin audiences are some of the most discriminating I have ever appeared before. Their knowledge of opera almost equals that of the Italian audiences. They have two seasons of opera in English every year which are splendidly patronized, and each performance is followed with an enthusiasm I have seldom witnessed elsewhere. Every person is there to enjoy the music, and although these seasons are great social events, this is merely secondary. One of the most interesting things about the opera seasons in Dublin is the fact that there is at every performance between the acts an improvised concert at which the well-known local celebrities are called upon to sing, which they do with a good will it really is a pleasure to witness. In my early days in Dublin I have sung at several of those performances. The caustic wit of these Dublin 'gallery

286

boys' is well known. I well remember a criticism of a tenor whose high notes were a little 'tight.' He was singing some operatic aria and the top note was not to the satisfaction of one of those self-constituted critics, who remarked in a loud voice, 'loosen his boots, and let his high notes come free.' Yet, the Dublin audiences are very discriminating, and eminently just. One of these days, when we have won the war, and I have made money enough to provide for my family, and a little bit more, I shall use that 'little bit more' to establish a conservatory of music in Dublin. And I will get the best professors in all branches of music for the Irish people, whose talents so deserve the best training possible to give them.

"I also gave much time to preparing for a joint concert tour I had arranged to make in September with that master-violinist, Fritz Kreisler.

"I have since come to know Kreisler intimately, and great as my admiration is for him as an artist it does not exceed my affection for him as a man. It is an opinion in which my entire family shares, and to Cyril and Gwen he is 'Uncle Fritz.' Incomparable violinist that he is, with qualities of tone, technique, heart and mind

287

which make him one of the most distinguished musicians of his time, Kreisler was then as now a supreme artist. He was sensitive in the extreme, yet essentially virile. And he was, and is, the sort of man to whom one felt instinctively drawn. To give him one's confidence is the most natural thing of which I can think.

"Kreisler and I appeared together in concerts for about four weeks, and my association with him was the beginning of a beneficial influence which grew steadily and still continues. I may say that I trace my first marked advance in classic song, so-called, from that time. Fritz was a constructive critic in the true sense, and during that tour gave me a piece of advice I have never forgotten.

" 'John,' he said after one of our concerts, 'always learn the music as the composer wrote it, be absolutely letter perfect, so to speak, and then put your own interpretation upon it.'

"In October Mrs. McCormack, the children and I sailed for New York. We reached Chicago the latter part of the month, and on November tenth, Nineteen Ten, I made my opera début in that city as *Rodolfo* in 'La Bohême.' "

John does not deny that he was less happy,

John McCormack and Fritz Kreisler.

*John McCormack (right) with the artist Augustus John at the
Dublin Horse Show, August 1924. Lily McCormack is next to
Augustus John, and McCormack's manager Denis McSweeney
may be seen at the far left.*

under the new order of things operatic, than he
had been when the company was the Manhattan,
with Oscar Hammerstein at the helm. He admired his Chicago public—that I know—and enjoyed singing to it, during the ten weeks he spent
in that energetic city.

"It is a vital city," he told me, "the very air
seemingly charged with dynamic energy. One
got it from the people passing in the streets; that
radiation of excess physical strength. It is an
American city, and as different from New York
(which is cosmopolitan, and therefore, to my way
of thinking essentially non-American) as water
is from fire."

"But . . . you liked the town?"

"I really cannot truthfully answer," he said
with his customary straightforwardness, "for I
did not come to know it as I do now. That
which I saw, and the people I met and passed in
the course of my work, all impressed me as the
right sort.   A buoyant people, self-confident and
taking a pride in their city.   They had musical
perceptions, also, less presumptuousness than
one might expect from so successful an array of
humans, and were always fair.

"The citizens took a proper pride in their first

permanent opera company, and gave us com-
mensurate support. There was a financial
deficit, which the public-spirited guarantors made
up, but when one realizes that the quantity of
opera was materially greater than the city had
been accustomed to it was, perhaps, too much
to expect a larger patronage than we got. It
takes time to build a self-sustaining clientele,
in anything, but Chicago did its loyal best; and
the day is not so far distant when the income
from a ten weeks' season will be equivalent to its
expense.

"The Philadelphia part of our season was interesting, for it was like meeting old friends.
There were two divisions of performances: Chicago having its season divided into two portions
(our opening and middle parts being held there),
with Philadelphia taking the second and the last
sections.

"We gave 'Natoma' that season, in which I
created the leading tenor rôle. I also sang
Cavaradossi in 'Tosca,' the part of *Hoffmann* in
'The Tales of Hoffmann,' and the other characters
with which I had been identified in New York,
Philadelphia and Boston under Oscar Hammerstein's direction. The Chicago-Philadelphia

290

personnel of artists was practically unchanged from that of the Manhattan company's, and Cleofonte Campanini held the post of general musical director.

"In December I sang in Boston, appearing twice in 'Cavalleria Rusticana' and three times in 'Bohême.' My reception by Bostonians has always been cordial and most enthusiastic. I regard them as discriminating judges of music and musicians, and quick to show how they feel. If I have a favorite audience in America it is in Boston.

"It was in January that I sang my first New York concert. I also appeared, a little later in the season, in other cities in what Dippel called a tour of his International Concert Company. It consisted of Carolina White (soprano), representing America; Marguerite Sylva (soprano), as the French representative; Nicola Zerola (tenor), for Italy; Rosa Olitzka (contralto), appearing for Russia, and myself for Ireland.

"During this International Concert Company tour I met a gentleman who has become very closely identified with my career. I refer to Mr. Charles Wagner. I was so taken with his frank and honest personality that in ten minutes we had fixed up a business deal which has been to our mutual advantage.

"His associate, Mr. Denis F. McSweeney, had been a McCormack 'fan' from the old Manhattan days, and I strongly advised—seeing Mac's natural aptitude for the managerial business—that he and Wagner get together. This they eventually did, and they make a splendid combination. I, of course, think they are the greatest managers in America.

"And whilst on the subject of my management, I wish to state here how grateful I am to them for their most dignified presentation of me. No one knows better than I how much their splendid cooperation has aided me in my hard climb towards success. Their kindly advice, their unswerving loyalty, their unshakable belief in my abilities and, above all, their absolute honesty in all our business relationship have been a pillar of strength to me. I want my public to know that I am grateful to them."

CHAPTER XXII

"Australia is a country," said McCormack, "which I deeply admire. Some of my most substantial successes were gained there, and the people have treated me as though I were one of their nationality. I had never been in Australia, so when Nellie Melba invited me to appear as her leading tenor in a season of opera to cover many weeks, to be divided between Sydney and Melbourne, I accepted.

"It had been a strenuous year, for after the Chicago-Philadelphia opera appearances and the International Concert Company tour, I went direct to Covent Garden where I remained actively engaged until the last week in July. I should have liked to 'loaf,' because I strongly advise giving the singing voice a complete and lengthy rest once a year. My engagements, however, forbade—until Mrs. McCormack and I went aboard the boat at Marseilles, bound for Sydney, Australia.

293

"Before leaving for Australia, however, I had the fortune to sing at a gala performance given in Covent Garden in honor of the coronation of King George V. All London was a-quiver with anticipation and the choice seats for the coronation performance sold for ten guineas each, with tickets only for those whose names were on a selected list.

"To my mind Covent Garden is the most perfectly appointed and efficiently administered opera house in the world. Such gala performances as I mention are a feast for eyes, as for the ears. Decorations costing fifteen to twenty thousand dollars transform the interior of Covent Garden into a place of splendor,—consistently artistic splendor. And the center half-dozen boxes are made into one, sufficient to accommodate twenty-five or thirty persons, for royal use.

"Every one of consequence, who was physically able to attend, was present at Covent Garden on that occasion. All the royal family were there; also the entire Corps Diplomatique, with their attachés, military and naval officers of every accredited nation, in full uniform, and the rest of those in London whose positions justified their presence.

"The starting hour was late; nine-twenty o'clock. At this time the king entered the royal box, which was a signal for the audience to rise. Then the orchestra played 'God Save the King.' Within an hour and a half the celebration was over—which meant that the performance consisted of acts from different operas.

"There was plenty of what we hear described as 'atmosphere' to this performance. In dignity and substance I doubt whether its equal could be provided anywhere else on earth. Yet there were touches of the sort we call 'human,' which I observed. For instance: when I made my first entrance my attention was attracted, instantly, to a box at my left. What appeared a searchlight caught my gaze, and kept it fixed upon that object—a strange, utterly inexplicable one, I thought. Gradually, as I became more accustomed to the brightness, which may have set my sight from normal focus, I was able to determine what the odd light meant. If you will believe it, it was nothing more than a huge corsage of diamonds (which must have been worth a fabulous fortune) worn by an East Indian prince; a fitting adornment for the occasion, which had no doubt been donned with as much indifference as I would put on a white scarf as part of my evening dress."

We were on the veranda of the New York Athletic Club house, at Travers Island. John sat facing the sweep of water and small islands which fronts that side, and his animation indicated his interest in the part of the narrative he was beginning.

"That trip to Australia was one of the most interesting in my life," he said. "Through the Straits of Messina we went, catching a view of Mount Etna in eruption; on to Port Said, the back door of the world; continuing, through the Suez Canal and the Red Sea, in heat that makes a New York heat wave feel like an autumn-day; thence to Colombo, a real Paradise. We stopped overnight at Gaul Face Hotel. Next morning we proceeded to Freemantle and thence over the Australian Bight, which is supposed to be the roughest sea in the world, for across it blows a wind that comes straight from the South Pole without interruption.

"We reached Adelaide in a mood of joyous anticipation, for I had been looking forward to meeting Cardinal Moran, of Sydney. He was a Prince of the Church of whom I had heard a great deal; and I had learned that His Eminence had expressed a wish to meet the 'Irish minstrel boy,' as he called me. But I never was privileged to see Cardinal Moran; he died the day I arrived in Australia, and our trip by train from Adelaide to Sydney was not altogether a happy one. I felt as sad as if I had known Cardinal Moran personally.

"The rehearsals for the opening performance were intensely interesting. Mme. Melba was like a child with a new toy, and insistent that everything be done to allow the presentations to be made without a hitch. The soprano did everything to promote a spirit of harmony among us, and it is no exaggeration to speak of us as 'a happy operatic family'; it was very like the feeling that prevailed at the Manhattan, in New York.

"The *première* performance was of 'Traviata,' and I consider it the best one in which I ever took part. The audience was said to have been the most representative ever assembled in Sydney.

It included nearly every one of importance—from the Governor-General and his staff down. Lord Denman was then Governor-General, a courtly gentleman, who took a lively interest in all things Australian and was deservedly most popular with the people. He came often to our performances with his charming wife and from time to time invited some of the artists to Government House to entertain them there. Mrs. McCormack and I enjoyed their hospitality on several occasions. The occasion marked Mme. Melba's first appearance in opera before her native people, who were as anxious that she should triumph as she was herself.

"And triumph she did, as she deserved. Mme. Melba is a great artist. I never tired studying her methods; to be near her, and observe what she did, was an education for a singer. That night she was superb; and the supporting principals, the orchestra and the conductor (*Maestro* Angelini, a thorough musician and a man of real charm) did their share in contributing to the success.

"The ten weeks' season in Sydney was notable in the history of opera in Australia. The performances were made *events*, and the attendances

John McCormack as Romeo in Romeo and Juliet, *as he appeared in Australia with Melba, 1911.*

John McCormack as Rodolpho in La Boheme.

were both large and composed of those who constituted desirable audiences. We all spared no effort, individually, which might aid in creating the effects desired. No petty jealousies arose to disturb our serenity; and nothing of serious nature interfered with our endeavors.

"Both the people and the press accepted me, almost unconditionally, from the outset. It was gratifying to find my popularity growing, which, of course, stimulated me to the best efforts of which I was capable. I was fortunate, also, in being in good health during the eighteen weeks of opera in Sydney and Melbourne; I disappointed only once. And that brings to my mind an incident which will show the spirit of good will existing between the principal artists.

"I was to have sung the title rôle in 'Faust,' but indisposition prevented. When the audience learned of this they began to chant: 'We want John McCormack, we want John McCormack'—and they continued this, in a good-natured way, during the first act of the opera. The one who told me about it was the tenor who sang in my stead, and we laughed together over the matter.

"The Sydney season closed brilliantly, and was

declared to have touched an exceptional artistic standard. Nor do I wonder that this was the verdict. The same care was shown by Mme. Melba in the choice of artists for the small parts as of those for the more important ones; and this resulted in an *ensemble* which would have done credit to any opera house in the world. My personal acceptance gave me both pride and confidence, and when we gave our Melbourne *première* I was prepared, in mood and vocal condition, to give the best of which I was capable.

"The reception we received in Mme. Melba's home city was so enthusiastic that I can think of but one appropriate word adequately to describe it: a 'riot.' News of our achievements in Sydney had preceded our opening, and the assemblage came prepared to hear and see an unusual performance. From their demeanor they must have been thoroughly satisfied. Mme. Melba, of course, triumphed unequivocally, and received a demonstration such as few artists have had in their careers. The most interested member of that audience was Mme. Melba's father. He sat in the first row, in a state of rapt attention throughout the performance; he must have felt proud of his daughter.

"Our repertoire, as in Sydney, was sufficiently extensive. The operas in which I sang were 'Faust,' 'Traviata,' 'Romeo and Juliet,' 'Madame Butterfly,' 'Tosca,' 'Rigoletto' and 'Bohême.' "

McCormack, at this juncture, allowed himself a smile. It preluded something of an amusing nature which he presently related.

"The one humorous incident of the season occurred during a performance of 'Bohême.' We had a soprano; a nice voice, but she hadn't had enough experience with the rôle of *Mimi* to render her letter-perfect in either music or action. Yet, circumstances made it necessary to cast her for this appearance, one evening. You remember my telling about *Maestro* Sturani giving me the music entrance cues during the last act of 'Bohême' in Philadelphia? Well, I had the advantage, on that occasion, of at least knowing the notes. This young woman had scarcely a bowing acquaintance, during that part of Puccini's opera, with any of the first soprano's notes.

"In the love scene in the last act between *Mimi* and *Rodolfo* I discovered my colleague getting deeper and deeper into musical difficulties. She began to skip whole measures, and mumble and drop her voice. Now a duet is satisfactory to the

301

hearers only when both parts are sung; but as the soprano increased her floundering there was nothing for me to do (aided occasionally by the basso) but to sing both tenor and soprano music —where the notes permitted. Briefly, I made love to myself during that portion of the opera, and found amusement in so doing.

"The season closed, in Melbourne, wonderfully—that just describes it. The stage, after the third act of 'Bohême,' was a rose garden, made so from the floral contributions of admirers. Mme. Melba addressed her hearers, showing how deeply she was touched by their tribute; and she did not neglect to praise her fellow artists.

"I never have so completely enjoyed participating in a season of opera. The people of both cities where I had so frequently appeared took me to their hearts. My type of voice was what they seemed to admire in a tenor. They do not care much, in Australia, for shouters. A sympathetic voice appeals to them most, and is preferred to the big, booming instrument.

"In the midst of preparations to proceed to the United States, where I had concert engagements to fulfill, I was approached by Mr. Southwell, a concert manager, suggesting that I consent to give two programmes in Sydney and one in Melbourne. As admirers had already begged that I sing to them I was in a responsive mood, and therefore commissioned Mr. Southwell to make the arrangements.

"These concert appearances filled my cup to overflowing. I had had ovations in opera, but they were no more pronounced than those given me on the concert platform. The newspapers were enthusiastic; and directly there arose controversies as to whether I was superior in one form of musical entertainment or in the other. So intense were the discussions—in the press and out of it—that the people allied with the respective issues divided themselves into two camps. I never knew which side, if either, settled the question to the majority's satisfaction.

"It was just prior to my Australian concert appearances that I met a young man who subsequently became identified with me in my career, a violinist of admirable talents and a splendid youth who has since heeded the call of his country and joined the Royal Air Force: I mean Donald McBeath. He was sent, with a letter of introduction from Mother Xavier of the Lewisham Hospital, to me at my house in Melbourne.

He was a tall, lanky boy of sixteen. He played for me an *Adagio*, by Ries, and splendidly; I became immediately interested and my interest has not abated.

"Mother Xavier, whose lovable character had made her adored throughout Australia, was exercising a sort of protecting guidance over Donald. His playing impressed me sufficiently to engage him for my three concerts; and I was glad this was so, because Mother Xavier did so much for others that any request she made the people always took delight in granting. Yes, and there was yet another reason.

"This good woman came from a town only twenty miles from my own Athlone—Mullingar, in County Westmeath. I had been to see her, and was so taken with the work she was doing that I asked if I could not, in some way, be of service.

"She smiled, and answered: 'If you could come to the hospital and sing a few of those wonderful songs for the nuns.' It was such a little thing, I thought, for her to ask, though she did not appear to think so. I quickly arranged to have Donald McBeath go with me, and Mother Xavier brought her nuns together. The pleasure these good people derived from that concert was many times worth the slight effort caused in giving it, so much so that I shall never go to Australia that I shall not give a concert for Mother Xavier and her nuns.

"I never had a more appreciative audience than this little body of workers in a noble cause. I'll concede that they may have been a trifle prejudiced, still they seemed discriminating, for they were enthusiastic over the better music no less than over the ballads.

"Sailing away from the Antipodes I could not refrain from pondering over my experiences of those five preceding months. Rewards had come to me, most bounteously; and I was unutterably grateful.

"Wonderful as the trip from Marseilles to Adelaide had been, another, scarcely less wonderful, lay ahead. Past the Fiji Islands we steamed; thence, under a canopy of clouds, to Honolulu —garden spot of the Pacific. And it was there that I was first made acquainted with that native instrument, the ukelele, which has since become so popular.

"On a winter's morning, in February, Nineteen Twelve, we landed in Victoria, British Columbia. We entered a cab, and the driver took us to the Empress Hotel. It was only a few blocks from the dock, but this shrewd young man went about, through street after street, until he felt he had given us ride enough to warrant the fee he intended to demand.

" 'Two dollars,' he blandly remarked, when we stepped out before the hotel.

" 'What for?' I asked.

" For the ride,' he retorted.

" But isn't that rather steep?' I wanted to know.

" 'Well,' remarked the cabby, 'I paid two dollars for a Victor record of yours this morning, and it's only fair to get even.'

"What did you do?" I asked, laughing.

"What could I do?" said John. "He had me, and knew that he had. So I paid him his two dollars."

CHAPTER XXIII

AMERICAN AND AUSTRALASIAN CONCERTS

McCormack came eastward across the American continent, that late winter and spring of Nineteen Twelve, by easy stages. He sang thirty-four concerts, and according to newspaper accounts they were important affairs. The tenor's return to the United States was welcomed in each city where he appeared by a large audience, which seemed happy to renew a musical friendship.

At the conclusion of this part of his tour he went to London, and resumed his annual appearances in Covent Garden. His voice and his artistry had developed; he was twenty-eight, and his experience and his travels had not only made him a more convincing singer but had broadened him, too, in knowledge and the understanding of life.

In the autumn of that year, after a summer at Hampstead with his family, McCormack pre-

pared for concerts in the United States under the
Wagner management.   But each leave-taking of
those closest to him grew more difficult.   Homesickness continued to be a malady he could not
elude; yet there was a comfort he took in the
thought of the companionship which Mrs. Mc-
Cormack had in her sister, Miss Josephine Foley,
and in Cyril and Gwenny.

"For," as an intimate friend of theirs told me,
"in the McCormack home Miss Foley has
thoughts of all others before herself.   She is
'Auntie,' and indispensable; a buoyant nature
that shows in the upturned corners of an expressive mouth, and a smile eternal in eyes that look
frankly into yours when she greets you.   A
personality one feels at once, with charm of manner in which sincerity dwells.   The visitor observes these things instantly; and returning
again to the McCormack household becomes convinced of them the more.   So, if she be momentarily absent, she is missed—and by Mrs. Mc-
Cormack and the children and John, even more
than by the guest, because Miss Foley has a
faculty of making things pleasant, in ways that
are gratefully smooth."

St. Louis marked the launching of that Nineteen Twelve season. McCormack and Wagner, his new manager, both had a desire to begin in the city where the inexperienced Irish boy had sung to appreciative audiences during the Exposition, more than eight years before. The assemblage that gathered in the Odeon packed the place to the doors. There were a score of encores, with men and women applauding until too weary to continue.

Each subsequent concert was but a repetition of that which moved the St. Louis throng to its demonstration. The McCormack hold upon the people grew, and with it his prestige. He was a personality, with fame spreading everywhere. I recall that it was about this time that the serious musicians and the ablest of the music critics recognized the McCormack voice and art as things of outstanding importance. Within a scant three years he was justifying the promise which discerning people at his first Manhattan appearances had believed that he held.

But had John been less the artist he was, had he been in the slighest degree unequal to touching the hearts of his hearers, he must have blighted the large hopes cherished for him. It is incontestible evidence of his qualities that he measured, in those days, up to the standard the people were brought to believe was his.

The music critics of recognized authority began to discover all this. But the programmes John offered confused them, because his resources and his unquestioned sincerity admitted of his offering more songs of so-called classic mould during a concert than were forthcoming. They failed to see (I know that I did) the purpose of John's methods, (which he has explained in another chapter): that the simplest songs must be sung, almost exclusively, for some time before those of finer character, in considerable number, can with safety be offered.

It is only additional proof of McCormack's faith in himself, and the course he was pursuing, that he continued steadfast in his mission to take to the people the songs they could understand —the songs they longed to hear. Yet with each reappearance in a city (and in many, that season, he sang twice and three times) he would introduce just a little more of the better music he was so judiciously bringing into its place.

Every important city heard John McCormack between the fall of Nineteen Twelve and the late spring of Nineteen Thirteen. The largest auditoriums possible to obtain were filled as often as he appeared in them, and the people went away—clamoring for more.

Again the tenor returned to London, for his Covent Garden annual engagement; and once more the public and the newspapers recorded the advance he had made in his art. In opera, as well as in concert, he continued steadily to progress, and the gratifying part of it was in the general recognition that obtained.

"That summer was one of happiness, happiness in being at home with my family, in the study I was engaged upon, the anticipation of my approaching Australasian concert tour, and my participation in affairs of absorbing interest. I had corresponded, some months before, with J. & N. Tait, a firm of established and highly respected Australian concert managers, and arrangements had been made for an extended tour, through Australasia.

"It was during this summer," continued the tenor, "that I sang at a concert given in aid of the Ovada Bazaar, held in Dublin."

We were on a golf course during this part of the narrative. I was curious to pin a story I had heard: that John had broken down when he sang

311

"Mother Machree" at a concert where his own mother sat in a hall, listening to him. He smiled when the question came, and teed his ball.

"It's not true," he declared. "The time and place where I sang the song—and to mother—was that concert I just mentioned. Mary Anderson was the moving spirit of the Ovada Bazaar, and she made a remarkable speech. When I sang 'Mother Machree,' which happened to be for the first time in Ireland, I confess to being deeply moved. But mother was nearer to tears than I. It was, I believe, the most eloquent interpretation of the song I had ever given; there was reason enough—in my mother's being there —and I think the audience sensed it, and understood the reason. Two years before, in San Francisco, when I first sang 'Mother Machree,' I felt a lump in my throat; the poem and the music always affect me."

John and I walked down the golf course towards the spot where his ball had gone. His friend Dick Lounsbery, with the two caddies, were beating the grass where it lay hidden. They located it as we drew near, and John remarked he "guessed" he would have to use his spoon.

"It isn't a spoon you want here," retorted the bright young man, "what you'll need are a knife and fork."

John laughed, but after his shot, made adequate rejoinder. He was not far from the green, for that drive had gone a distance. He approached like a professional, sending the little white sphere to within ten feet of the cup. His partner had been overruning the greens, and John found his chance.

"That's the way," he exulted; "anyone can smash 'em *double-forte*, but it takes a golfer to hit them *mezza-voce*." After holding out the tenor continued with his narrative.

"Having engaged McSweeney as my personal representative for the Australasian tour, I sent him on well in advance of my arrival in Sydney, where it was planned I should give my opening concert on September 4. Shortly after his arrival there, McSweeney cabled that a small-pox scare had Sydney by the heels. He informed me that nearly all the theatres were being affected by this fear of the epidemic, but that in spite of this the feeling was that it would not diminish the attendances at my proposed concerts.

"I therefore sailed, as before, from Marseilles;

313

taking with me Mrs. McCormack, Miss Foley, Vincent O'Brien, and Cyril and Gwendolyn. The trip was a second enchanting experience in beholding those sights I have previously mentioned. Mrs. McCormack and Miss Foley found a delight similar to mine, and the children, in so far as they were able, were interested.

"Shortly after arriving at our destination, the Mayor of Sydney—at a reception given me—said he was glad I had reached the city, because he felt that no one would do more to allay the fears of the people than the Irish singer 'who had already proven how deeply he was able to move the people with his rare singing of songs everyone wanted to hear.'

"That, naturally, encouraged me to do everything in my power to satisfy my public. The Messrs. Tait, and McSweeney, assured me that I was certain to have all the patronage the Town Hall would accommodate; and they were right. But the opening concert found me half sick from the effects of the vaccination to which it had been considered wise I should submit. I was in that condition, though it was not generally known, throughout the three succeeding appearances.

"Donald McBeath, who had improved in his

314

violin playing, appeared with me, and acquitted himself most creditably. The newspapers all asserted that my singing was better, even, than it had been when I first sang in Sydney, on my earlier visit. As for the audiences, I was truly overwhelmed, not only by their demonstrations during and after the concerts, but when I appeared to get into the vehicle which should carry me to my hotel.

"It was at one of these Sydney concerts that Cyril and Gwen heard me sing in public for the first time. They sat, with their mother, in the audience; and from time to time I looked to see how my endeavors were affecting them. I was anxious most naturally to see the effect produced on their youthful minds, and I can't tell you how delighted I was to watch the rapt attention they paid to each song. But Cyril was disappointed because I had not sung his favorite—'Molly Brannigan.' He came with Mrs. McCormack and Gwen to my dressing-room, as the audience was leaving the hall, and expressed his childish regret. I was sorry, too; but it happened that Vincent O'Brien was ill. This made it necessary to get a substitute accompanist, who had not had time to rehearse the music of Cyril's pet song.   At a later concert, however, the boy had his wish fulfilled; he told me, on the way home, that it sounded better in the 'large place' than in our music-room, which was where he had always heard it."

Melbourne, Adelaide, Brisbane, Rockhampton, Newcastle, Towoomba, Bendigo and Geelong welcomed the tenor with no diminution of the enthusiasm which Sidney audiences had shown.   He gave several concerts in each city, and still the people continued going to them—usually in numbers too large to permit all gaining admission to the hall.

At Adelaide, after the farewell programme, a crowd numbering several hundred gathered about the stage door.   When McCormack came out a spokesman made his way to us and said: "Give us one more matinée, John, to-morrow."

"But there's no time to let the people know," replied the tenor.   "Time enough," retorted the spokesman.   So John consented. His announcements were carried in the morning newspapers, and before noon every ticket in the house had been sold.

"It was like that throughout the tour," continued John.   "The receptions I got at the stage doors as I went out from a concert became a regular occurrence. And the night of my Sydney farewell the enthusiasts assembled and, as I came from the hall, began singing 'For He's a Jolly Good Fellow.' The people used to crowd round my car and ask for souvenirs, one young lady going so far as to steal the cigarette I was smoking and take it as a souvenir. I wonder if she still has it."

A humorous incident happened at the closing Melbourne concert. McCormack's final song was Balfe's "Then You'll Remember Me," from "The Bohemian Girl." The words in the last phrase are those of the title of the aria. They had barely died away when a man called out, from the balcony, "How could we ever forget you, John!"—a charming compliment, you will admit.

"A most loyal people," continued the tenor, as he recalled those enthusiasts in that part of the world, "and I know of none to whom I would rather sing. Everyone was so considerate. I shall never forget Lillian Nordica, who was present at one of my Melbourne concerts. I discovered her, early in the performance, among the audience,—stunning in appearance. And I know that her presence stimulated me to my utmost to win her appreciation. I was touched on receiving from her a laurel wreath, nearly three feet high; and some time after, when I met her at a state ball at Government House, where she certainly looked every inch a queen, she said that my singing of a song she had never fancied, 'Kathleen Mavourneen,' was one of the most satisfying interpretations she had ever heard.

"It was in Sydney—to go from music to medicine—that I met one of the ablest physicians I ever knew. He was Dr. Herbert Marks, and he helped me during some throat difficulty I had because of the climate there. One of his remedies was some oily preparation, which could be dropped upon a handkerchief and inhaled. One evening, during the summer following, at a Covent Garden performance of 'Madame Butterfly,' chancing to look down from the stage at the nearby portion of the audience, I caught sight of Dr. Marks sitting in the front row. It was a complete surprise, for I did not know that he had contemplated a trip to England.

"In a spirit of greeting, and reminder of those Sydney days, I took from my pocket a handkerchief, and held it to my face. The doctor became convulsed at this, and sat silently shaking in his seat for several seconds.

"But Mrs. McCormack, who was also in the assemblage, had also learned of Dr. Marks's presence there,—and here is a coincidence. She had barely received word from home that Cyril had been taken ill, and that 'Auntie' was endeavoring, unsuccessfully, to reach our family physician. So Mrs. McCormack sent word to Dr. Marks, asking that he come to her in the foyer—which he did.

"She took him direct to Hampstead, where he found Cyril to be ailing, though not seriously. He attended the lad, prescribed for him and then returned to Covent Garden . . . but not without having missed the whole of the opera's second act.

"However—to continue with that Australasian tour. I had been there but a few weeks when a letter reached me from that great artist, Lilli Lehmann. It had been forwarded from London, to which the soprano had sent it from her home. It is one of the most treasured communications I ever received; written in beautiful French, and inviting me in words I shall never forget, to participate in two of the proposed Mozart performances which were to be given the following summer, in Salzburg, the home of the master composer.

"My good friend, 'Tony' (Antonio) Scotti, had, Madame Lehmann wrote, told her of my Mozart singing. He had spoken of me at such length, and in such a way, she declared, that she would in no circumstances be satisfied until I advised her that I would sing *Don Ottavio,* in 'Don Giovanni,' and the leading tenor rôle in Mozart's Seventh Mass, these being two of the works it was Madame Lehmann's intention to perform. She concluded her letter with the remark that it made no difference in what language I replied, so long as I wrote 'yes.' I sent her a cable, and did not hesitate to make it a long one, assuring her of my delight in accepting.

"I consider that invitation to have been the most striking musical honor ever bestowed on me; nor can I conceive of one greater to achieve. Madame Lehmann's letter recalled my experiences in Boston, during the preparation and the performance, in the Boston Opera House, of 'Don Giovanni,' which I was privileged to sing under that eminent conductor, Felix Weingartner.

"It was said that Weingartner pronounced me

the greatest living singer of Mozart; but such a statement is, undoubtedly, without foundation in fact. It would be too sweeping, and though I am sure that no other singer approaches a Mozart composition with deeper reverence, I should certainly hesitate to accept such superlative endorsement.

"I do recall, with the utmost pleasure and satisfaction, that during the first general rehearsal of that Boston 'Don Giovanni,' Weingartner, after my singing of 'Il mio tesoro,' put down his baton and applauded; which he repeated in the performance itself. After the third act of the performance he came to my dressing-room to personally congratulate me.

"With these recollections," resumed McCormack, "I was elated at Madame Lehmann's invitation, and the remainder of my Australasian tour found me devoting considerable thought to that forthcoming Salzburg festival—which was prevented, it was to turn out, by the outbreak of the war.

"At the Melbourne races," said the tenor, "I met one day Clarke, the Australian pearl king. There is a tale, I understand, which has been circulated to the effect that he gave me a large pearl fabulous in value, which Mrs. McCormack wears at the center of her necklace. It is scarcely within the limits of truth, however; for although Clarke did say that he wished to leave with me a keepsake in memory of the pleasure my singing had afforded him, the pearl, though a beautiful one, was not large—nor is it the center one in Mrs. McCormack's string, though it forms part of it.

"For hardship I recall nothing so vividly as the railroad accommodations of northern Queensland. The roads were narrow-gauge, the sleeping-car berths both short and shallow, and being generally behind schedule and without dining-car service we often were called from an unfinished cup of coffee, to get on board a train before it pulled out of the station. Whenever I think of these times I can see myself, deserting a half-empty coffee cup, and scurrying, a sandwich in one hand, a banana in the other, for the car platform. But the trip in this part of the country was worth while, for the audiences were as 'shamelessly enthusiastic' as every other one.

"In New Zealand, through which we traveled extensively by automobile, my experiences were varying and of great interest. The people greeted me, and sent me on my way, with the same evidences of feeling which I had encountered everywhere else. Throughout Australasia there is shown the same outward recognition for an artist well liked which the Latin races display. Some of the keenest listeners in my New Zealand concerts were Maoris, who are a most interesting people, with a lively imagination and musical tastes.

"One of the things I remember most distinctly is our visit to the Rotorva, the show-place of the Dominion, and the finest I have seen, anywhere. The guide described the various spots, as we reached them, in English that was a strange mixture of beautiful words with those wholly ungrammatical in their use; it was a picturesque description.

"There was a lake in this show-place; its waters appearing absolutely pink from the reflection of the sunken terraces, and formed by geysers and hot streams. Long before there had been some sort of volcanic disturbance which had left its effects. Even the fish in this lake—affected, no doubt by the pigment of the clay—were pink.

"It is small wonder that I should hold the experiences of that concert tour in such pleasant recollection.

"I have often thanked God that He let me live and sing in this wonderful age of progress when distance has been practically blotted out by telegraph and telephone and when even the 'men who go down to the sea in ships' are no longer out of touch with the world but are constantly in communication with their friends at home. I see you are wondering what is the reason of this digression. It is an interesting story and in many ways unique. On our way to the United States, when about two days out from Honolulu, I received a wireless message something to the following effect: 'Have heard you are passenger on *Niagara* which arrives here Thursday morning; do give us a concert in Honolulu. [Signed] Adams.' I had met Mr. Adams, a charming wide-awake American business man. Mrs. McCormack, McSweeney, and I held a council of war at which we decided we should give a concert. Then we approached the Captain as to how long we would remain in Honolulu and he replied, 'Mr. McCormack, if you give me a good seat and sing "Mother Machree" and "I Hear You Calling" I will hold the ship for you.' 'Done,' said I.

A wireless to Adams and a concert fixed in less time than it takes to tell it! We certainly live in an age of progress. The newspapers published on the day our boat arrived carried striking advertisements of a 'very special' concert by John McCormack, and recounted the unusual circumstances under which the programme would be sung. Whether it was the novelty of the mode of arrangement, or my name, or a combination of the two, I only know that the tickets were entirely sold before noon on that day. We gave our concert, to the evident delight of the large audience, and went our way with the consciousness of having done something unusual.

"It is interesting for me to recall at this point my many meetings with that great benefactor of mankind, Signor Guglielmo Marconi. When one considers how much more terrible, if possible, those disasters of the *Titanic* and the *Lusitania* might have been, in fact how much more 'frightful' this cowardly U-boat war would be without the God-given genius of this splendid Italian patriot, I feel I have been honored in grasping his hand, and that every civilized nation—mark my use of the word *civilized*—should perpetuate his memory and deed in marble and bronze. Of course," said McCormack with a smile, "I have another reason to love him and his achievements. You see he loves Ireland, his mother was Irish —a student of singing in Italy when she met his distinguished father—and he married an Irish lady, but be that as it may, my earnest prayer is 'God bless Marconi.'

"I sang sixty-two concerts during that Australasian tour. I haven't been back since, but I am going. For they are wonderful people out there, and they know what they like."

CHAPTER XXIV

THE AMERICAN CONQUEST

"After that Australasian tour," remarked McCormack, "it was America once more. I can assure you that the sight of land, after our long voyage, was welcome to our eyes. Mrs. McCormack, O'Brien, McBeath, McSweeney and I watched from the deck of the ship the approaching shoreline. It was late February when we landed in Victoria, and cold . . . b-r-roo!"

"But," I interrupted, "where were Cyril and Gwen? Did you leave them aboard ship?"

"Yes . . . in Adelaide, several weeks before, when we thought it best to send them back to Hampstead. Miss Foley went with them, so we held no worries for their care and safety.

"Back in the United States our audiences were waiting for us; and we presently took up the filling of the score of concert engagements which Wagner had prepared. After Victoria and Vancouver we appeared in Seattle, Portland and other Pacific coast cities; every concert brought a

327

crowded house, with the people welcoming me in a fashion that warmed my heart.

"Nothing at all like the concert I once gave in Scarborough (England) when there were thirteen persons present, by actual count.

"However, that is ancient history which was never repeated. The newspaper writers began to regard me as useful 'copy,' to be regularly used, and I didn't object. I found myself interviewed in every city; though not as an editor in a New Zealand community once did it. *He* came with himself too prominently in mind, and after listening to an extended discourse upon his peculiar greatness I excused myself for something more to my liking. Still, I had, it seemed, offended his critical majesty, for after my next concert he wrote that my voice was *nil,* my use of it atrocious and my enunciation impossible to understand."

"Touched your weakest spot," I suggested.

"Yes," said John with a grin, "like the fellow who once remarked that Caruso hadn't much of a voice.

"Right across the country, eastward from the Pacific coast, our concerts attracted throngs, so much so that we found it necessary, with regrettable regularity, to turn people away. We invariably secured the largest auditorium available, and had extra chairs placed upon the stage, but even then there wasn't room enough to accommodate all who sought admission—and I was genuinely sorry. I always am, in such circumstances. I enjoy a 'packed' house, but I do not like to feel that anyone who has taken the pains to come to a concert hall to hear me is unable, from physical limitations of space, to do so.

"As audiences in San Francisco, Los Angeles and other communities of the American far west greeted me with declarations of being glad to have me back again, so did Salt Lake City, Denver, Kansas City and every other city wherein I faced an assemblage. Larger and smaller ones appeared to be of the same opinion: they wanted me and my singing and my songs. And I was delighted to respond to their desires.

"From the middle west we entered the realm of the east, and in good time New York, Philadelphia, Boston, Washington, Baltimore and other centers listened to what I had to offer, and pronounced my artistic wares to be of a desirable nature."

John paused, there. Mrs. McCormack and Miss Foley appeared to remind him of a social engagement they had for that evening; so when they had departed he continued with this part of his story, somewhat hurriedly, though with care for sequence and fact.

"We crossed to England, in the late spring, and I prepared for my Covent Garden opera season. It was not long before there occurred the incident which was made, by Austria and Germany, the basis for their subsequent declaration of war. The man in the street did not appreciate, perhaps, the full gravity of the situation, but when late July arrived those of us who were in a better position to know were very grave. Rumors of war had begun to circulate; the very air seemed charged with currents of dire foreboding.

"I was in Ostend when the first formal declaration of war came. And the day the German soldiers crossed the Belgian frontier there was a general rush of foreigners to seek places of comparative safety. I had given a concert the night before, in Ostend; but, like the others, I felt no desire to linger. London impressed me as a wise objective, especially as Mrs. McCormack was with me.

"I shall never forget the day we spent on the

330

dock, in Ostend, waiting to board a steamer that should carry us across the English Channel to Dover. From eight o'clock that morning until six in the evening, Mrs. McCormack, Edwin Schneider, and I waited; we finally got away.

"But the impressiveness of what we were to see will never leave me. Nearing Dover our boat ran in between a lane of British destroyers. It was my first full appreciation of the majesty of Great Britain's navy, of the titanic power it wields. As we proceeded through the protecting destroyers one of them came near, and the captain called to the commander of our boat to move in as closely as possible to Folkestone. There was the feeling of something terrible impending.

"It was intensely real, because there arose before me a vision of the trip we had planned, down the Rhine, on the way to Salzburg, where we had planned so soon to go. Schneider had been telling me all about the scenery and my anticipations were keen.

"When I reached home I found there a cablegram from Madame Lehmann, which said: 'Sorry we will have to postpone our Mozart festival until after the war.' It would have been a performance of 'Don Giovanni,' worth hearing, for besides Madame Lehmann, as *Donna Anna*, Scotti was to have sung the title rôle, Geraldine Farrar the *Zerlina*, with Carl Braun, Andres de Segurola and myself completing the more important membership of the cast.

"The summer was one of sorrow and anxiety over the war into which so large a part of the civilized world had been plunged. We, in England, were of course very close to where the battles were raging. And the import of the consequences could not be denied."

The autumn of Nineteen Fourteen brought McCormack back to the United States, and into full artistic and popular stride. He was an international celebrity, with a very large income from his singing, and phonograph records.

Cities and towns of all sizes and inclinations, and in every part of the United States, wanted this illustrious tenor. Even communities other than the largest found two (often three) appearances insufficient to satisfy the popular demands. The majority in any town wanted to hear John whenever he opened his mouth to sing. So three, often four, concerts in a single community within a period of seven months came to be an accepted condition.

New York, Boston, Chicago, Philadelphia and a few other centers provided so many concerts within brief periods of time that experts shook their heads in undisguised amazement. Nothing like it had been known before; so these wise persons marveled and, asked for a solution, gave the matter up.

Large cities, smaller ones, and others of even lesser populations appeared to find a greater enjoyment in McComack's singing than ever. This was Edwin Schneider's first complete season with the tenor as his accompanist, and he tells of the estimate in which John was held in words that make an accurate mental picture.

There were many notable concerts that season—in all parts of the United States. The newspapers began to recognize that John McCormack had become "an institution," and accepted him as such. The magazines accepted him as "a personality" who could "not be advertised," and they sought him for "feature articles" with increasing frequency.

I think at that time that one might say McCormack had gained an indisputable place in his profession; that he had become a fixture, who would be taken (with the ever-renewed and enthusiastic demonstrations of his hearers) as a necessary matter of course.

To recount the experiences of the tenor in the United States since that period seems unnecessary —at least, to any considerable extent. The public is familiar with the fact that he sang continuously, save occasional appearances with the Chicago Grand Opera Company, in concert. He had previously appeared in New York with that organization, during its occasional Tuesday night visits to the Metropolitan Opera House; but it was to the concert platform that he devoted his chief endeavors.

On Christmas Eve, Nineteen Fourteen, John had thrilled an audience of one hundred thousand by his singing, before Lotta's Fountain, in San Francisco. Out of doors, in the heart of the business district, this annual ceremony, sponsored by the San Francisco Press Club, is an event. And McCormack's singing that Christmas Eve gave the newspaper men something to write about.

So, John continued in his career: mounting steadily, being honored outside as well as within the field of music; meeting personages and building a life of usefulness far wider than that commonly falling to the lot of a musician—regardless of his eminence.

When John established a record by giving twelve concerts in Greater New York—as he did in the 1915–1916 season—and packing both Carnegie Hall and the Hippodrome (with its 5,000 seats) beyond their legitimate capacities the public ceased to wonder. It was the matter of course attitude, all over again.

Seven concerts he gave to Bostonians that season; six in Chicago; three each in Philadelphia and Washington. And when a single artist can go three times in a season to a city no larger than Springfield, Massachusetts, fill completely the largest auditorium there, and cause so many people to ask for tickets that they cannot be supplied, his position is unique. Numerous other instances, of approximate impressiveness, might be cited if any purpose might be served.

One charity concert, in the New York Hippodrome, netted $14,000. Another in the same place a few years later, for the benefit of the Catholic Orphan Asylum of Kingsbridge, brought in $36,000.

That was the way of it. The 1915–1916 season established a quantity, as well as a quality, record for John McCormack.

But because he had won his place McCormack did not relax his artistic efforts, nor bask in the sunshine of self-content. He studied harder than ever, and to each public appearance he gave his strictest attention. He was barely thirty-two, and great as his achievement had been he realized better than anyone else the possibilities which lay ahead.

For, as McCormack has already said, there is no stopping-place in art. He must go either ahead or drop back, and it was not his intention to retrogress.

Symphony orchestra conductors now began to take notice of John McCormack, and one by one they invited him to appear at an important concert, in the interpretation of some vocal masterpiece. It was then, I am moved to think, that the serious-minded members of the country's corps of music critics got the complete artistic measure of John McCormack.

His programmes, too, were steadily being

John McCormack, Jean de Reszke, and Lily McCormack at the de Reszke villa near Nice, April 1921.

*John McCormack, Bishop Michael J. Curley, and General Sean
McKeown of the Irish Free State Army, Athlone, 1923.*

strengthened in artistic character; and when he went to Boston, and gave four concerts devoted exclusively to the gems of song literature, any skepticism was swept aside.

On one of these occasions H. T. Parker, critic for the Boston *Transcript* and one of the severest in the land, wrote; "Idol of the popular audiences, if you will, but on the way also to be the idol of connoisseurs of song." It was an opinion, without a doubt, which was and is shared by the majority of the leading music critics in the United States.

But McCormack prizes most highly, I believe, the treatment he has received at the hands of Dr. Karl Muck. Enemy alien though he is, the latter's position in the world of music is supreme. John accepted the engagement to appear for the first time with the Boston Symphony Orchestra with considerable apprehension. He knew Muck's reputation as a disciplinarian. It was natural that he should have held an idea of stupendous musical demands being made upon him.

"So anxious was I to let Dr. Muck know that I was letter-perfect that I may have been stilted in my delivery of the Mozart aria (a *Rondo,* called 'Per pieta non Ricercate,') at the rehearsal.

" 'It is not necessary for you to take no liberties which will give ease and beauty to the music,' said Dr. Muck. 'Interpret as your good taste and feeling impel, and I will be with you.'

"After the first public performance, the following season, when I sang a Beethoven aria that Dr. Muck accompanied superbly, I stopped in the wings, and found the conductor beside me. I was still in the transport which the work and masterly support of the orchestra had given me. I could hear the critical audience applauding, but I had thoughts for only one thing; that was the accompaniment.

"I turned to the sober-faced musican standing beside me and told him that never had I had such a thrill as his conducting and the orchestra had supplied. And Dr. Muck, with a faint smile, made me an answer I shall never forget. 'You gave me a bit of a tear yourself, John,' was his remark, and that was compensation for all I had undergone."

CHAPTER XXV

"The United States is the country in which I have sung most continuously; the land where my career has been developed and whose people, in greatest numbers, have taken me to themselves as though I were their own," said McCormack. "I had felt, for a long time, the desire for citizenship, and in the latter part of Nineteen Sixteen the decision was made.

" 'America for me and for mine,' I thought, and I determined to apply for citizenship papers."

We were sitting under a canopy, on the west lawn at Rocklea, watching a tennis game. Two of the players were ensigns, in the U. S. Naval Reserve, on leave. Tanned and clean-limbed they were, average specimens of our fighting-boys in blue and looking their parts.

"Stalwart lads," said John, "both of them; quick in mind and eye, and sportsmen. Will they give good accounts of themselves? You can find the answer in the newspapers, any day.

Brother citizens of mine, they will be, in a few months more—when I get my final papers in January.

"It was January eleventh, Nineteen Seventeen, that I took my preliminary steps towards naturalization. Independence Hall, that historic structure in Philadelphia, was the place. Could there have been one more fitting? I chose it deliberately. That is what the word 'independence' means: liberty, freedom of thought and action, human rights untrammeled—and all, in their unrestricted fullness, to be had in these United States."

He stopped there, and watched the ensigns at their play. Irishman that he is, and with a true Irishman's love for his land and its people, McCormack is also an American. Those of you should know who have seen him in his Liberty Loan campaigning; who have heard him in speeches he has made since the United States entered the war, and seen his eyes light as he has sung for the American Red Cross and Knights of Columbus funds.

For John is a fighter for whatever he has given his heart to. He was most anxious to join the service and he has not yet given up hope.

When he stood before President Wilson, tendering his services to sing to the American soldiers on the western battle-front wherever he might be sent, the President replied:

" 'We cannot all do the same things, and those of us who stay at home and religiously perform our duties here as Americans are doing just as much for the cause as the soldiers in the trenches. But I would not wish for one moment that a spirit of hate should enter into our hearts, for were that to occur we should be swerving from principles which are among those for which we stand, and any such spirit of hate would rob us of the efficiency which at this time we need.

" 'I know, Mr. McCormack, that you are fond of sports, of contests between boxers. You are aware that when a boxer sees red he endangers his chances of winning. So we must not allow hate to enter our hearts, and somebody over here must help to that end by keeping the fountains of sentiment flowing.' "

What McCormack did for the Knights of Columbus and the American Red Cross is in itself a story, to which we shall presently come. Just now, to round out the notable moments in John's life during Nineteen Sixteen and Seventeen, there are two events to be recorded: the banquet tendered him by old-time associates of Summerhill College, at the Biltmore Hotel, in New York on May fifteenth of the former year, and the conferring upon him of the degree of Doctor of Literature by Holy Cross College, of Worcester, Massachusetts, sixteen months later.

Seventy-five men were of the party which assembled at the Summerhill dinner to McCormack, the only laymen present, excepting the guest of honor, being the Hon. W. Bourke Cochran and the Hon. John C. McGuire (both Summerhill alumni), Charles L. Wagner, Denis F. McSweeney and Thomas J. Shanley.

The Right Reverend Michal J. Curley, Bishop of St. Augustine, was to have delivered the principal address. McCormack anticipated, eagerly, having his old friend there—especially in the capacity planned. But his duties interfered, and Bishop Curley, at a late hour, was obliged to disappoint. He sent for the occasion a letter, however, to be read by his nephew, the Reverend William Fallon, and in it he wrote:

"I regret my inability to be with you in person at this great gathering, but I am there in spirit, and from my heart of hearts I wish my friend, John McCormack, continued prosperity and success. True to his splendid Irish faith, to the grand old-time Celtic traditions, he is hailed to-day as a credit to Irish Ireland, and centuries from now his name will be written on the pages of Ireland's story as her greatest gift to the world of song."

After Bourke Cochran and others had spoken, the Reverend William Livingston, pastor of St. Gabriel's Church, New York, delivered his address. It was in part as follows:

"Now that so many true and beautiful tributes of esteem have been paid to Mr. McCormack; now that so many flattering words of praise have been wafted to his ears; now that so many fragrant garlands of affection have been laid at his feet, may we not consider for a moment the rather serious question of our personal duty to him in the days that are to come?

"Great men have always been surrounded by a guard of honor on special occasions, and by a bodyguard in times of danger, when protection was deemed to be either prudent or necessary. If then we are so proud to call ourselves Mr. McCormack's guard of honor to-night, should we not feel bound by a high and holy obligation to call ourselves and to be his devoted bodyguard at all times in the future? If it be true that 'death loves a shining mark,' as Young said long ago, it may surely be said that jealousy and ignorance always turn their attention in the same brilliant direction. In these days of ours, even as in former times, every man who attains distinction is subject to the calumnies of the envious and the suspicions of the unthinking. The character of George Washington was bitterly assailed during his lifetime, though now no man dare raise his voice against the Father of our Country. Even Our Blessed Lord did not escape the tooth of malice and the tongue of calumny, though He came to teach the law of love for all mankind. Surely then, if that law of love is to be observed by the laity, we of the clergy, whose office is to preach charity, should be the first, not only to practise that divine virtue, but also to rebuke those who may seem to forget its existence. Surely then, as Irishmen and priests, we shall be on guard at all times, ready to defend the good name of one who is so dear to us, even as we would defend our own. We have placed that name on a throne to-night; let it be ours to see that no man dares to tear it down.

"Again, it may be safely asserted that from the beginning of time men have had different opinions as to the best means of attaining a great end. Such a difference of opinion exists among our people to-day. Some men are positive that constitutional agitation is the only safe road that leads to Irish freedom. Others assert that this road has led to merely another form of slavery and will lead to worse in the future, namely, the gradual but utter extinction of Ireland's undeniable intellectuality, Ireland's age-long love of freedom and Ireland's world-famed fidelity to the 'faith once delivered to the saints.' This difference of opinion is not disunion and it is not a thing to be ashamed of, no matter what be said to the contrary.

"Mr. McCormack is doing work for Ireland to-day that no other man on earth can do. He is convincing a hitherto unbelieving world that Irish music is eminently fit to take its place among the compositions of the great masters, that its soul and expression should receive due consideration from all true artists, and that its inspiration should be a potent factor in the musical productions of ages yet unborn. As a man he has a very clear conception of duty to his native land.

JOHN McCORMACK

As an artist he must be a thing apart, dedicated and consecrated to a great cause. Therefore, it is but voicing your holiest sentiments when I say in your name that to the greatness of his name and to the glory of his achievements, present and future, we pledge him here to-night our warmest support, in loyal, unswerving and affectionate devotion."

A further evidence of his appreciation of the tenor was forthcoming from Father Livingston in the poem, entitled "McCormack," which is as follows:

Where Shannon's lordly waters sweep along
In foaming majesty from fair Lough Ree,
Athlone's old bridge still lives in storied song,
And keeps men dreaming of the years to be.
Its stones are gone, its glories passed away;
But song-bird memories are waked to-day.

Near that old bridge came first an infant's cry,
A lad's sweet treble, then a youth's soft tone,
Which flamed in fervor as the years ranged by,
And made the hearts of all mankind his throne.
Northward it flashed to rouse the sleeping thrall,
Southward rang out its silver clarion call.

Across far seas that soul-enchanting strain
Flowed on, melodiously so clear and strong,

346

FOR AMERICAN CITIZENSHIP

Till Music crowned him in her loved domain
  The master singer of true Irish song.
With lays whose tenderness is half his own,
  He charms the world and glorifies Athlone.

With all the honors that have been heaped upon him, McCormack still blushes when a new one offers. The occasion of the Holy Cross College Degree was no exception. He fidgeted throughout preliminaries. And when the Rector, Father Dinand, S.J., began his conferring address John was frankly embarrassed.

"To sing his country's songs," began Father Dinand, "caring naught who made her laws, was the sentiment of the seer who voices the common feelings of his fellow men. The soul of the nation passing through the entire gamut of change must sound the depths and at times reach to heights of passion, hence the songs that tell this story will ever be the embodiment of the nation's life, while laws will but point the pathways of the nation's progress.

"Sculptured marble, deftly wrought, silent must stand and ever mute, what though you strike it and cry out 'Speak!' Bronze, verdantique with years, can never be the sacred depository of the living soul.

347

JOHN McCORMACK

"To a heart fashioned in the land of tender emotions, to a mind schooled in the isle of scholars, the gift of sweetest song was vouchsafed to fill up the measure of creation in the man who could interpret for the world the hidden depths of his country's treasure-soul.

"In fullest appreciation of his deep study of the Celtic and the Romance literatures, in hearty acknowledgment of his God-given mission as an educator of the world in the wealth of music and folklore of his native land, and as an earnest of affection for the gifted son of Erin's soil,—Holy Cross College confers the honorary degree of Doctor of Literature upon John McCormack."

I was rummaging, one evening, through McCormack's collection of papers: documents and letters and clippings of articles which the tenor had placed at my disposal for such information as might demand incorporation into this book. There were heaps of them, and I had sorted the lot, and read until my eyes ached.

One, however—an extract from the San Diego *Sun*—attracted and held my attention. It was so typically pertinent that I reread the article, alleged to have been written by a cub reporter on

348

that newspaper, who confessed to knowing nothing about music, yet disclosed a singular capacity for peering into the depths of human nature.

I do not seek to contradict him, he may have been what he proclaimed; but my opinion is that he was an old hand at the newspaper game, who knew a story when he saw one, and how to write it as well.　And as for the cub reporter part, that, to my notion, was a bit of camouflage on the part of a city editor, just to dress the tale for his readers' tastes.

The writer began his story by stating that the regular music critic of the paper (who, if there was one, probably covered fires and the police-court, besides) was indisposed.　The cub reporter admitted, without shame, his unacquaintance with music or how a music review should be handled, and—but here is what he wrote:

"The fact that I don't know the difference between an arpeggio and a coloratura soprano is what doubtless led to my selection to 'cover' John McCormack's concert at the Spreckels last night; it's a way city editors have—to shovel out an assignment to the man who knows nothing about it.　But, as a matter of fact, I knew a little something about the particular subject in hand, so to speak, for several times I had heard a record of McCormack's singing, 'I Hear You Calling Me,' and had wept honest unashamed tears over it, and on the fifth playing, had threatened to break that record; because I felt sad enough already.

"Then some fellow over in the Spreckels Theatre, who had heard McCormack sing somewhere in the East, told me I would enjoy the affair, that he sang a number of the old songs we all heard in our younger days, the songs everybody loves to hear repeated, and that cheered me up, for I concluded that this Irish tenor must be a fairly popular entertainer instead of a highup god, whom the highbrows worship, even though they understand not.

"As to that, however, I had some doubts when I saw the programme, that this Irish tenor— whom the phonograph people say they made famous—much as Mr. John McGraw might speak of Mr. Christopher Mathewson in baseball—that this Mr. McCormack was going to start by singing a recitative, an aria by the justly celebrated Mr. Handel.

"And when I heard him sing this I still had some doubts, for it all sounded miles away from anything like what Sousa or Leo Frankenstein have written. And, besides, I noticed the most applause came from the chaps in dress suits and the ladies in dress to match. In fact, their applause was furious, not to say superior.

"But the encore was a little song which invited a beautiful lady to sleep on her lover's bosom and to lose herself in him, and that, to my feeble and non-artistic understanding, seemed much more human and much more worthy of ordinary human applause. By the way, McCormack is a fine, manly-looking fellow, with the kindest of smiles, and when he sings he stands with his feet well apart, his head tipped up toward the balcony, and his hands clasped in front of him.

"After his first encore, he sang 'Love's Quarrel,' followed by a song in French, of which I actually understood some few words, and then the great, rich, noble song 'The Lord Is My Light,' whose fine chords of accompaniment made you know that at some time a musician had been able to picture a great, reverent thought and had done it powerfully and nobly. McCormack sang it that way, too. Then some lilting Irish songs, with the twang of the ould sod in them and love and romance, and a bit of mischief as well. Then, by and by, 'I Hear You Calling Me,' and

I went to hide the tears that came from my eyes and met a music expert—a fellow whom I had regarded as high-browish and with superior knowledge. He has a fine tenor voice and uses it for money. Rather timidly I asked him how McCormack stood among great singers? And he said: 'Lord, man, if I had that voice—if I could only reproduce those tones—I'd give my socks, my shoes, my shirt—honest!' And he gulped apologetically.

"At the end they all stood up and applauded and waited, and McCormack came back again and sang to that great audience, one of the largest ever in the Spreckels. I'd go again without being sent."

CHAPTER XXVI

MC CORMACK AND AMERICAN WAR FUNDS

'Tis a good soldier who does as he is bid. John McCormack became a soldier in the fall of Nineteen Seventeen; enlisted to swell the exchequers that provide the means for our soldiers and sailors to fight with, and to succor them when succor is needed.

"Could any man with red blood in his veins do less?" demanded John of me as we discussed the matter. "I'll never forget how I felt while I stood with others in a vast crowd, watching the first contingent so soon to embark for some point 'over there.'

"Young they were; among the pick of our youth in all the land. And they were marching before us for the last time before facing the enemy—some of them never to . . . come back. Mrs. McCormack was with me. She felt as I felt. I never see the men pass by with our banner at their head that I do not get a great lump in my throat.

" 'One has to be close to them, to really under-stand,' she said in lowered voice. I turned to look into her face; her lip trembled. She was right. Nor were we the only ones in that throng of New York spectators, who felt the tug of the heart, and a strange clutching at the throat.

"It is no effort for me to sing 'God Be With Our Boys Tonight,' for it is a prayer that comes from somewhere deep down inside me—almost unbidden to my lips."

McCormack has sung that song many times in the last year. Other songs he has also sung, without compensation save that which he felt his duty; and from that singing has come from the public approximately half a million dollars for investment in Liberty Bonds, and two hundred and forty-nine thousand dollars contributed to the funds of the American Red Cross, the Knights of Columbus, the Sixty-ninth New York Regiment, the Ninth Regiment of Massachusetts, and other funds.

I learned, quite by accident, that these large sums represent not only the net receipts from McCormack's efforts, but also the gross. For when the tenor has sung there have been no incidental expenses to be deducted from what the public has paid to hear him. He and Managers Wagner and McSweeney and Accompanist Edwin Schneider have not only given their services but have paid the attendant traveling and living expenses.

Not a penny of the money was handled by Wagner and McSweeney in any of the McCormack concerts for the American Red Cross and the Knights of Columbus. And to fill the San Francisco and Los Angeles engagements McCormack and his management personally took care of the railroad fares, among other items, from the Atlantic to the Pacific coast and return. But in addition to all this, where public-spirited citizens did not do so, McCormack and his business associates have paid the rent of halls, and the cost of printing and advertising.

"For weeks I had been impatient to do something to help the country in the part it was playing to defeat the Allies' enemy," said McCormack. "It was in November of Nineteen Seventeen, after I had seen the President. My personal interests were matters of secondary consideration. I must do something, I felt, and at once.

"Soon thereafter I lunched with John D. Ryan,

355

of the American Red Cross, at his home on Long Island. 'What is it that the American Red Cross most needs which I am able to assist it to get?' I asked. 'Whatever it may be, I am at the Society's service.'

"Mr. Ryan's eyes shone. 'The Red Cross needs two things,' he replied: 'money and the spreading of its propaganda. Many men can raise money, but few men—or women, either—have the power to stimulate the public into making cash contributions and, also, to make known to the people what the Red Cross represents and its accomplishments. You are one of those few, because you have the capacity to reach the public through its hearts.'

"I was willing, if need be, to contribute one hundred thousand dollars," said McCormack, "but I realized what spreading the propaganda meant."

" 'In that event,' I answered, 'you may rely upon me to sing as many concerts as are necessary to net the Red Cross one hundred thousand dollars. And, to the best of my ability, I will spread its propaganda.'

"On the following seventeenth of December," continued John, "I gave my first Red Cross con-

356

cert. It was held in Washington, on an evening possible for President Wilson, Mrs. Wilson and others of the presidential suite to be present."

Concerts in New York, Philadelphia and Boston followed, and the cause brought enthusiastic audiences into every auditorium. Chicago provided its quota of people and dollars, and Denver, San Francisco—where $25,147 was realized from the sale of tickets and McCormack phonograph records, which John contributed and autographed—and Los Angeles followed.

At McCormack's Boston appearance, at the big Red Cross Rally, held in Tremont Temple, the throng that sought admittance could not be wholly accommodated. General John A. Johnston, chairman of the meeting, aroused the audience—which had previously been in a tumult through John's singing of "The Star-Spangled Banner," "Keep the Home Fires Burning," and other patriotic songs—by calling for a rising vote of thanks to the tenor. General Johnston termed John McCormack "the singing Prophet of Victory!"

"It was an experience that thrilled me," admitted John. "Much as I believed I understood what spreading the propaganda meant, and stimulating an appreciation of the great accomplishments of the Red Cross, it was only in the field of activity that I got close enough to its heart to feel its real beats."

I am aware that John performed his service for the American Red Cross with no consciousness of sacrifice. I know that his own affairs, during that period of service, concerned him least of all. Absorbed in the work, he lived it with a patriotic simplicity that was its appealing characteristic. I recall speaking with him, in the Pennsylvania Railroad station, in New York, just before he left for the west to fill one of these Red Cross concert missions. And he was disinclined to speak of his personal efforts in the undertaking he had assumed.

"It is the cause, not the men in it," he said, "which we must consider and concentrate upon. We are all soldiers, enlisted for specific purposes; each having his particular part to perform. My share in what is being done is only the accomplishment of what my abilities allow me most effectively to do. One man fits in here, another man at some other place; and the women, too— they are doing their respective tasks nobly."

He regarded himself no more than part of a

human machine, assembled for humanity's sake. It was the attitude McCormack holds these days, which points his thoughts towards the big things in life, and is making of him a singer able to touch hearts even more poignantly than ever before. He held it during his Red Cross service; and the people got it when he stood before them—spreading propaganda with his song.

If ever it were proved, conclusively beyond any doubt, it was proved by John McCormack during his enlistment (he feels that he still is enlisted, under waiting orders) that music is no longer among the non-essentials. "In these times," he asserts, "it has been demonstrated that music is as necessary to victory as munitions and supplies . . . for it is music that is helping to get them, by keeping, as President Wilson said, 'the fountains of sentiment flowing.'

"The song," asserted McCormack, "that has been hallowed and sanctified by feelings so much greater than any ever roused by mere musical and verbal perfection is such that there is no longer anything in the world with which to compare it.

"When I sing 'God Be with Our Boys To-night' I am not offering musical intervals of much or little charm, or words of literary or non-literary value. I am singing something that everybody left in this country is singing with me. Every people the world over has put itself into its war songs and made those songs immortal.

"And there will be more songs; they will spring up suddenly, no one will be able to tell why. They must be simple, and sincere, and must have that indefinable quality which makes everybody who hears them want to 'join in.'

"But those are the songs our singers must keep singing—it's our branch of the service, and we dare not neglect it. I think every singer in this country should be at work for the war."

John did not cease his patriotic service with the successful conclusion of his efforts to secure for the American Red Cross one hundred thousand dollars. The Knights of Columbus required money for its war fund.

"What do you want me to do? How much money can I assist, through my singing, in securing?"

Fifty thousand dollars was the amount, and McCormack's endeavors in New York, Boston, Baltimore, Buffalo and Chicago yielded this sum.

He gave concerts, also, for the dependents of

the Sixty-ninth Regiment of New York and the Ninth Regiment of Massachusetts.

John will continue in his work, whenever necessity requires, because his heart is in it—and he stands ready to respond to the call.

CHAPTER XXVII

SELLING LIBERTY BONDS

John McCormack never took a course in salesmanship.   He has no intimate acquaintance with what some experts in that line term "the science of selling."   He might learn, if he were so disposed, for Edwin Schneider, his accompanist and close friend, asserts that John has a mind like a sponge.

But John is an artist, not a scientist, and it is therefore not surprising that he should have applied art to his appeals to the public to which he disposed of many Liberty Loan bonds.   The tale, however, that he sold two millions dollars' worth is not correct.   He seeks no credit for anything he has done to assist in prosecuting our share in the war; what he does insist upon, though, is exactness, not exaggeration, in statements regarding whatever service he has performed.

"I do not know the precise quantity of Liberty Bonds I have been instrumental in selling," he said, "perhaps a half million dollars in value.

One person, alone, took one fourth of that amount at a single purchase, and I want it understood that it was a voluntary contribution which came unsought and from an unexpected source— after I had finished with the actual assignment given me.

"It was during the Second Liberty Loan, when the drive was in need of every impetus that could be applied, that I was asked to aid. McCreery's department store, near Fifth Avenue in Thirty-fourth Street, was the place in New York where I was sent. It was an autumn morning, the air was crisp, and I had abundant enthusiasm.

"Why not? I had something of sterling value to offer; the inducement, from a monetary viewpoint, was sufficient to interest anyone of discernment having money to invest. But more than that, my prospective customers stood on the common ground of patriotic unity. It wasn't 'Will you buy?' it was 'How much in Liberty Bonds to-day? Our country needs your support!'

"Stability in values and sentiment were joined when I appealed to the people who gathered about my booth, in McCreery's. I had as associate an official bond-salesman, whom the government provided. We decided upon a plan of campaign —I believe that is customary, in selling.

"To every purchaser of a one-hundred-dollar Liberty Bond it was agreed that I should autograph any phonograph record of a song I had sung. For whoever would buy a one-thousand-dollar bond I was prepared to sing a song, and allow the purchaser the privilege of choosing the selection.

"You see, we surrounded our selling proposition with every inducement possible to make it attractive. According to business analysis, it had a triple appeal: value, sentiment and the choice of either my autograph or a song, depending upon the investment.

"It didn't take long for us to get started. We secured a crowd, quickly. The arrangement was that I should serve for the one day only; it was an endeavor in which many personalities well known to the public had been asked to aid in a special drive. The government wanted its Liberty Loan to be oversubscribed, and was entitled to the enthusiastic support of everyone capable of selling and buying.

"I had seen patriotic and capable men engaged in appealing to people to respond to the call of their country by doing their duty to the limit of their ability—to buy bonds. And I admired and felt with those who possessed the power to reach the hearts of their listeners. For that is what this war means to us over here: our hearts must be reached, and kept beating with the sort of responsiveness which will 'keep the fountains of sentiment flowing.'

"Many times, during that autumn day in Nineteen Seventeen, I was moved by some incident. Some one patron, to whom the buying of a one-hundred-dollar bond meant some personal sacrifice, would disclose an unselfish loyalty which made my own heart throb. And there were more than a few of this sort. For them I signed my name on my phonograph records with real joy; and I signed it often.

"I was happy to sing—for the one-thousand-dollar buyers, who were numerous. It got to be like encores at a concert, after a time. And thus enthusiasm grew. As the day wore on, and our sales mounted, I addressed those who were within sound of my voice in the store."

The New York newspapers, in their news stories published the following morning, pronounced McCormack's speech as one filled with sentiment and devotion. They laid particular stress upon the unusual effect upon a throng of people who blocked the aisles, listening to the plea of a singer—who also had unquestioned powers of oratory.

"At times someone would appear, and inquire rather skeptically, if I really *would* sing if five thousand dollars in bonds were subscribed. The firm had advertised the terms upon which I would supply the autograph and vocal bonuses, yet there were people who, arriving late, evidently felt that my voice might have given out.

"I assure you it was inspiring to me to feel the response from those men and women who came and were susceptible to an appeal. It fired me with gratitude that the singer and the song are what they are. My professional experience had long convinced me of this; but it has taken the Red Cross, the Knights of Columbus and the Liberty Loan work I have done to show me the flame of truth at its brightest.

"In the end," declared the tenor, "I actually bought bonds for myself from myself, and I was happy in being able to do so."

During the Third Liberty Loan push John helped the government to lift it over the top. In

John McCormack and the soprano Lucrezia Bori, as they sang together on January 1, 1926 over radio station WEAF in New York.

John McCormack on his concert tour of the Orient, 1926.

the midst of his Red Cross campaigning, at a concert he was giving, in Providence, a short but vital speech he made stirred his hearers to an extent that caused a liberal opening of their purses in the purchase of bonds.

Mayor Gaynor spoke to the vast audience before McCormack appeared. He told them of what the tenor had already accomplished; that $85,000 of the $100,000 he had pledged himself to raise was already in the treasury of the Red Cross. And he appealed to them to buy Liberty Bonds.

McCormack's entrance caused a demonstration. It was some time before he could start his programme. He closed it with "God be with Our Boys Tonight," and he left his hearers silent, for a moment, before they could bring themselves to their applause.

But when John returned to the platform it was as speaker, not in the capacity of singer. I think it is sometimes more interesting for a throng to listen to spoken words from one who uses the voice in song—if the occasion be peculiarly suited to it. In this instance the people sat, many holding their breaths, waiting for the tenor's opening words.

"I know," said McCormack, "that the sentiment expressed in that prayer, 'God be with Our Boys Tonight,' finds an echo in your hearts. As the body without a soul is dead so, also, is faith without good works of no avail. The good work of our boys over there is going on, we know, because of their faith that we over here are standing behind them; they know they can depend on us. If you have faith—and I am sure you have—back it with your contributions that will prove that you are doing your part as well as our fighters are doing theirs. Buy Liberty Bonds!"

"I had known that John had some oratorical gift," admitted a close friend of the tenor, in talking about that occasion, "but he actually thrilled me that afternoon. Nor was I the only one so impressed. I concede to being prejudiced, yet I do not overstate in asserting that I seldom have been so moved by John's singing as I was during that spoken appeal of his in Providence."

"I remember a very interesting experience," John continued, "and I hope I will not appear boastful in telling it, eleven days later, in Buffalo. Walking through the rotunda of the Iroquois Hotel I was stopped by a lady. She told me that a blind gentleman living in the hotel, who was further afflicted through being an invalid, had never heard me sing.

" 'He has so often expressed the hope,' explained the lady, 'of some time being able to listen to you, Mr. McCormack—if only in one song. In New York we know that you sang for whoever purchased a five-thousand-dollar Liberty Bond. This gentleman . . . well, if you would sing—just one song—is willing to buy one hundred thousand dollars' worth of bonds.'

"It is contrary to my custom ever to sing before going on the platform on the day of a concert. Yet this was so marked an exception that I replied, 'Certainly I'll do it.'

"So a piano was wheeled into the room on the second floor of the hotel, where a Liberty Loan luncheon was to be served; and there the invalided and blind gentleman was taken. I sang 'God be with Our Boys,' and true to his word the patron bought one hundred thousand dollars' worth of bonds."

At the meeting at the Metropolitan Opera House in New York, on the evening of September 27, 1918, when President Wilson delivered his great war address at the launching of the Fighting

Fourth Liberty Loan, John McCormack sang "The Star-Spangled Banner."

No patriotic call finds him hesitant. E. T. Stotesbury, the banker, sent him one, in May, Nineteen Eighteen, when the final touches were being put upon the campaign of forty-eight eastern Pennsylvania counties to sell $115,000,000 in War-Savings Stamps. It was pledge-week, and Charles M. Schwab and four thousand Philadelphians were in the Metropolitan Opera House, where Mr. Stotesbury presided as chairman.

McCormack's singing was a factor in that meeting, which netted a very large subscription for War-Savings Stamps. But the incident that seemed to make the impression that night was in Charles Schwab's words, as he stepped to the spot where the tenor stood waiting to sing. With one hand upon John's shoulder Schwab said:

"I want to thank my old friend, John McCormack, for coming here to-night. He is a great artist, but great as is his art his heart is greater; and greater still than his heart is his patriotism. God bless you, John!"

CHAPTER XXVIII

THE AMERICAN SINGER

The day was sultry and the humid heat-waves had sent us to the pierhead, where the *Cyril* lay like a sea-thing dozing on the glassy surface of the water. Besides Mrs. McCormack and the two children, we were, Miss Foley, John, his master-accompanist Edwin Schneider, and myself, a party of seven, all rather moist and turning appraising eyes waterwards where possibly bodily relief might be had.

Our wilted attitudes made us look an amusing lot, or would have had there been in any one of us ambition to summon a sense of humor. But with the shore left behind and the *Cyril* tearing along at twenty knots we found a breeze other than that of the motor-boat's own making. The lowered temperature, which always prevails on water, gradually restored our interest in externals and we prepared to take notice.

I sat alongside John, who held the wheel and

371

worked the controls—all like those of a motor-car. The others sat aft, in wicker-chairs, under a canopy.

"From time to time someone rises to deplore the managerial recognition given to the American singer in his own land and to ask if in fairness he should not have wider opportunities, and receive a more general acceptance from the public," said the tenor.

"I believe that I am amongst those who feel that the American singers have not only demonstrated their capacities, but that they are now reaping benefits from them. In concert and in opera we see and hear them, during the music season, so continuously and under such favorable auspices and they are accomplishing such admirable things, that in my opinion the American singers may in all truth be said to be coming into their own.

"Inspection of the roster of the Metropolitan Opera Company will disclose an amazingly large percentage of Americans, a number of them first-principals. The same is true of the Chicago Opera Company, and of other, if smaller, opera companies in the United States. In opera the American who has ability to achieve is being accorded opportunity, and I have no doubt that as there is an increase in the number of those who possess exceptional qualifications for their tasks we shall witness a corresponding gain in the quantity growth of their triumphs.

"The concert field certainly reveals the Americans prospering and accomplishing much artistically in their own country. Men and women both are appearing everywhere. In recital, oratorio and miscellaneous concert the native artists are not only challenging successfully those of foreign birth, but the greater number of the desirable engagements are theirs.

"There are persons, I know, who contend that American audiences prefer a singer having a foreign-sounding name; who assert, and rather violently at times, that the adage about 'the prophet in his own country' is in full working order where the American vocalist is concerned. But with all due respect, I cannot agree. For I think the day of such possible bias is past and that the period of ascendancy for native singing-artists is now well under way.

"If we consider the great American singers, pronounced that by the press and the public, their number will compare very favorably with those of other lands.   Possibly not in opera, for our vocalists engaged in that branch have begun but recently to develop in appreciable numbers.   But in concert American singers win the greater part of the many engagements to be had, and I should be surprised if the next decade does not bring opera-singing Americans of the first rank to the fore in numbers that will satisfy their most valiant champions."

John drove the *Cyril* to starboard of an outlying rock and headed a few points astern of a thirty-footer which lay gracefully ahead.

"There's many an American singer like that sloop yonder: capable, personally impressive and succeeding in the chosen element.   I rejoice that singers born in the United States have such undeniably exceptional talents and that they are putting them to proper advantage.

"Nowhere in the world have I heard as many splendid natural voices as in this country.   You may find them in every city and town, in villages —even upon the countryside.   The quantity of American singing material now being developed is colossal.   I would not wish to intimate that the major part will bloom, but enough will in time to allow favorable competition with foreigners.   And from it there will emerge, I feel, more than a few sterling artists.

"I believe we must go far to find foreign-born artists whose successes equal those that have came to Lillian Nordica, Emma Eames, Mary Garden, Geraldine Farrar, Olive Fremstad and Louise Homer—to name a few whose operatic reputations are preëminent.   Doesn't it indicate that where exceptional abilities are present in a singer the singer achieves and is recognized?   I might go on and name other native artists who have triumphed, and are triumphing, if it were necessary; but if anyone will stop and mentally go over a list of those known to have prospered artistically and in the public's estimation the proofs will appear in themselves and clearly.

"In both the Metropolitan and the Chicago companies there is scarcely a performance wherein at least one American singer, and oftener more than one, is in the cast.   A generous number of first-rôles are allotted our singers; if there be some who would like to see increased representation in this respect I believe some compensation is provided in the truly predominating appearance of Americans in parts of secondary importance.

"Sopranos and mezzos and contraltos, tenors, baritones and bassos who are Americans may be heard in leading rôles in both of our largest opera companies. And a comparison of the frequency of their singing and their number with what obtained in these respects a dozen years ago will show the growth of both to be astonishing. In these circumstances is it not within reason to assume that another ten years will place the American singer in a stronger position operatically than that now occupied, and add to the quantity which is winning on sheer ability? "

Dead ahead at that moment we saw something running low in the water. It was half a mile off, not readily distinguishable and our attention was drawn to the object by a cry from Cyril, whose sharp eyes first saw it. "A submarine!" he exclaimed. And so it proved.

John twisted the wheel and the *Cyril's* bow swerved to starboard. That brought within our area of vision what we had not noticed until then —another craft several hundred yards astern of what appeared to be a submarine. Looking we discovered a patrol steamer. She rode high enough for classification; her appearance slightly resembling a destroyer. Up forward we could make out a gun and about it a group of naval boys very evidently on the job.

Our motor-boat, as John opened wide the throttle, leaped ahead still faster, every minute carrying us closer to that low-lying thing of gray which was now unquestionably an American submarine of the K type, running awash. She was moving leisurely, and our flag floated from a mast. Several figures, in uniform, were discernible on the bridge; one surveying us through a glass.

We ran as close as we dared, swerved sharply to starboard again and passing on circled the stern of the patrol. We waved, got our answer from the crew on deck, and continued our course. As John slowed the speed of the *Cyril* he turned to me and spoke.

"Doesn't it give one a thrill to see those defenders? A sense of grateful security; of confidence in what this country is doing, here and over there? If we can develop a fighting-force in the short time we have, and give them the necessary support on sea as well as land, it should be reasonable to assume that American singers can find their places, and the best ones too, just as surely in opera.

"It needs only the serious study required to

win foremost operatic positions, and the other essentials that go with serious study. For natural voice and operatic talent unquestionably abound in this country. Nor do I feel that the public will be any less loyal in extending recognition and support to its opera singers than to its soldiers and sailors.

"When we scrutinize American singers in the concert field there is really little to justify any complaint that they are without prestige and plenty to do. The public, moreover, seems ready and waiting for them, for it welcomes them again and again. Everywhere I go in the United States I hear, on every side, expressions of approval for the achievements of singer after singer who has been born in this land. And if we would look for evidence of who they are and what they have done it is necessary to go no farther than to point to Alma Gluck and Reinald Werrenrath—and there are others, besides."

A cloud drifted over the sun just then, and looking overhead we saw from the west other clouds, black and quick-moving. "A squall," announced John; "we shall have to run for it." When we had docked and reached the McCormack veranda, the tenor finished with his opinions.

"Personally I have the highest admiration for American singers and for their future. They have voice, musical natures, intelligence, industry and perseverance. They are coming fast and will not be denied, and to those who are not over-impatient and learn that progress cannot be forced there is a reward and a public of their own people who will greet them with open arms."

CHAPTER XXIX

SONGS FOR THE CONCERT PROGRAMME

Mrs. McCormack, her sister and the two children had gone to a neighbor's to play tennis, the weather had turned cool, and I descended from the study to the veranda for a breath in the pure air and a general look around. I was standing there when John appeared, fresh from a trip to the city, as exuberant as a small boy.

"Some new songs," he announced, "dug out of the library—and several you never heard."

I didn't enter a denial. John is rather sure of his facts.

"I had the same experience, last year, in the Boston library. I met Philip Hale, the critic, and showed him songs he had never seen." The tenor surveyed me triumphantly. Hale is one of our musical scholars; few have a chance with him—a veritable human encyclopædia of music. I entertained no desire to match my knowledge with his, so, by manœuvering, I extricated myself from that position by encouraging John to talk.

THE CONCERT PROGRAMME

"After all, what's in a song?" he demanded. "A message people can understand. Melody, first, set to text that conveys something to heart and mind. One of the difficult tasks of my profession, and as important as the actual singing, is the choice of material for my programmes, and its arrangement. Programme-making has been declared an art, and that it is. Occasionally some erudite musician attempts to treat it as a science, and discovers something gone wrong. The solution is easy: one cannot apply the square and other measuring instruments to human emotions. Not, at least, where music prevails.

"I build my programme in a set way," said the tenor, "and never vary from it. The formula is this:

"First, I give my audiences the songs I love.

"Second, I give them songs they ought to like, and will like when they hear them often enough.

"Third, I give them the folksongs of my native land, which I hold to be the most beautiful of any music of this kind—this is song propaganda.

"Fourth, I give my audiences songs they want to hear, for such songs they have every right to expect. If I were to speak to an audience before beginning a programme I probably should say something like this: 'I thank you with all my heart for being here, and I'll do my best to make you glad you've come.'

"And whilst on the subject of audiences I want to say that they have rights the artist should at all times respect. We hear occasional objections to what is termed 'the encore nuisance.' I hope I shall never come to regard in that way the desire for additional singing of those who come to a concert to hear me. It really is a tribute which one should esteem; I know I do. It is as if they said: 'That is beautiful; please give us more.' I know I should feel lost were encores not requested through applause, and I wish to say that if the day ever comes when my hearers do *not* want me to give them encores I shall consider it time to stop singing.

"We have, I believe, two kinds of music: one kind for our feelings and another for our purely intellectual side. You frequently hear some musician praising a musical composition which has neither inspiration nor mood. 'Splendidly written,' pronounces the musician, overlooking the paucity of the content. But technique never will cover, for the people, any lack of melody.

THE CONCERT PROGRAMME

"The first duty of any artist to his public is to consider its tastes. He may cultivate them, if he can, but he must do so wisely—so that the people may not be made aware that they are being educated. To them that is distasteful; Oscar Hammerstein admitted that it was unfortunate that he should have designated his preliminary season at the Manhattan in the fall of Ninteen Hundred Nine as 'educational.' He admitted it, too, in a curtain speech at the close of his effort.

"My way," confessed the tenor, "is to stimulate—by an easy and imperceptible route—in the audiences I sing to, the desire for some songs that are of the best. It is a delicate procedure. One must go cautiously, and go slow. An exceedingly small part of the public truly seeks a concert which has as offerings only the songs of the masters. And as my audiences are invariably of great size, with the majority having simple musical tastes, I have those tastes to respect. After years of endeavor I have succeeded, gradually, in incorporating into a programme from six to eight song compositions of genuine musical substance; and I have managed to hold the attention of each audience during the interpretation of these 'better' songs.

"And this is what has happened. Little by little, the 'better' song has come to be comprehended and then thoroughly understood. All the while I have given them generously the simple songs, songs that many pronounce inferior. They may be that, musically. I admit that many I use are not 'classics,' but if they give pleasure to my hearers do they not serve a useful purpose? I think so.

"I am aware that some so-called 'highbrows' charge me with singing 'popular stuff.' So I do, and I am proud to be able to sing it so that this 'popular stuff' performs its mission: a mission that banishes sadness from darkened hearts, that turns the thoughts in the way they should go, that lifts and encourages—or sends a tear into the eye. If a song that appeals to our better nature happens to have a sentimental touch which is simple enough to reach the simplest heart, is it any the less a song having a purpose than some song, more finely made musically, which touches only the few? From an æsthetic standpoint I concede the connoisseur's objection, but two varieties of tastes require my consideration, and I must heed them.

"If a professor of mathematics were to jump,

The main entrance to Moore Abbey, County Kildare, McCormack's Irish estate from 1925 to 1937.

John McCormack on the concert platform. Edwin Schneider,
the singer's accompanist for most of his career, is at the piano.
A scene from the 1930 Fox film, Song O'My Heart.

or to attempt to jump, his class in arithmetic to calculus without any intermediate steps his pupils could not understand. To their minds calculus would be as blank as to the poor whites of the South. I recognize that the bulk of my audiences must be introduced, by degrees, to the finer composers. By this method, hearing a song or two at a time, they unconsciously gain some comprehension of this class of music. In a phrase: though not so informed, they are being musically educated.

"Six years ago, when I began extensively to appear in the United States in concerts, my object was to please my auditors. I have stated before, in this book, that the greatest things are the simplest. That sounds paradoxical, in a way; but I will explain by saying that the most difficult phrase to sing is one in which one tone is joined to another in a manner that allows no break— what we call *cantilena* or *legato*. So, with the song, it requires the more consummate art to interpret the pure and melodiously simple song than that which jumps about, and thereby allows for the concealing of defects.

"I felt, six years ago, that I could develop a following only by giving people what they wanted to hear; thereby prompting those people to tell their friends of the pleasure they had thus derived, and by this process I would, in time, find numerous adherents and be serving them in a useful way.

"My success as a singer of songs had always been rather pronounced. So many people had told me that my singing gave them great pleasure that I finally concluded that, perhaps, my mission was to extend that singing so that the largest number possible might hear.

"That first season of Ninteen Twelve and Thirteen decided me. My audiences grew in size and in appreciation and I then felt it no assumption to devote myself, primarily, to giving my following what was wanted.

"Further evidence which seemed to confirm my feelings in these respects were steadily piling up. Some of it came from serious musicians—Fritz Kreisler, and others—who frankly told me that I touched them with my interpretations of those simple ballads, which have been unjustly called meretricious. I needed no more than such admissions, from musicians brave enough to make them, to strengthen my determination.

"Lest there be a misunderstanding—I want to

make myself clear on the subject of the simple song, which has sentiment. By such songs I emphatically do not mean trash of the order which many Americans know as 'popular.' The songs like those of Stephen Foster are what I refer to; and their beauties are unquestioned because they have endured and because they unfailingly arouse our sincere emotions.

"If a man or a woman does not happen to understand a Bach fugue it does not follow that the man or woman has no perception of musical beauty. The musical potentiality may be there, without having been cultivated. Give it food and light and air, in the form of understandable songs sung in a language that the hearer knows, and the hearer comes to appreciate and, presently, begins to acquire musical intelligence.

"But—and this I hold to be vitally important —the song must be sung to people in their own tongue, and with an enunciation that makes every word understood. In the United States English is the language I use; and no inconsiderable part of the enjoyment my audiences derive from my singing is attributable to this ability to 'get' each word. For without conveying the words—*every* word—the heart of the song is not there. And when you take the heart away from anything you kill it."

So extensive had been the disucssion as to Mc-Cormack's own enjoyment of the simple songs he uses that I was moved to ask him, and to want information, too, on the character of songs he best likes.

He did not hesitate. From his chair he rose to his feet, quickly, and began to pace between one spot and another—which is a habit when he is discussing a subject that interests him. "I like the songs of simple melody," he declared, "and with simple harmonic construction. I mean, of course, the finer examples of such songs, in which the melodic line has genuine beauty and the treatment is of proportionate value.

"But I take the musician's enjoyment in compositions of breadth. Take, for purposes of illustration, a comparatively unknown oratorio of Mozart's—'Davidde penitente.' This is one of the several unique works that I have discovered this summer (1918). And it is one of the most suavely glorious compositions I have ever studied.

"There is a tenor aria—called 'Bei dir, o Quell des Lebens'—which taxes the resources of the

388

singer to his extreme limits. One must sing it; there is no opportunity for slighting so much, even, as a single phrase. Broad *cantilena,* dramatic emphasis . . . and vocal agility, too. There is little in the direction of pure singing which Mozart does not demand of whoever would interpret it adequately.

"And the trio ('Wohl dem, der auf den Herrn') written for an unusual combination of voices: two sopranos and tenor. That is a trio which cannot be sung save by those who have voice, musicianship and art.

"Mozart drew his material for 'Davidde penitente' from his last unfinished mass. He wrote the Italian words below the Latin and added two new airs."

But McCormack admires every fine song classic, no matter what the school. Schubert, Beethoven, Bach, Schumann, Hugo Wolf—and the representative French, English and American composers. His taste knows no nationality; it is towards the merit of what has been written, that his taste inclines. And anyone who has heard his delivery of "Waft Her, Angels," and other oratorio masterpieces, must appreciate his versatility.

In McCormack's judgment the greatest song ever composed is Schubert's "Die Allmacht," for which an adequate English translation is "Omnipotence." "It is a flood of exaltation," declared the tenor, his eyes shining, "the outpouring, in music, of a poet's soul. Still, my personal preference—over any other song—is for 'Die Mainacht' (A Night in May), by Brahms. Then there is 'Der Dichterliebe,' with the tender love poems of Heine as the musical basis; and there is much else, besides.

"I might go on, rather extensively, in a discussion as to songs, songs of every nationality; but it would make reading for the musicians, I fear, rather than for the general public—for which this volume is primarily intended.

"America, I am glad to say, is making strides in its creative musical side. Many gifted composers are of the United States. And all they need is time, and a recognition which will encourage them, to place their works eventually alongside some of the great works of their colleagues of other lands.

"As in my plea for giving a chance to the American singer, I feel, quite as keenly, upon the opportunities that should be placed in the way of American composers. Their efforts should invite an outspoken attitude of willingness to hear what is new; not an attitude of expecting something of inferior character.

"If the people will but remember that it takes a country longer to develop its creative side than it does its interpretative they may come to a clearer appreciation of the situation and, that reached, govern themselves to a constructive rather than a destructive end.

"After all," said John, looking with unseeing eyes across the sloping lawn towards the water, "we should try, in this life, to help one another. There is too great a tendency to criticise for the sake of saying something 'superficially smart.' And it only hurts, and does no good. Americans are admittedly fair sportsmen—and I should like to see a trifle more of that fairness exercised in the treatment of their own musicians: composers as well as singers and instrumentalists.

"Personally, I do not care for the music of Debussy, because I miss the note of sincerity in his work. Yet I would feel guilty if I were to find fault with what he has done in words ungracious. Ravel I do admire, immensely, and Strauss; there is a master.

"But when I get to talking on this subject I never fail to think of what George Bernard Shaw said, replying to the question, 'Who is the greatest musician?' 'Beethoven,' said Shaw, 'but Mozart was the *only* musician.'

"We are, however, on the right road—so far as the American in music is concerned. It will be some years, no doubt, before he gets his dues, yet they surely will come; for the American has the musical talent."

CHAPTER XXX

MC CORMACK ON CRITICS

"Now—for the music critics!" I said, as John and I came out upon the veranda at Rocklea one August morning. "Shall we have them shot at sunrise, or frizzle 'em in boiling oil?"

"Oh, let's give them a banquet and invite all to sing, together, 'The Soldiers' Chorus' from 'Faust.' "

"Then you don't hate them?" I queried.

"On the contrary," replied the tenor, settling into his chair, "they light the way for me. There are exceptions; once in a while you find a self-opinionated youth who wishes to teach the world, who misuses his power—who incorrectly assumes his functions to consist chiefly of emphasizing one's faults, of exaggerating faults of slight consequence. Some few critics, also, occasionally attend a concert or opera performance in a belligerent mood; or, feeling out of sorts, lapse from their habitual fairness.

393

"But the majority, I have found, strive sincerely to judge without prejudice or bias, and write their reviews accordingly. They wield an unquestioned weight, the critics, and are an absolute necessity—some would say a necessary evil—and I believe most of them try to give, as accurately as they can, an honest estimate of what they hear.

"Constructive criticism, offered by one skilled in the craft, is of inestimable help to the artist; and no singer or instrumentalist who earnestly seeks to progress in his art will resent an intelligently and kindly expressed opinion upon technical and interpretative musical achievement which happens to take issue with that achievement. And, to be honest, we resent it mostly because it hurts our vanity.

"The critic may, in the estimation of the artist, be right; or his views may be open to question on the part of the artist. After all, it is only one person's opinion, and may differ from the opinions of that critic's colleagues. But I always read, with an open mind, whatever a music critic writes who, I feel, in the reading, has written constructively and out of adequate knowledge."

394

McCORMACK ON CRITICS

"Do you regard it as an essential part of the music critic's equipment to be able to perform the thing about which he writes?"

McCormack dropped his head to one side and regarded me with gravity. Ready with his reply he waited to frame it in certain desired phraseology. "No, I don't think such a thing is necessary, but it must have been wonderful," said the tenor reflectively, "for Schumann to have been able—as we know he was—to write of a new composition, adversely, and say with the full authority which was his: 'Now if *I* had written that composition it might have sounded better to have done so-and-so.' Think, too, of the advantage the composer thus criticised must have derived from such constructive criticism. Such a music critic, granting he possesses the judicial temperament, has an advantage over others not so fortunate. There can be no dispute, I think, as to that; yet a critic may not have such a gift and still be highly competent.

"To be endowed with the capacity to weigh impartially all the evidence pertaining to a musical performance, eliminating one's personal preferences and dislikes, is ideal. We'll accept that as an established premise. Now—where such qualifications exist in a critic, and to them is added the natural faculty of recognizing excellence and mediocrity instinctively, we have the perfect critic.

"I remember a story I once heard, and a true one. It happened in Chicago, years ago. A distinguished American composer, at that time music critic for a Chicago evening newspaper, reached his office one afternoon and in the hallway met the critic for the morning newspaper which was under the same ownership. The critic for the morning paper had just been appointed; moved over from another position on the staff of that publication. He was an able editor, a splendid writer; but he admitted, frankly, that music was to him as Greek might be to a baby.

"The composer-critic had read his associate's review of a performance, given the night before, by the American Grand Opera Company. Theodore Thomas had been the conductor; the work, by Delibes. The composer was asked by the newly appointed critic: 'How did you like last night's performance?'

" 'I thought it exceptional, as I did the opera,' he replied.

" 'So did I,' retorted the unskilled music judge.

396

" 'But,' ejaculated the musician, 'you roasted everything, from Delibes down.'

" 'Oh, I had to do that; I went there to criticise.'

"Nevertheless," declared the tenor as he straightened up in his chair, "I respect the opinions of every critic who goes about his task with good intent and makes a respectable job of it. I may differ from him, in details, possibly, at times, in essentials; but so long as I discern sincerity in his trend, and intelligence, I will concede that he has the same right to his ways of thinking in the matter as I have to mine. For, after all, it is a difference of opinion that provokes the discussion (or thought) which leads to progress.

"Now and again one encounters the 'cocksure' reviewer; the one of positive utterance, who considers himself infallible, and takes himself, also, with far more seriousness than his importance should allow. He writes to catch certain of his readers with clever phrase; hitting here and there with unkindness, and very often taking the heart of a struggling artist who might be corrected were the reminder of remissness put in a helpful way.

"Still, his kind is beginning to disappear. He

is of the old school, grown ancient in his trade and myopic through having too long looked in a groove because of the blinders of traditions he has worn.

"Give me, if you will, the joyous reviewer; the one having in him human responsiveness and appreciation, who has the courage to say 'great' if he really thinks so, even though others hold a contrary view. He may be either old or young; I care not, so long as he goes to a musical performance in a plastic mood, ready to be convinced if the music and performer have merit.

"But, as I said in the beginning, I genuinely admire the critics, as a body. They have given me my dues. We send them tickets for a concert, voluntarily ask them to come and write about it, and it is we who must take our chances. And I wouldn't give a fig for any man who, admiring my voice and art, refused because of his admiration to say I had not done myself justice if such were the case. For that happens; singers are human beings, and not being machines they cannot, and should not, be expected to perform with mechanical accuracy which does not vary.

"Especially do I respect the representative critics, serving on the leading daily newspapers in the large American cities, who have expressed their growing regard for my voice and art and programmes. These men, all of them splendidly equipped and speaking from an abundant knowledge, are the recognized authorities. They are not infallible, because, like the singer or instrumentalist, they are only human. They speak well and at other times they also speak not so well of great artists: of Caruso and Kreisler and Hofmann. So it is with pride that I have discovered my own position and powers enhancing in their estimation; for that is a reward to any artist who conscientiously wishes to be accepted as such by those who are presumed to know."

It is a fair summing up of the critics and their functions, which McCormack has made. I can conceive of none, in the whole corps of the country, who will justly dispute the essence of what he has said. And at no time in his talk did he mention by name any critic whom he in particular admired, or one who may have drawn his disfavor.

Yet, much as he respects those whose musical education and geographical opportunities give them an advantage over their less fortunate colleagues, John has a weak spot in his heart for the writers attached to dailies outside the larger sphere; for the men and women who perform other newspaper duties than those exclusively musical, and whose writings are out of the heart rather than a musically trained mind.

It would be interesting to incorporate in this volume a hundred representative critiques. They would make illuminative reading, to many. But space is a consideration to be heeded.

CHAPTER XXXI

EDWIN SCHNEIDER

One of those drizzly rains, that tend to stir the reflections of a thoughtful person, was falling over Noroton. McCormack sat on the veranda, at Rocklea, engaged with Edwin Schneider in an informal discussion on songs. The pianist excused himself when the subject had been ended, and went into the house. When he disappeared, the tenor turned to me.

"Do you wonder that I'm fond of him? A combination of man and musician," he said, "which is out of the common run. I've known him, intimately, for five years. We've wintered and summered together, and our friendship tie tightens. That is the real test—to develop the feeling of comradeship as well as artistic unity, with one who is almost constantly alongside.

"I've said that my intimates are few: a comparatively small number of persons, living in different lands. Perhaps it is just as well, for those I feel close to I like to be with as much as I can,

401

and this precludes a large friendship even where one's inclinations move in that way. But there is one man whose companionship I particularly enjoy—Edwin Schneider.

"He is totally different from me, temperamentally. Almost always serene, an optimist every day of every week and, for all his virility, gentle. Schneider is what I should term a *gentle*-man. A scholarly musician, too, and a student; and with original ideas. Thank fortune, he is not a hidebound adherent to tradition! He has vision, and he likes the things musical which I like. So, you see, we fit: in music as well as in less artistic things of life.

"It was a fortunate day for me, when I met him, because he has exerted a positive influence upon my career. No one has had a greater faith in my capabilities, even when I was in doubt about some part of them, myself. From his point of vantage, and with his intuitive faculties and discernment, Schneider has not infrequently observed that it was wise for me to attempt what I hesitated attempting. And never has his judgment been at fault.

"His confidence in me, always so reassuringly calm, has been like a tonic. Knowing that he recommends only that which he honestly believes, I invite his opinions. We differ in matters, of course, and that is as it should be. Still, in whatever is vital I think we are not often at odds.

"Before Ted" (that is John's name for Schneider) "came to me I questioned the suitableness, for my voice and style, of certain songs. I recall, in particular, 'J'ai pleuré enrêve.' My previous accompanist had said: 'That isn't for you.' But one day, chancing upon it, Ted suggested that we try it over. I repeated what this other pianist had said. It had no effect, however, upon Schneider. He only said, with a smile, 'I think he is mistaken.' So we went at it."

My recollection was that this song was one which McCormack sang exceedingly well; almost made for him. I said so, and John nodded.

"That's just it," he continued. "Schneider's perceptions were correct. And that experience gave me added confidence in him. Nor was that instance the single one of its kind; others occurred. Ted studied my methods; he sought to discover what was best suited to me, in the way of songs, and was forever conscientious to aid me in developing my resources.

"Sympathy, such as that, and understanding

bring the singer and his accompanist into that
spirit of harmony which contributes to a oneness
of effort.   There is a saying one often hears
about accompanist that he 'follows' well.   That,
to my mind, is no compliment to an accompanist;
for he should never 'follow,' nor yet 'lead.'   Always, should he be *with* the singer with the pianoforte part of a song; feeling as the singer feels
(in so far as he may be able to do so) and main-
taining the spirit of the music and that reflected
in the poem.

"I always feel that we go well together in a
song.   If I want to 'give' a little here, or 'take'
a bit at another place, Schneider will be with
me . . . will sense what I am about to do so
quickly as to give the audience the effect of instantaneous action by each of us.   I do change
an interpretation, now and again, no matter how
'set' it may have been as sung scores of times before.   Every artist does, who feels what he interprets; that is what keeps him from being a machine.   It is a comfort to know that when these
changes occur—and they may come many times
in the course of a concert—that the chap at the
piano, who supplies the musical background, will
not drop you suddenly, with a thud.

"The critics everywhere have recognized these rare qualities in Schneider. He has a singing touch, and a *legato*. His accompaniment is something built in right proportions, like a piece of architecture which leaves the eye satisfied. You never find Ted's accompaniment obtrusive; he gives the singer the required tonal substance for the voice, but not too much. And his *pianissimi* is not so vapory as to be lost on the hearer.

"He colors the tone, too. Sonority, when we want it; a rich, pulsating tone, one with less 'red' in it, another having mellowness but not so deeply tinted. Again: crispness, the brilliance that brings people erect when we seek a definite sort of climax. He uses the pianoforte for song accompaniments as the painter uses the pigments upon his palette. His technique, likewise, is ample; and his musicianship sound.

"I met him, in Chicago, one morning when I went to call on that splendid American singer, Clarence Whitehill, who was preparing, in the Blackstone Hotel, for a recital he expected to give. I liked Schneider's way of playing during the first song Whitehill sang; before I left I discovered characteristics which appealed tremendously to me. Making inquiry, I learned that

Schneider had played for Marcella Sembrich, Johanna Gadski and George Hamlin. I learned, too, of his thorough pianistic training, much of it gained in Europe; of his recognition as a solo pianist and as teacher.

"But the difficult art of song accompaniment—and it *is* an art, which, by the way, few pianists acquire—was Schneider's by instinct. The singer gets that the minute he starts a prelude. What my estimation of his ability is may be gathered from the fact that we have been together for five continuous seasons; nearly five hundred public appearances we've made together, and that tells the story.

"In the summers we ransack the music stores in search of unusual song compositions, and libraries. And Schneider knows the song literature of many countries. He makes something of the accompaniment as distinctive as the melody for the voice because of his comprehensive knowledge of song literature. Every composer is something more than an acquaintance; for Schneider does not rest content until he plumbs that composer.

"His equals as a 'coach' are few because of these qualifications I have mentioned. Having gone to the root of every school of song composition he continues to that end with each member of each school. When he has finished one may be sure that Schneider knows; he isn't guessing, or relying, too largely, upon an accompanying talent.

"He composes well, also, and several of his songs are among the most satisfying on my programmes."

Schneider rejoined us at that moment, just as McCormack finished speaking. The tenor left us, on some errand within, and I was glad of the opportunity to get his ideas on John—those intimate ones which he, of all persons, was able to supply.

"I came to McCormack," said Schneider, "a worshipper at the shrine of his voice and art; I have played for no one else since that spring of Nineteen Thirteen. I have watched him grow, and seen his capacities expand with as much gratification as though he were a brother. His triumphs—though his alone—are mine, also.

"It has been one of the most interesting experiences in my life to observe his 'education' of his audiences, because educate them he has.

"The presentation of Schubert, Schumann and

Franch at his concerts was followed by the introduction to most of his hearers of Brahms and
Hugo Wolf, and the modern German songs and
the Russian and French. He insisted on using
the best English translations obtainable, because
he rightly places emphasis on an understanding
of the text. And in many cases we together
made our own translations, especially those of
Rachmaninoff's songs.

"Handel and Mozart have a direct appeal upon
John because of their lyric and florid qualities;
and I cannot now think of a better exponent of
these two masters. But his grasp of Irish folk-
songs, and his interpretation of them, are things
I never cease to admire. He has opened to me
the wealth of this music, and it has made it possible for me to appreciate why the Irish are so
musical and so endowed with sympathy and sentiment.

"This summer, like each of the preceding
ones I have spent with McCormack, has brought
hundreds of unknown songs to his notice; and
we have gone through them with open minds that
seek to find whatever we consider worthy of public use. Since the war began, John has been
chiefly concerned in exploring the song literature

of France, Russia and Norway, and many fine compositions has he discovered.

"There is, of course, a mass of 'popular' music sent to him in manuscript form—most of it, I am sorry to say, unsuitable for John's purposes.

"The budding Schubert has certainly weird ideas of the songs that suit McCormack. I remember how we laughed over two wonderful specimens, called respectively 'In the Subway,' and 'Has the State of Montana Gone Dry, Mary Anne?' The author of this last priceless lyric announced himself as a great poet and was sure with the co-operation of a great singer, he could make what he called 'the big noise in the music world.'

"I can add little or nothing to the critical and public estimate of John McCormack's artistic worth. For me he is a supremely great artist because of his sincerity. Nor do I place either voice or the singing talent above this quality; for without that depth of feeling which is his, John could not, and would not, be the singer we know him to be.

"For rapid study I know no singer who is McCormack's equal. During his first Covent Garden season, John learned in exactly six days

the rôle of *Don Ottavio* in 'Don Giovanni.' He
began to study it on a Monday and sang the music
the Monday following. Nor have I yet met one
who reads at sight with his facility or whose musicianship rests upon a more substantial foundation. He is as painstaking as he is thorough, and
delights to run through any soprano aria of the old
masters. He is a master of vocal agility and his
execution of florid phrases is accomplished with
the ease and surety of a coloratura soprano who
is mistress of her art.

"To play for John, in both rehearsal and public performance, is an inspiration. He develops
in the accompanist the spirit of what is best and
truest in the art. From him I have learned
much; I expect to learn more. Having been
with him so continuously for five years, I have
come to know the man as well as the artist. And
I have felt what one friend feels for another in
seeing him win what he has deserved.

"As I see him now I feel that he is coming into
the fullness of his powers. He has done much,
but he will do more. His artistry is ripening and
his vision enables him to foresee all that he
should. Because of these things I anticipate
from John McCormack certain accomplishments

that will make his name still more widely acclaimed—for he is the sort of singing artist the world brings forth but once in a long, long time."

CHAPTER XXXII

REFLECTIONS

It was a few days after the Rt. Reverend Bishop Curley had confirmed Cyril and Gwendolyn McCormack, in late June of Nineteen Eighteen, in the tiny stone church in Noroton, that he spoke of John McCormack and his voice in a way I shall never forget. He termed it a service of the voice—the dedication of soul and heart and mind and utterance to a lofty purpose. That, I think, is the most expressive description I have ever heard of the man and his mission.

The Bishop had been recounting some of the attributes of his boyhood chum; had been giving me illuminative information which could not have been gathered from any save one who had grown up with John, and enjoyed, always, his absolute confidence. Much that I have been enabled accurately to set forth in this volume about McCormack—and which he, himself, never would have hinted at—was thus made possible.

412

REFLECTIONS

With Bishop Curley it was a labor of love; for to him John McCormack is the sun in the sky.

The service of the voice. That phrase, more fittingly than any other I know, opened the gates of my understanding. It clarified one's mental search for the element, or elements, which have lifted McCormack above others who have also had voice and the gift of song. For to him there was given all things necessary to make him what Bishop Curley, in his gently suggestive way, meant me to grasp that he is—the prophet of song.

Out of his knowledge gained in his college days; of his studies, among the many he mastered, of Irish literature; and of the folk-songs of his native land, too, John brought an abundance of the mind to each interpretation and joined it with that of the heart. Neither, without the other, could have served; and to these two the adding of the McCormack voice made a trinity.

All of this Bishop Curley made plain to me. I comprehended, then, why the people (and the musicians, also) receive a McCormack message, why he interprets the poet, no less than the composer; and what it is that stirs the pulses when he sings. The service of the voice—in speech and song—is the thing John McCormack has been given to do.

Having grasped these matters it did not surprise me, when one who had been in that gathering on the lawn of George Washington's home, at Mount Vernon, Fourth of July, 1918, told me of the effect John had made upon them when he sang "The Star-Spangled Banner." I was able, thus, to gather the full of McCormack's simple statement when I asked him what President Wilson had said to him, after he finished.

"I stood very near to the President," said the tenor, "while I sang. Never did patriotism surge within me as on that day. One felt the dignity, the majesty, of the occasion. And the President's speech left my soul fired. I saw nothing, heard nothing, felt nothing but the grandeur of what the poem meant. My eyes were closed all the while I sang.

"There was a brief silence at the end. Then President Wilson stepped a few paces to where I stood, and took my hand and pressed it— fervently, it seemed to me. 'I never heard "The Star-Spangled Banner" sung, Mr. McCormack, as you just sang it! And I thank you from the bottom of my heart.'"

REFLECTIONS

And it is somewhat odd, in view of what Bishop Curley told me, that President Wilson, on the way down the Potomac, aboard the Presidential yacht, *Mayflower*, should have discussed, at length, with McCormack the subject of voice.

I should have liked to hear more extensively from John concerning that experience, but he hesitated to say more than just those few words. To him, no doubt, it appeared something to feel rather than to discuss.

We were approaching the last stages in the preparation of this volume when McCormack touched upon that Independence Day Mt. Vernon experience of his. Mrs. McCormack, Miss Foley, Cyril and Gwen and Edwin Schneider had gone to the tennis court, and the tenor let his thoughts drift to matters he had not already spoken about.

Never having been in his New York City home, in Fifty-seventh Street (near Central Park), I had not seen some of the art treasures he has there.

"I had always wanted to have about me some really fine canvases," he said. "My natural love for the beautiful had been cultivated during my studies in Milan; you will recall I spent much of my time in the Galleria. The influence of everything in painting, sculpture and architecture that is beautiful benefits the singer, just as the best in literature does.

"To one who is as sensitive to environment as I, it is helpful to have about as much representative of the arts as one consistently can. I have a fondness for rare violins, too. But some of my paintings give me the deepest pleasure. One room, alone, is given over to Rembrandt and other masterpieces. There hangs the portrait of 'Rembrandt's Sister.' Rembrandt did it in Sixteen Forty-two. There is much history surrounding it—Gwen and Cyril can tell you all the details.

"My 'Nymphs Bathing' is one of the best specimens of Corot I have seen. I always admired Blakelock, too, and when I found an opportunity to pick up a representative canvas I didn't hesitate long. There's a nice landscape by J. Francis Murphy, and a quaint painting, of two peasants, by David Teniers. I have other canvases, not so fine as some of the rest, but containing for me a wealth of sentiment; they are by Mary Carlisle—scenes of Ireland, with the flowers of Ireland almost with the radiance of their natural colors.

"They are all friends, now; sometimes they seem fairly to talk to me. Then there is the portrait Walter Dean Grosbeck did of Mrs. Mc-Cormack; the 'Romeo and Juliet' statue which Rodin made, and one in which his genius shows in each detail. Two marble busts, as well, of Cyril and Gwen, which Mario Korbel did two years ago."

"A pretentious start," I ventured.

"Interesting," agreed McCormack, "and giving one a pleasure in the ownership which, somehow, doesn't come when you see works in a gallery which are just as fine. For the beauties in a picture, or any other masterpiece of an art, arise through understanding. At first you form its acquaintance, then you become a 'friend.'

"Take the original manuscript of Eugene Field's 'Little Boy Blue,' which I bought for my kiddies: a glow comes over me when I take it in my hands, to read. And both Cyril and Gwen learned the words from those very words which Field penned with his own hand.

"A genuine pleasure comes to me," said Mc-

417

Cormack, "through the letters I get from members of what I might call my 'invisible audience'; those who hear me oftenest through the phonograph."

One can understand the tenor's feeling, in this respect. Of all singers, his "invisible audience" is largest; probably the most loyal. The total of McCormack records sold each year by the Victor company is astonishing; some idea of their quantity may be gathered from the fact that John's last year's royalties from this source is considerable—the tenor preferred not to state the sum.

In every land one may find McCormack "fans" —which is a proper word to apply to those who go regularly, each month, to purchase the newest McCormack record. The tenor's contract stipulates that he shall make five records of new songs every year, but he always exceeds that number.

C. G. Child, in charge of the department which has to do with the artists singing for the Victor Talking Machine Company, might explain why he wants more, and yet more, McCormack "master-records"—from which those sold to the public are made.

418

John McCormack in 1929. A photograph taken on the set of the 1930 Fox film, Song O'My Heart.

John McCormack, an informal portrait taken shortly before his retirement from the concert platform in 1938.

REFLECTIONS

"I always enjoy my trips to Camden, (New Jersey), for Child is a staunch friend and sympathetic. Making a record is no easy accomplishment. Infinite patience is required to secure a 'master-record' which has no flaw. On occasions I re-make a record several times before Child and I are satisfied; and during these difficult moments he is always by my side, encouraging and helping as he so well can.

"The 'Jocelyn' lullaby, of all the records I have made (I believe they number one hundred and twenty), is my favorite. Somehow it seems to lend itself completely to phonographic reproduction, and the obligato, by Kreisler, discloses that artist at his best. Then there is 'The Trumpeter.' 'Mother Machree,' 'Mavis' and 'I Hear You Calling Me' are all popular with the public; so is 'Ah! Moon of My Delight.'

"Every little while," said the tenor, "some experience I have with one of my 'invisible audience' makes my heart beat faster. Three years ago, in Hartford, a gentleman was brought to my dressing-room, after the concert. He was one of Connecticut's representative business men. He had, he said, a message to deliver personally to me from his mother, who was an invalid and unable to attend my concert. Having obtained a programme, in advance, of what I was announced to sing, she arranged one of her own (to be performed through the medium of my phonograph records), had printed copies made, issued tickets of admission to her home to her friends, and began the 'invisible audience' concert at the precise minute my own, in Hartford, was scheduled to commence. My caller had a request to make of me: he wanted an autographed photograph, for his mother."

The tenor seemed a trifle sad this day. When he talked about some few, who are dead, he sobered, but he would brighten, in recalling to his mind his experiences with certain living personages.

"I am a devoted admirer of Theodore Roosevelt," said John, "and his autographed picture which hangs in the hall is a gift I prize. He is a tremendous force, and I think he more faithfully typifies America than any man I have met. One of the most difficult tasks I ever undertook was writing my letter of condolence in his loss of his brave son, Lieutenant Quentin Roosevelt. Yet the reply he sent me was characteristic of his capacity to accept with the fortitude of a great nature what must have been one of his severest blows.

"Another great man for whom my admiration is unbounded is His Eminence, Cardinal Gibbons. And an incident at one of my concerts which he attended will always make me feel closer to him than had it not occurred. He makes it an invariable rule never to remain at a function or entertainment later than nine o'clock in the evening. On this occasion, when he prepared to leave the auditorium, he discovered the time to be twenty minutes of ten; and I am told that he remarked that he had forgotten, in listening to my singing, all about the hour." The same thing happened at Ocean Grove August 17, 1918, when Cardinal Gibbons attended a McCormack concert.

"I lost a friend," said John with a trace of longing in his voice, "in the death of Archbishop Ryan. I lunched with him only a short time before he died, and I remember clearly the brilliance of his mind, which fascinated me as I sat there, and his gift of repartee. Few others possessed it in the degree he did."

Later, with the inclination to talk returned, McCormack perceptibly brightened.

"Former President Taft is a man I deem it an honor to know. His friendship means something, to me particularly because of the way we met. It was during my first appearance with the Manhattan Opera Company in Washington, on which occasion we played for a week to the varied and brilliant audiences always characteristic of the national capital, that I received in my dressing-room a visit from Mr. Taft's then military aide, Captain Archie Butt. Butt and I afterwards became intimate friends, and his death was a shock from which I did not easily recover.

"I remember, as though it were yesterday, what Archie said as he stood and delivered President Taft's message. 'The President would like you to lunch with him to-morrow at the White House.'

"At first I could not believe that I had understood correctly, and informed my visitor that there must be some mistake. I can see him now, standing before me with a smile, and replying: 'No, there is no mistake. The President would be pleased to have John McCormack take lunch with him to-morrow.'

"It is not exaggeration when I say that I was

dubious even as I made my way through the presidential grounds to the White House itself.

"During the years that I knew Archie we lunched together, often, when he came over to New York. It was usually in the Waldorf-Astoria grill. The last time we met in this way he said to me: 'It's peculiar, John, how friendships grow out of chance meetings; I believe we shall be friends all our lives.' And shortly after, when I endeavored to reach him by 'phone during a brief stay in Washington, I was told that he had just left for Rome. Not long after, as we know, he was among those who lost their lives in the sinking of the *Titanic*. But there is a great consolation in the thought that he died as he lived—a true American gentleman.

"Among the men who are doing things to-day, and have done them in the past, Melville Stone, general manager of The Associated Press, is prominent. His mind is tremendous, his judgment and discretion such that the foremost in administering the affairs of many nations give him their confidence and hold his opinions in profound respect. I am proud to have Mr. Stone as friend, and of the honors tendered me I count the dinner he gave me at the Lotus Club, in New York, as one of the highest."

John spoke feelingly of many people that afternoon. For nearly all he held kindly thoughts, and for some affection. A few he mentioned in a regretful way, though without censure. I sensed that the tenor would rather have had them persons of a different sort; and I think he was sorry for them. He showed, during my many talks with him, a commendable attitude of tolerance toward those he might have felt tempted to criticize. There were few instances wherein he disclosed in speech displeasure with another's actions, and at those times he would conclude with some such expression as, "But that is his misfortune; I suppose one should make allowances."

I left him, when I started for New York, seated alone on the veranda. He didn't rise. His gaze was directed towards the beach where the swimmers were. I called a "So-long, John!" as I reached the screen door, which caused him to look over at me and smile. "So-long," he replied, "see you Thursday."

CHAPTER XXXIII

CONCLUSION

It was morning, on the twelfth day of August, Nineteen Hundred Eighteen. The prostrating heat of the week previous had broken, leaving those of us in and about New York somewhat limp and with an eye to approaching September and a hope that it would bring permanent coolness. I had taken an early train leaving the Grand Central Station for Stamford. At ten o'clock I had finished my shaky ride, in a small car of a famous make, from the Stamford station to Rocklea. I stepped out upon the ground and across under the shallow portico which shelters the McCormack doorway.

Gwenny caught sight of me, from the living-room, and saved my touching the bell. She came and opened the door, her face aglow and her eyes snapping in the vigor of perfect health of a ten-year-old miss.

"Papa's waiting," she announced, "and an

425

oyster barge's burning over at the island across the Sound and we're going over and you'll have to come along and—"

She declaimed it all in a breath, her features rosy from much and sudden physical effort which had sent her into a costume appropriate for the anticipated adventure. But time, evidently, was an essential; for she bolted with her sentence unfinished and leaped from the veranda and ran across the lawn. I had followed less impulsively and had half crossed the living-room when Cyril burst upon the scene, duplicating the excitement of his sister.

"She's burning!" he cried, "and the men jumped overboard. Come on!"

I counseled a curbing of his impetuous spirit to which he flung, over his shoulder, a reply I did not get. But I paused, at the doorway leading to the veranda, and watched. Hard after the children ran the two smallest dogs, Towser, the woolly dog, and Go-Go, the Peke. Then, from around a corner of the house, shot a streak. It was Nellie, the Belgian police-dog. Evidently the chase, in its entirety, was on. But, it appeared, my reasoning was premature, for a voice greeted me from behind and I turned to see Mrs.

CONCLUSION

McCormack and Miss Foley making hurriedly for the veranda exit.

With less visible excitement the ladies apprised me of the news and followed it with the information that they, also, were about to embark upon the expedition, in John's small boat which had a "kicker."

"What!" I exclaimed. "You, too?"

"Yes," replied Mrs. McCormack, "we *two!* Will you make it three?"

"I'm a hard-working man," I objected.

"That old book, I suppose. But come along, anyway. John will wait."

I remembered the carrying capacity of the boat, and reminded Mrs. McCormack. I would be excess baggage, I opined, endangering the sea-worthiness of the craft. McCormack, hearing our voices and coming to investigate, appeared now before us.

Mrs. McCormack, Miss Foley and I stole glances at one another and they waved their hands and departed, leaving John and me standing there. He watched them hurrying after the advance guard and laughed. "Regular children," he murmured, "like the others."

We went outside, where Schneider sat with

427

his legs looped upon one arm of a wicker-chair, lolling over the morning paper. "Drop it," commanded John, "and get to work"—meaning to join us in the concluding efforts of "copy" revision and the providing of the final material for John's book. Ted wriggled into a semblance of physical normality, wished me "howdy!" and obediently prepared to give himself to the task.

For two hours we battled: John and Schneider and I alternately agreeing and disagreeing. It was over at last, and I put into my portfolio sundry sheets of paper and a sheaf of publisher's proofs.

After luncheon, during which the sea-faring members of the McCormack family hurled at us details of their investigation of the still burning oyster-boat and the escape of its crew, John and I fared forth for a jaunt. His Ocean Grove (New Jersey) annual concert was five days off, the period of serious preparation with Schneider for his approaching season near at hand, and the tenor was in a serious mood.

"It flies," he said soberly, meaning time. "It seems but yesterday that I finished last year's work; and an hour ago that I sang 'The Star-Spangled Banner' before President Wilson and his distinguished guests at Mount Vernon, on July Fourth."

"Are you sorry?"

"No. I wouldn't say that. I love my work; I'd be miserable without it. And my people—they're mine, you know . . . in a way, just as I am theirs. But each autumn it is harder to leave my family. I've never outgrown homesickness, and never shall. It grips me as firmly, in another way, as in those college days at Summerhill."

We trudged along the smoothly paved road, in silence, for a considerable stretch.

"Bishop Curley sent back his last batch of proofs. He made a few changes, but he approves what we've done. I'm glad of that."

I was glad, too. We have been fortunate, John and I, in having the scholarly and sympathetic guidance of His Lordship, as editor.

"You're relieved, I suppose, that it's over. A lot of bother with the work; and not so easy, either."

I wasn't relieved, in the least. Truthfully speaking, I felt a bit blue. The many hours we had spent together had been happy hours, and fruitful ones. And I had come to know the real

John McCormack. The sky was a turquoise blue, with only a few flecks of fleecy clouds, and I raised my eyes as if to glimpse nature's canopy—though really, covertly, to steal a glance at the big Irish-American at my side. He strode on, with head thrown back; I could fancy him almost ready to sing.

"I shall . . . miss you, John."

He swung a trifle out of his course, and I caught his gaze squarely.

"Will you?" he said, with a rising inflection.

"I've been a nuisance, more or less. Popping in at odd times, and fussing things about—during your vacation."

His tone held a gruffly suspicious edge when he replied. "Well, what's a nuisance, more or less? It's all in a lifetime." I smiled inwardly at this, holding my tongue. "And the book had to be written . . . some day."

There arose, then, before my mind's eye the swarm of letters I had read; those communications which he treasures far more than he is willing to admit. I shouldn't have censured him had he felt a conceit. For they might easily have spoiled him, together with the recognition his audiences have accorded him in the flesh.

CONCLUSION

Not that he is without his weaknesses, for he has them. But at heart he is still the unassuming boy he was before Distinction tapped him positively on the shoulder. And I remembered, at that point in our walk, what he had told me about his planned retirement; at forty-five, he had said. "Eleven years more," I mused; "four more than the small number which he only has needed to make a career already incomparable."

Big though his accomplishments have been they will be bigger. Those of us who have watched McCormack grow know this. It needs no more than steadiness of head and purpose, and these he seemingly has. His voice is not yet at its best, strange though this may appear. A richer quality will come, as John's experience ripens; and its use will develop its resource, its responsiveness to the singer's commands.

Nor is McCormack's art at its zenith. Wait and see, if you, who read, doubt. Hear him now—admitted master though he be—and hear him six years hence, at forty. Recall his advancement over the last six years, then visualize what it is likely to be when he touches the milestone that makes broader men of all who are men.

Caruso will be fifty-one then; John McCormack forty—forty, with the richest period of his singing career unfolding in that coming half-decade, and hundreds of thousands upon hundreds of thousands of people hanging upon the tones he so unstintingly gives.

I hope that final day may be long delayed—which shall mark John McCormack's farewell. I shall not want to be there, wherever it happens to be. For I doubt, if it be arranged as such, that John can really sing. The last concert will have to be something completed and done, without John's knowing it is that. Otherwise he will not finish what he begins. It isn't in him, with his nature, to go through with an ordeal such as that would be. He'd break and go to pieces, right there with his audience—which would break with him, too.

But if he were voluntarily to cease his singing, now (which he will not do), he would still leave behind a career unapproached by any singer since Jenny Lind. I doubt if even that illustrious songstress has done as much to make people love music as John McCormack. With eleven working years ahead, McCormack will leave a name likely to be untouched by any other who has gone before and, in all reasonable likelihood, almost unattainable by any singer who may come after.

It was some time later. We had finished tea, on the veranda, and I had shaken hands with everyone. John and the others went out with me to the car, where Wilkinson sat waiting. "I won't go with you to the station," he said. "Any other time, but . . . I don't like farewells. Staying here, behind, it won't seem that."

We shot off, Wilkinson at the wheel of McCormack's Rolls-Royce, down the driveway. I turned as we reached the gate, just before we would roll out, and from view. John took a step or two in my direction. He waved a hand as I caught sight of him—and I waved in reply.

I thought then, of that bit of verse Bishop Curley had discovered, somewhere up in Massachusetts, last June. He thought it fitted McCormack so perfectly. It ran:

"Something more than the lilt of the strain,
Something more than the touch of the lute,
For the voice of the minstrel is vain
If the heart of the minstrel is mute."

THE END

433

INDEX

INDEX

INDEX

INDEX

INDEX

INDEX

INDEX

INDEX

INDEX